PIGGYBACK and CONTAINERS

A westbound "piggyback" train, on Southern Pacific's Donner Pass Route, crests the eastern slope of the pass. In this scene, the train exits a concrete formed snow-shed, with Donner Lake in the distance. In order to reach Norden, the train pokes into a tunnel on the left. A TTX flat with two American President Lines containers on chassis brings up the rear of the train. — DONALD DUKE

PIGGYBACK *and* CONTAINERS

A History of Rail Intermodal on America's Steel Highway

David J. DeBoer

Golden West Books
San Marino, California • 91118-8250

PIGGYBACK AND CONTAINERS
A History of Rail Intermodal on America's Steel Highway

Copyright © 1992 by David J. DeBoer
All Rights Reserved

Published by Golden West Books
San Marino, California 91118 U.S.A.

Library of Congress Catalog Card No. 92-39181
I.S.B.N. No. 0-87095-108-4

First Printing - November 1992
Second Printing - July 1994

Library of Congress Cataloging-in-Publication Data

DeBoer, David J., 1938
    Piggyback and containers: a history of rail intermodal on Americas's steel highway / David J. DeBoer.

    p.   cm.
Includes bibliographical references and index.
ISBN 0-87095-108-4
1. Piggyback transportation — United States — History.
2. Containerization — United States — History.   I. Title.
HE2316.D43   1992   92-39181
385'.72 — dc20   CIP

Could this have been the first piggyback and terminal crane?

Golden West Books
P.O. Box 80250
San Marino, California • 91118-8250

TO

Intermodalists — past, present and future.
And to my bride Sandy, who has suffered
us all.

General Motors Electro-Motive Division devised this 75-foot experimental "Depressed Center Trailer Car," back in the summer of 1954, utilizing the Ryan hitch. This car was designed to handle two 35-foot highway semi-trailers. — G. C. MILLER COLLECTION

Acknowledgements

For those of you who have read and enjoyed history, it appears that writings fall into certain categories. Most histories have been written in what I would call "the inexorable events of history" mode. Things happen, people are swept along by it, react to it and events take place. It is, for all intents and purposes, an event-driven view of history.

Through my college years, two professors taught me a much different perspective of history, and, consequently, I had a great zest for the subject. The two gentlemen were Homer Oliver "Bobo" Hendrickson, professor of American History at Albion College, and Alexis Labonov Rostovsky, professor of Russian History at the University of Michigan. Both were rigorous historians in their field. Their approach to history, however, was based on a much more humanized view. They explored such things as what the people were like, what they looked like, why they did what they did, how they interacted with others and what caused us to understand them in an historical context. To these two men, I owe a great debt of gratitude. They not only developed my love for history, but they also nurtured it.

Within the past ten to 20 years other historians have been writing in the same genre as these two professors, the same gentlemen who made the lecture hall such a joy for me. Modern chroniclers of railroad history such as Don Hofsommer and Maury Klein are writers who also have the talent to explain how and why people affect history. In essence, they put flesh on the dry bones of history, and make it easier to digest.

I met both Don Hofsommer and Maury Klein through the Lexington Group at one of the wonderful, eclectic gatherings. Herb Bixler was the person who introduced me to that group some years ago. Ned Breathitt will no doubt be pleased to note that this organization was originally formed in Lexington, Kentucky, in 1942, and its membership consists of professional railroaders, railroad writers, railroad book publishers and railroad artists. It is a group that I thoroughly enjoy being a part of.

At one of the meetings I presented a brief overview of double-stack container cars. Afterwards, one of the members approached me and suggested that with my knowledge on the subject I should write a book about it. My response was to the effect that, "I would rather do it than write about it."

Later, over dinner, another fellow member took a more significant approach. He said, "You've been around intermodal a long time, and probably have a lot of friends who were in it before you." "Sure," I replied. He then asked, "How old are they?" To which my response was, "Oh, I guess most are in their seventies."

After he had finished his remarks, I looked at him and said, "I see your point. Somebody ought to do it." And just as quickly, I realized that without ever intending to do so, I had just volunteered.

So to all of those who mentored, helped, taught and drove me in intermodal, such as Bob Austill, Fred Boone, Chico Clark, Scott Corbett, Laurin Cowling, Bill Edson, Tom Fante, Tom Finkbiner, Bill Greenwood, Charlie Groton, Bob Ingram, Phil Kantz, Charlie Kaye, Norm Kirsch, Rob Krebs, Jack Lannigan, Jim McClellan (AKA "Old McMillan"), Bill Manos, R.C. Matney, Don Orris, Francis Phillips, Bob Reebie, Reggie Short, George Stern, Bill Thomford, Gordie Volkers and Bob Wharton, and to the "intrepid three," Larry Cena, Stan Crane and Dick Spence, this book is for you.

To all those who have helped fill in many of the dark corners of intermodel with photographs, recollections and sources — I say thanks. There are also many fine works that were used in preparing this manuscript. Some had opposing views to those expressed here, and many will provide an additional flavor. Secondly, there was a trove of unexpected material that became so valuable it needs separate recognition. At this time I will go on record as saying (thankfully) that Gordon Miller is the only person I have ever met who is a bigger pack rat than me. His collection of early photographs and intermodal memorabilia seems endless. I can also attest to the fact that it is very heavy stuff, having carried a good part of it from Chicago to the San Francisco Bay area and then back again. Pete Bambach provided valuable material on Gene Ryan, who was his father-in-law. Jack Lanigan gave freely of the material on Drott. Pat Cannon's NRIA oral history project was invaluable. Jim Nix was a real help on early Le Tourneau. Jim Taylor and I traded date corrections, and he also solved the mystery of the fourth president of Trailer Train. Jim Panza culled the Trailer Train company files and found some real photographic gems. Gary Towell provided a valuable unpublished manuscript on U.S. Freight. Scott Corbett supplied material on Raygo. Bob Yates gave his usual sound counsel on economics. Rocky Canzoniero whom I have known for many years, but now know even better, is a walking historical experience.

The man who must be credited with instilling in me the love and appreciation of railroad history was John W. Barriger, III. He was an avid book collector, and a speaker on all aspects of railroading. "Papa John" was a mentor to hundreds in the railroad industry, and shared his knowledge unselfishly with the juniors, thereof. In many of us he created what the Japanese will understand as an "on." That is an obligation to pass along that which has been shared with you.

Albro Martin, the Lexington Group's unofficial "Grand Old Man," shared his understanding of economics and the sweep of history. His great command of the mother tongue has been a joy. To Paul Moore, a railroader and publisher of most of the railroad tools of the trade, many thanks for suggesting the appendix scale drawings.

A special thanks to my critical manuscript readers, Bill Edson, Bill Schafer and Gordon Volkers, who came to the rescue in a way that only an author can fully appreciate.

I wish to thank the "Old Buffalo" group of the Steering Committee, Ed Frey, Roy Hayes, Bob Jabins, Paul Johnston, Bob Krehmeyer, Dennis Larsen, Jimmy Plant and Tommy Thomas. Also, our Association of American Railroads helpmates, Dan Croes and Tony Perticari, who through the years were always there and provided me with help on the history of early AAR Committees.

To all of the young intermodalists — those of you who will be responsible for the fourth part of the intermodal history — I hope every one of you will enjoy reading this history just as much as I had the pleasure and enjoyment of writing it.

A Union Pacific container train winds its way through the Nevada desert, east of Garnet, as it speeds eastbound with two "Centennial" 6900-class diesel locomotives on the head end. — UNION PACIFIC MUSEUM COLLECTION

Table of Contents

	Introduction	10
1.	The Less Than Carload Problem	13
2.	It's Soup — The First Generation	21
3.	The Amazing Mr. Ryan	27
4.	Commercial Implications	33
5.	"Load 'Em Up"	43
6.	Technology — Never Weres, WannaBes, and Sorta Weres	51
7.	The Birth of Trailer Train	67
8.	Intermodal Gains a Voice	73
9.	Trailer Leasing	77
10.	Terminal Mechanization	83
11.	United Parcel Service — The Little Brown Package Car	99
12.	Trailer Train and Gene Ryan	105
13.	Santa Fe — Super C and the Coax Train	111
14.	Federal Railroad Administration	119
15.	RoadRailer	129
16.	New Technology	135
17.	Deregulation — Free at Last	147
18.	Putting Technology to Work	151
19.	The Movement to Domestic Containers	167
20.	End of the Beginning	175
	Appendix	179
	Bibliography	184
	Index	188

Painted a brilliant red, bright yellow, and gleaming of chrome silver, are the colors of Santa Fe's intermodal locomotives. In 1990 over one million double-stack and trailers accounted for more than 35 percent of the road's revenues. This eastbound "pig" train was photographed at Sullivan's Curve of Cajon Pass, back in July of 1989. — MIKE MARTIN - SANTA FE RAILWAY

Introduction

This is a book about *intermodal*. But what is *intermodal*, and what does the word mean? Don't try to look it up in *Webster's Third New International Dictionary* as it is not there. Also, forget the encyclopedias as it is neither listed under *intermodal* nor under railroads. *Piggyback* is listed, but not *intermodal*! A Santa Fe intermodalist stated that his interpretation is, "Being or involving transportation of a container by more than one carrier during a single journey."

Webster's 1976 edition which is nearly a foot thick does list *piggyback*. It is defined as, "The process of loading, transportation and unloading of truck trailers on railroad flatcars or cars of special design." It also defines the word *container* as, "A possible metal compartment in which freight is placed for convenience of movement esp. on railroad container cars." Such is a lesson in semantics. No doubt *Webster's Fourth International Dictionary*, to be published in the year 2000, will define *intermodal*!

Neither the railroad nor the container are classified as inventions, they are merely the putting together of ideas already in existence. A railroad, after all, is merely a track on which some kind of mechanical power is used to draw cars. Both tracks and motive power were well-developed inventions before the dawn of the railroad era. They simply had not been put together.

The story of intermodal is also the combining of ideas already in existence. The container concept dates back to early Roman days. Also, the Liverpool & Manchester was using roll-on, roll-off containers for the hauling of coal by railroad in 1830. The intermodal story has not been told and is worth telling as it has revolutionized today's modern railroad industry. Intermodal now makes up over 40 percent of many Class I railroads total freight revenue.

Following World War II the message was clear. If railroads were to grow they had to win back traffic from the highways. The question was could they do it and could they make a profit? For over a century the railroads had been boxcar oriented. All freight, except liquids or bulk items such as chemicals or grain, was loaded in boxcars. As rail traffic began to take a nose dive in the late 1960's, the assumption was that what moved in a boxcar could also be transported in a box. There were strong indications that a domestic container would emerge as the standard rail vehicle of the future. Hard-line railroaders believed you were dealing with the enemy when it was suggested that railroads could carry truck trailers on flatcars. The growth of piggyback was at first a slow and hard fight, but the most surprising development of all was it ended up being new traffic and was not at the expense of the boxcar.

The piggyback concept dates back to the beginning of railroads in the 1830's. Probably one of the most colorful uses of piggyback was when P.T. Barnum used end ramps to load and unload circus wagons on and off flatcars way back in 1872. This gave rise to the term "circus loading," a common early Trailer-on-Flatcar (TOFC) practice. The piggyback revolution as we know it began in 1935 when the Chicago Great Western began to shuttle common-carrier truck trailers between Chicago and Dubuque on flatcars. The piggyback revolution has been on the rise ever since.

Who would have dreampt that a trucking executive would develop a land and water coordinated system for the transportation of freight! Malcom McLean witnessed the military containerization of war goods during World War II, and strongly believed it was a sound idea. He attempted to sell his system to the railroads and steamship lines, but it fell on deaf ears. So he purchased an old military tanker and converted it into a containership. The container revolution caught on like a wildfire. McLean's line would eventually become Sea-Land. As containerships began to proliferate in the 1960's, so did containers moving across the continent by rail.

What system of land transportation is geared to transport huge volumes of freight across the United States? Yes, the railroad. Marine containers began to appear on railroad flatcars in the 1960's. It was quickly found that intransit time could be saved by running containers coast-to-coast, rather than by ship through the Panama Canal. Thus, the "land bridge" was born. It was an intermodal movement in which containers were transferred from a ship to a train on one coast, then transported across the country to another port and placed aboard an awaiting vessel. A variation of the "land bridge" concept was the micro-bridge" where a container is transferred from a ship to a train at one port, then moved by rail to its destination.

When marine containers began to move by rail, they had to share space with truck trailers on piggyback flatcars. However, there are now dedicated trains of containers, and perhaps an even more revolutionary breatkthrough for container traffic was the development of the double-stack container car, the first car designed exclusively to carry containers.

Today's railroads are no longer a great general carrier, but rather are specialists in the transportation of bulk freight. Traditional seaports like New York, Los Angeles, San Francisco-Oakland and Seattle-Tacoma, where swarms of longshoremen would load and unload the giant ships, are now eclipsed by container terminals. The famous Panama Canal has lost its importance, and who knows what will happen when Panama assumes complete control of this waterway. The boxcar is on the endangered species list and may soon join the ranks of the stock car, caboose and steam locomotive.

Containerization is essentially a phenomenon of international trade and the development of worldwide marketing. It is an entirely new ballgame in which the railroads of America take part. This book is the intermodal story, revealing how it grew from the seed planted in the 1930's by the Chicago Great Western. Who said that the railroads were not modern enough to meet this worldwide challenge?

David J. DeBoer
Walnut Creek, California
October 1992

A scene from a more tranquil era. Here is the famous "Farmers Train" operated by the Long Island Rail Road in the 1890's to take goods loaded in wagons on flatcars to Gotham City. — DONALD DUKE COLLECTION

A Container on the Highway

Strange and wonderful intermodal ideas are not unique to the 20th century. Here's an early woodcut of a device for loading containers on railcars. — RAILWAY REVIEW

Chapter 1
The Less Than Carload Problem

Early intermodalists pointed to the Long Island Rail Road's haulage of farm wagons from Long Island to New York City in 1884, as the earliest form of piggyback. At that time the procedure was to load the wagons on flatcars and the horses and passengers on separate cars and then, the train was off for "the city." This service started to taper off in 1890 and by 1894 it completely disappeared.

Jack White of the Smithsonian, in a throughly researched article on the roots of containerization, probed back as far as Circus Maximus in Roman times. He urges the barrel as the oldest form of containerization. A British reader of *Railway Age* urged the Birmingham & Derby Junction Railway carriage of containers on flatcars, citing a tariff issued in October 1839, that quoted fares for passengers (first and second class), horses and carriages. He also points out, as an early example, the 1830 engravings of a goods station with containers being transferred to wagons in the Liverpool and Manchester areas.

For our purposes, the origin of rail intermodalism will be traced back to the first continuous use by rail of another mode's line-haul vehicles. However, other early experiments that had significant impact will also be explored.

In the overall scheme of things, intermodal was the new kid on the block, but it resided in a very old neighborhood. To understand the difficulties faced by early intermodalists, one needs to consider the historic context in which it occurred.

Railroads through the years hauled large amounts of heavy things, usually over great distances. This, they did very well. However, merchandise traffic fell out of this category very early on. Through the years it proved to be a source of great frustration for many operating people. The failure of railroaders to properly address the problem of merchandise traffic was twofold. First, much of the merchandise moved by rail was less-than-carload (LCL) — that is, the freight moved in small amounts — often only one or a few boxes at a time. In the beginning that meant taking your box to the local depot and presenting it to the agent. He would then prepare a waybill, collect the charges (or bill the receiver) and load the shipment aboard the baggage car of the local passenger train. The box was then routed to its destination, similar to the way a passenger was handled. As time went on the LCL business outgrew the space available in baggage cars. It required both specialized LCL boxcars and specialized LCL "sheds" — large warehouses in major cities where the LCL freight was sorted and moved "cross dock." This meant transferring the freight from an original car to a

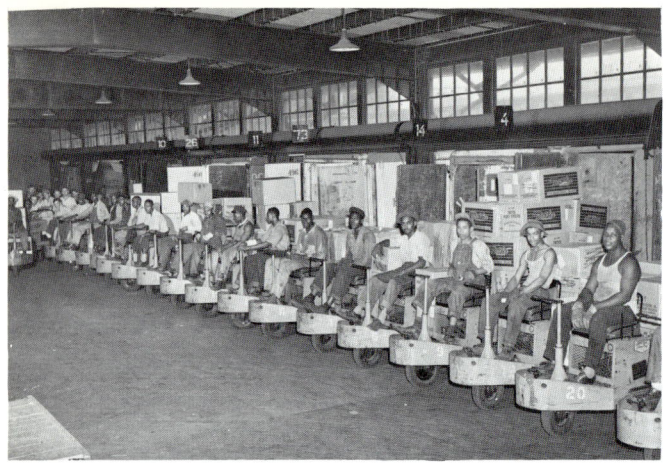

This is what the interior of a small LCL shed looked like. The 28 men lined up for this photo shows the labor intensity of railroads handling less-than-carload freight. — ROBERT KREHMEYER COLLECTION

An LCL car being loaded with a checker (background) and hand stacking. One can see why this was a labor-intensive business. — ROBERT KREHMEYER COLLECTION

destination car or an intermediate facility car. The process was the forerunner of the hub and spoke system which airlines, truckers and intermodal systems use today.

Unfortunately, several other elements inserted themselves, bringing the system to grief. One of the earliest problems was, of itself, strictly internal to the railroad. It was management's rigidity and system of keeping score. As the system grew, railroads began to measure such factors as efficiency which at first was important, then became critical and finally became ingrained. Things such as head count (employees working a location on a division or for a function), tons per car and gross ton miles per freight train hour became standards against which railroaders not only measured themselves, but also each other. These measurement criteria had a tendency to favor "efficient" commodities, i.e., those loading heavy, moving in large quantities throughout the year and traveling over long distances without "special services." LCL did not meet the first or fourth criteria and sometimes it also fell down on the third.

When dealing with LCL, operating people were faced with what they considered to be a monster. In tight times it was easy to cut back on their labor in the freight sheds since LCL cars loaded light, and LCL freight produced a "poor" tons-per-car measurement. However, when there were many LCL cars in a train (or worse, a full LCL train) this produced a poor gross ton mile per freight train hour measure. This situation led to a built-in bias against LCL within the operating department, since the operating department received no credit for the higher LCL revenue. We will see this same bias carry over to intermodal later on.

Alfred H. Smith's New York Central first embraced the concept of using wooden, and later steel, containers for handling LCL freight, following World War I. In this scene, container is being lifted from a truck at Rochester, New York, in the 1920's. — SMITHSONIAN INSTITUTION

New York Central's early container service was called the L.C.L. Company. Freight and bulk commodity containers were carried in gondolas. — GORDON VOLKERS

In an attempt to overcome LCL costs, the New York Central, in 1921, experimented with a container system. The containers were small (6x9x7.5 feet), heavy (2,800 pounds) and carried only 6,000 pounds of lading. They were designed to help overcome low equipment utilization, light loadings, high loss and damage claims and very expensive cross-dock railway labor.

Alfred H. Smith, the Central's president, was immediately attracted to the prospects of cost reduction for LCL, and, consequently, he became personally involved. The containers were originally carried in 60-foot gondola cars, equipped with express car trucks and brakes like those used in passenger service.

Service grew rapidly, attracting all types of freight. It ranged from department store fashion merchandise, U.S. Mail, freight forwarder parcels and, ultimately, to bulk goods. The latter included milk, lime, coal, cement and bricks. The LCL Corporation was established to supply the necessary boxes for such shipments. It was not long before other railroads and freight forwarders started to use their product. By 1935 LCL Corporation had more than 3,900 boxes in service.

After unsuccessfully attempting to buy into the LCL Corporation in 1928, the Pennsylvania Railroad established a similar service in 1929, calling it the Keystone Container Car Co.

The PRR containers were placed on flatcars and held in place with cast steel brackets. Unlike the Central the PRR handled most of the containers through freights houses without removing them from the cars. Nevertheless, both systems grew very rapidly.

The rapid growth of the container business was due, in part, to their unique pricing system. In those days truck pricing (and LCL on rail) was based on a class rate structure. Briefly, this arrangement took into account "rating elements" such as the value of the goods to be transported, the difficulty in handling, the danger to other goods and the distance. The class rates were designed specifically for goods moved in small lots that required cross-dock handling. Goods moved in larger carload lots were priced on so-called commodity rates which were generally much lower.

The Central began pricing LCL Corporation freight on a FAK (Freight-All-Kinds) basis, that is; the cost of shipping a whole box was figured strictly on mileage variations regardless of content. By 1927-28 the system began to gain real momentum. When the PRR entered the business it also used FAK rates. In 1931 Pennsy ordered 3,250 containers.

At this point, however, the roof fell in. Some of the competing railroads and truckers filed a complaint with the Interstate Commerce Commission (ICC). The Commission, on April 14, 1931 in its first decision ever on an intermodal concept (Docket No. 21723, *In the matter of Container Service* 173 ICC 377), found major flaws in the FAK rates, including Fourth Section violations (i.e., the long-haul, short-haul provision of the Act), and ordered the carriers to refile using class rates. The dead hand of regulation had now been placed on intermodal. It was not to be lifted for another 50 years.

The Pennsylvania Railroad also initiated "Steel Box" service. This 1931 Pullman Company photograph shows details of locking in a metal container to a flatcar. — SMITHSONIAN INSTITUTION

Acme Fast Freight Line, a large freight forwarder, used these Kellet containers made of steel and plywood to handle LCL loadings. The containers had sprung floors inside the containers in order to hold the ladings tight. — SMITHSONIAN INSTITUTION

The problem of high labor content for LCL traffic began to be compounded by increasing labor unit costs. As railroads and their economic power grew in the late nineteenth century, so did the power of rail labor. Railway labor was the first to organize an industry, first to exercise major political power and first to pass social legislation (Railroad Retirement was the precursor to Social Security).

During World War I the railroads experienced a major increase in carloadings. Unfortunately, the traffic was forwarded to the ports of embarkation in an uncoordinated manner. The ports became jammed and car shortages resulted. The carriers quickly called for emergency meetings in order to try and solve the problem. The solution, however, was very slow in coming. On December 28, 1917 the Federal Government took over the railroads, establishing the U.S. Railway Administration, and did not relinquish control until the passage of the Transportation Act of 1920.

The rising crescendo of labor's demand fell on sympathetic ears at the United States Railway Administration. Labor precedents that survive even to this day were established under McAdoo's Federal stewardship. General railroad labor rates went sky high.

Unfortunately, as a high revenue, high labor content service, LCL became an early, high visibility target for the railroad clerks. Originally an agency function, LCL initially appeared to the clerks as a natural area of growth and opportunity. They pursued it with vigor.

At the same time the young competitive highway mode arose, and with it the beginnings of the International Brotherhood of Teamsters. By the 1940's the Teamsters picked up and delivered LCL freight to rail LCL sheds, and as a result were thoroughly familiar

At Cincinnati's railroad terminal, a container is brought out to the street by an overhead crane and then lowered onto a delivery truck. — SMITHSONIAN INSTITUTION

with the job opportunities that lay in this segment of railroading. As trucking firms became larger and began to build LTL (Less-Than-Truck-Load) terminals, the railroad's LCL shed work began to look more like Teamster work to the IBT. Teamsters began to flex their muscle in union representation elections. The clerks, also busy with LCL, countered with work-rule protection which added jobs to the railroads LCL payroll. Often because of the "compromise" of having both unions in the LCL sheds, the railroads not only found themselves overmanned, but also inflexible and overpaid when compared to their trucking counterparts. This drove LCL cost to levels that left post World War II rail management totally convinced that its only solution was complete abandonment of LCL service.

California's first piggyback operation took place on the Oakland, San Leandro & Hayward Electric Ry. back in 1893. The wagon is dragged aboard the flatcar by a chain on the locomotive. — ERLE C. HANSON

As the railroads grew, so did the nation's economy. Often because of the railroads expanded economic levels and opportunites, expectations were raised to a point beyond that which a fragmented, regulated rail system could possibly deliver. This brought about the seeds of competition from a fledgling trucking industry. While at first this did not seem serious, the competitive threat increased rapidly. By 1940 almost five million trucks were on the road, and ten percent of the intercity freight was being transported by them. When the time came and trucks began to emerge as a serious competitor to railroads, the ICC stepped in and threw up a competitive umbrella in order to protect the trucking mode from predatory railroad pricing. Although seemingly well intended, the regulatory structure that emerged locked into place a system that made the railroads unable to compete for truck competitive freight.

Within the railroad rate structure, non-rail competitive local short-haul moves had to bear high rates in order to cross subsidize competitive (and thus lower priced) long-haul moves. The railroads, as common carriers, were not permitted to pick and choose their traffic. Instead, it had to haul any traffic over any distance that was presented to it, and still make an overall profit. It sounded good in theory, but impractical in the real world.

Truckers soon found that short-haul markets were easy pickings. They usually first took the branch line to branch line moves. Their next preference was the move from the major city center to the branch line. They patterned their tariffs after the railroad LCL class rate tariffs (often using ex-rail personnel), but would shave the rates and still give better service. This practice allowed the trucker to cherry-pick traffic that was most desirable and leave the rest on the rails.

Railroaders approached this problem with mixed emotions. While some of the LCL traffic was willingly surrendered to the truckers due to the large losses it incurred, the truckers were still able to cut into the LCL traffic where the railroad could make money. It became rapidly apparent to the railroads that those stations which were losing money on LCL still never lost *enough* traffic to enable them to abandon service altogether. While some of the traffic that lost money eventually went away, that which remained only incurred larger losses on the declining traffic base.

As we have seen in the early steel box container program of the New York Central and the Pennsylvania Railroad in the 1920's, railroads were always on the lookout to change the cost structure of LCL. In essence they were trying to find a way to more effectively compete with the newly emerging trucking industry.

While the Class I carriers were searching for answers to the LCL question, their smaller interurban brethren were faced with a similar situation. In their freight business, in addition to high LCL costs, the interurbans were faced with the problem of restricted clearances. The lines were lightly built, often to streetcar standards, and had primarily been designed to handle lightweight passenger cars between cities. Operation into city centers presented unique problems. In the case of the Chicago, North Shore & Milwaukee operations were conducted over the Chicago Elevated which dictated stringent clearances.

Like the Class I's, the interurban's initial response was to use small containers. The Cincinnati, Lawrenceburg & Aurora, the Detroit United, the Boston & Worcester, the Rockford & Interurban and the Cincinnati & Lake Erie all experimented with containers of various sizes.

It was Sam Insull's North Shore that put into place the major innovation which proved to be so critical to the Class I's over the last half of the twentieth century.

The North Shore had established a freighthouse on the north side of Montrose Avenue, and then contracted with truckers for their pickup and delivery. This type of setup was extremely expensive for the North Shore, especially in the very competitive LCL market. In 1920 it discontinued this operation, and established a downtown freighthouse at Franklin and Austin streets. Moves, however, were still made by truck from Montrose Avenue. While this type of operation was somewhat cheaper than the former system, the losses were still too large for the North Shore to ignore.

Thus, in 1926 the North Shore converted 26 of its old trailers and ordered 22 new special flatcars from Standard Steel Car. Consequently, they initiated ferry truck service between Milwaukee and downtown Chicago. Service was later extended to Racine, Wisconsin. An early major user of their service was

North Shore's truck ferry service for truck trailers was established in 1926, shortly after the line's new Skokie Valley Route opened for service. In this scene, two box motors handle a six-car trailer train with three containers per flatcar. — DONALD DUKE COLLECTION

Two North Shore trailers ride a Standard Steel Co. flatcar built in April 1926 to handle the line's new "Merchandise Despatch" service. The cars, in the scene above, each carried two trailers. — WILLIAM D. MIDDLETON COLLECTION

In 1926 the North Shore established its own downtown freight house below Chicago's elevated. The trailers were smaller than regular highway trailers because of tight clearances on the "L" and underneath the elevated structure. — WILLIAM D. MIDDLETON COLLECTION

Sears, Roebuck & Company.

The depression placed additional competitive pressures on the North Shore, and in 1932 it responded to the decrease in business by opening its ferry truck service to common carrier truckers and private shippers. Business increased from 2,967 trailers in 1932 to 6,504 in 1933. In that same year the regulatory agency of the "Progressive" state of Wisconsin prohibited the common carrier truckers from using the service. They based it on the grounds that it was being used to avoid the state's gross ton-mile highway-user fees. The ironies of the wrong headed, albeit historic regulation screamed out even decades later. This caused business to drop to only 75 trailer loads in 1935. The order was lifted in 1936 when traffic increased to 733 trailers. By 1943 traffic had risen to 18,314 trailers, the zenith for the service.

After the war, highway improvements, opposition from the Teamsters, the general availability of fuel and tires and a short stage length, all combined to reduce traffic to an unprofitable level. On April 28, 1947 the North Shore cancelled its tariff and withdrew its ferry truck service.

In the mid-1970's a company ran an advertisement, showing a mother bending over a pot on the stove and a young boy asking her, "Is it soup yet?" An explanation is due as to why the 1926 North Shore's service did not qualify as "intermodal soup."

First, the trailers that were used had to be specialized in size to meet the severe Chicago Elevated clearance restrictions. Secondly, the service did not continue to the present time (including by successor companies). So, while clearly critical to the process, intermodal "creation" would wait for another decade.

It did not take others in the interurban fraternity that long to see the value of the service. In 1927 the Chicago

The Cincinnati, Lawrenceberg & Aurora Railroad introduced one of the nation's first "intermodal" services because its standard gauge cars could not operate on Cincinnati's broad-gauge streetcar tracks. In this scene, a 5-ton container is being lifted from a truck and placed aboard one of the railway's electrical motorized flatcars. — ROBERT G. LEWIS COLLECTION

A photograph of Chicago, South Shore & South Bend Railroad's piggyback trailer pit at South Bend in 1934. The tracks were lowered for a direct drive-on. — WILLIAM D. MIDDLETON COLLECTION

South Shore & South Bend initiated "Ferry Truck" service with overnight service between South Bend and Chicago. It lasted into the middle 1930's before being discontinued.

The Depression of the 1930's put a multiple squeeze on the railroads, and it embodied three elements. The largest and most obvious problem was the massive fall off of economic activity, and the attendant reduction of rail revenues.

The second issue occurred in the cost area. For railroads, revenue cuts of 50 percent were not uncommon. However, costs rarely fell as rapidly as the revenues which resulted in a serious lack of cash, leaving little for productivity improvements. This in turn placed additional pressure on costs as rail assets aged over the decade of the 1930's. Finally, in addition to the natural loss of revenues due to the fall in the economy, truckers were getting hungry and began cutting into rail revenues even further.

Cleveland's Lake Shore Electric operates this Bonner Rail Wagon in overnight service between Cleveland and Toledo. Inside bearing trucks permitted the truck trailer wheels to straddle the special flatcar. — WILLIAM D. MIDDLETON COLLECTION

Circus loading an open top trailer with a tarp at the Chicago Great Western ramp in Minneapolis. This little midwestern carrier started the first use of piggyback, using standard highway trailers, in July of 1936. — WILLIAM D. MIDDLETON

Chapter 2

It's Soup — The First Generation

Intermodal was just waiting to be born. Apparently, what was needed in the Class I ranks was a railroad that was broke — and knew it. It had to be a road that needed revenues so badly that it would be willing to throw the book away. A perfect candidate was the Chicago Great Western Railroad. John Barriger had characterized it as "...a mountain railroad in a prairie country serving a traffic vacuum."

It was never a strong road. Prior to the Depression it had been acquired by the head of Standard Steel Car Company who placed it in a holding company, and bled off all its meager assets. And then in 1935 it went bankrupt.

In any case the "Great Weedy" suffered no pretentions of its larger brothers. Their situation never included learned discussions of traffic theory. This property needed one thing — cash flow. Probably, more to the point — it knew it.

Innovation is often the result of such a problem. The Traffic Department forces in Chicago had noted the success that nearby interurbans had accomplished with the truck "train ferry" service. Maybe it would work for them.

They wired a report to the Bankruptcy Trustee Patrick Joyce (who also was the purchaser of the Great Western, and the one who had put the railroad in bad straits in the first place), but found he was too busy fighting fires to handle their project. So he, Joyce, passed the "train ferry" project off to an able young assistant named Sam Golden. Golden was a tall, affable and very bright young man who had come to the railroad from Standard Car. He had graduated from Wharton School, and established a reputation at Standard Car as a good numbers guy as well as an innovator. Interestingly, it was Standard Steel Car who supplied the North Shore and the South Shore with the flatcars for their ill-fated Ferry Truck Service.

Even though he was a non-railroader, Sam Golden quickly recognized the need for help from the railroad itself. He tapped two stalwarts from the CGW's Oelwein Shops, the Car Department Superintendent G.P. Hoffman and L.E. "Pat" Hilsabeck, the general car inspector.

Hilsabeck was particularly valuable to the cause, having spent the previous season escorting Ringling Brothers and Barnum & Bailey Circus around the property. During that time he was able to observe the "circus loading" techniques and the methods they used for equipment tie-down while out on the road. This information would later come in handy.

Golden who needed to "get the show on the road" decided to try a live experiment with highway trailers.

He went to the Chicago-Dubuque Motor Transportation Company in hopes of borrowing a highway trailer, chocks, chains and binders of the type used by Ringling Brothers. Accomplishing his mission, he was able to outfit a standard 40-foot flatcar for the test. The trailers, loaded circus style, were backed up a ramp and onto the end of a flatcar. Then they were backed across bridge plates between the cars. The car was run in the Oelwein-Dubuque local for several trips without mishap. This new chain-down method eliminated the previous need for specialized flatcar equipment used by the interurbans.

The truckers watched the experiment with great interest. As the railroad demonstrated physical handling capabilities, the Chicago-Dubuque Motor Transportation approached Golden and told him that they would be interested in a Chicago-Dubuque service if Great Western would provide ramps (the inevitable name for an early intermodal terminal), cars and reasonable rates.

In 1933 the rate problem had proven to be the stumbling block for the New York Central and the Pennsy — the eastern colossi. However, in 1935 Congress had seen fit to pass the Motor Carrier Act, and the CGW, desperate for revenue, fixed a joint rail-motor carrier tariff. The effort passed muster, and the Oelwein Shop forces were asked to outfit ten standard flatcars. In order to do this the shop forces used chains and binders that they had on hand, plus screw jacks from Templeton, Kenly & Company. Using this patented securement system, the great experiment was launched. It was adopted, at least in part, by most roads into the 1950's with royalty payments going to the Chicago Great Western.

In the summer of 1935 the CGW moved Chicago-Dubuque Motor Transportation Company trailers between the trucker's corporate namesake cities for a charge of $42 per trailer. But by the time the leaves were changing color in the fall, the truckers had returned to the highway.

Golden was not discouraged. He was sure that if this trucker and this lane didn't work, surely there had to be another trucker and another lane that would. Besides, he already had ten cars equipped with chains and binders.

Golden turned the Traffic Department's sales force loose. It was not long before the same Chicago people who had spotted the interurban experiment were locked into the Illinois-Minnesota Motor Carrier Conference. Tariffs were filed with the ICC in May of 1936, and arrangements to borrow an additional 40 flats were made with the Chicago & Eastern Illinois Railroad.

Service started on July 7, 1936, and the era of intermodal as we know it today began. Service from the beginning was run in dedicated trains as second sections of passenger service. For the most part the securement devices that had originally been designed by Hoffman & Hilsabeck remained unchanged. The only modification was to go from a single to a double screw jack arrangement for the front of the trailer. As other railroads introduced intermodal service during the next 20 years, the basic CGW system for trailer securement was used with some modifications.

The CGW approach to tying down trailers has been characterized by some as "belt and suspenders" and by others as "bombproof." The acid test of the securement system occurred five months after the startup of service. A cornfield meet happened between the CGW's intermodal flyer and a Milwaukee Road passenger train at New Hampton, Iowa, north of Oelwein. The passenger train was traveling between 50 and 60 m.p.h at time of impact. The wreck left five dead, six injured and both engines destroyed. Although the center sills on some of the flatcars buckled, the trailers remained in place. However, some of the trailers' noses and doors were blown out by the shifting loads.

Even with the CGW's experience other railroads' mechanical and operating departments were still not convinced, and wanted to make absolutely certain that trailers were secure on the flatcars. In later trains trailers that had obviously been in a derailment emerged looking like they had been smitten by the hand of God. Note is made, however, that all securment devices were still in place.

This virtual paranoia with another mode's vehicles led each road to slightly modify the CGW loading tie-down approach. These modifications in turn led to the need for the ramps to match up specific trailers with specific flatcars being returned. However, all of this was to come later. In 1936 the only road handling intermodal traffic was the CGW, and all moves were single line hauls.

In the month of August 1936 the trailer business produced 870 loads for CGW. While seemingly successful, two factors emerged at this early date to cause the other Class I roads to give pause. Comments eminating from transportation types about the high horsepower per ton requirements and "efficiency" were to be expected. An interesting objection came from the Minneapolis Traffic Association and the St. Paul Chamber of Commerce. It was their contention that the new service would deprive the area of boxcars for grain loading at harvest time.

In any case the Chicago Great Western, in its pioneering effort, would remain alone for more than a year. Beginning in 1937 the Denver & Rio Grande

The New Haven was the second Class I railroad to initiate piggyback service in December of 1937. Here a New Haven piggyback train using standard flatcars, running between Boston and New York, crosses an inlet at Cos Cob on the 4-track electrified zone of the main line. — JIM SHAUGHNESSY

Western, for a time, operated trailers between Denver and Grand Junction with its own LCL freight, and in 1938 the Rock Island established a brief trailer service. But in December of 1937, another perennially troubled road, the New York, New Haven & Hartford, joined the "Great Weedy" as the second Class I to seriously try "train ferry" service.

As it entered the intermodal scene, the New Haven situation was very different from that of the Midwest pioneer. On the East Coast the New Haven with its short-haul routes from New York to New England suffered from many forms of competition. Interurbans, buses and airplanes gnawed at its passenger business and trucks ate steadily into its freight service. The New Haven's initial response in the passenger area was to co-opt the competition through purchase. They bought interurbans, bus lines and even attempted to buy an airline. Nevertheless, the truckers soon began to cut into their freight revenues, causing the New Haven to try some other tack that would not have such a severe impact on the balance sheet.

In the latter part of 1936 a contingent from the New Haven went west to visit the Chicago Great Western's intermodal operation. The group included Trainmaster Jim Farley, Traffic Department officer Dan Sundel and Operating Department representative Rocky Canzoniero. They were impressed with what they saw.

Upon their return Farley and Canzoniero set to work establishing terminals — Farley on the north end of the railroad and Canzoniero on the south end. Master Mechanic George Goebel worked with truckers to add lashing rings to their trailers. Meanwhile, Sundel concentrated on the commercial end.

The New Haven needed revenue — and needed it badly. Everyone agreed that the truckers, using joint rates, offered the best source for a quick revenue boost and, thus, the New York-Boston run looked like a natural. But Sundel still wanted to maintain contact with some of his large on-line shippers such as Sears and Pepsi Cola. The New Haven developed a rate for the truckers that allowed them to have one empty trailer for each load they shipped. Shippers were not as fortunate. They only had rates for loaded trailers. The first non-common carrier trucker business, although small, was from the beginning developed by the New Haven. This would set into motion a whole new chain

of events. Offering both common carrier truck and shipper service, the New Haven initiated Trailiner service on December 15, 1937, and planted yet another basic intermodal seed. In 1938 the New Haven handled 1,506 piggyback loads.

Piggyback service on the New Haven went into a bit of a shell during World War II, but fortunately had already gained a real foothold. Service between New York and Boston was expanded to New York-Providence and New York-Springfield. For this service the New Haven Shops built 325 50-foot flatcars.

After the war things picked up where they left off. Loadings in 1949 totalled 17,679 trailers. Physically, however, the business was not much different from that of the Chicago Great Western. The 50-foot cars loaded one "long" 28-foot trailer or a mix of two short 24-foot or 26-foot trailers. They were secured by the standard screw jacks, chains, binders and trailer rings developed by the CGW.

By 1952 business had grown to the point that the New Haven bought 200 new flatcars to handle the increased volume. But in a tip of the hat to the "practical" naysayers, the New Haven spokesman noted that "The cars are capable of being converted quickly and easily to regular railroad interchange service if desired." Clearly, even on the New Haven, not everyone was a believer.

In 1953 New Haven found it necessary to buy 100 more flatcars — this time they were the new lightweight Clejan cars. Their new business now included storage

Boston & Maine handled the Endy Brothers Show, one of the nation's first piggyback operations, as it pulls into Deerfield Junction, Massachusetts, back in 1948. — DONALD ROBINSON

Looking like it was smitten by the hand of God, this trailer appears to still be completely secure on the flatcar. The trailer rides on a 50-foot flatcar equipped with a kingpin grabber so it probably belongs to the Pennsylvania Railroad — GORDON C. MILLER COLLECTION

mail for the U.S. Post Office. It had become by far the largest rail hauler of trailers in the U.S. with 50,000 trailer loads handled that year alone.

The next carrier to dabble in intermodal was the Chicago, Burlington & Quincy Railroad. This, however, was no surprise since from its inception the CB&Q had been an innovative railroad. As was the case with most of the other rail carriers who had gone into intermodal, their basic motive was also the reduction of LCL costs. The trucking company organized in 1935 was to be used as a delivery agent from LCL sheds to branch line points. By 1939 the "Q" had begun to test piggyback. In the summer of 1940 they began to offer regular piggyback service between Chicago and Kansas City. The truckers supplied trailers, chains and binders and did the loading and unloading services. Burlington had a basic hook and haul arrangement.

Intercity trucking by 1940 had increased 400 percent from 1920 and had put five million trucks on the road. With the imminent approach of World War II, however, the "Q" concentrated on moving tonnage. Piggyback had to take a back seat. While service had been operated by the Burlington on a continuous basis since 1940 only 800 trailers were in operation by 1954. Thus, although the Burlington was considered a pioneer in piggyback, they still started about even with the rest of the Class I's in the mid-1950's.

Having watched its two neighbors, the Chicago Great Western and the Burlington, get into the piggyback business, the Chicago & Eastern Illinois decided to take the plunge in 1952. Always considered to be an "average" carrier, the C&EI did serve as the place where young, yet to be famous rail executives like John Budd, Downing Jenks and John Barriger cut their teeth.

The C&EI was never a leader or innovator in technology or on the commercial front, but it did generate several thousand carloads of trailer freight. For a brief while it was ranked as the nation's third largest piggyback carrier just behind the New Haven and the Chicago Great Western, but ahead of the mighty Burlington. This was, perhaps, the only time that the C&EI would ever be a big fish in a small pond.

An early Chicago, Burlington & Quincy piggyback load being switched at Fort Collins, Colorado, by Colorado Southern 2-8-0 No. 644 in 1957. The flatcar is equipped with solid bearings and still appears to have a "disaster cable" attached to the rear of the trailer frame (above the "C" of CB&Q of the car reporting mark). — ROSS GRENARD COLLECTION

In happier days, Gene Ryan (right) poses with New York Central officials on a summer day in Buffalo, New York, alongside Star Service Trailers. Note the Fruehauf trailers. Don Fruehauf was an early intermodal booster. GORDON C. MILLER COLLECTION

Chapter 3

The Amazing Mr. Ryan

As piggyback began its early rise it was not difficult to identify those on the railroad who were supportive — they were generally that small group off in the corner at whom the rest of the railroad was throwing rocks. In that generally hostile environment some notably staunch defenders of intermodal arose both outside the railroad and outside the intermodal industry.

Such a person was Gene Ryan. Ryan, the natty, silver-haired heir to a wealthy family-owned cabinet-making company, decided to eschew the family business and go to work for General Motors. He worked as a Zone Manager for the Chevrolet Truck Division and later for GMAC. While he was successful and highly regarded at General Motors, the pace at GM was just to slow to hold his interest. He decided to strike out onto new ground. This ground would be where he could apply his considerable sales talent and his leasing knowledge acquired at GMAC. It had to be to a company where he could run his own show.

Ryan spent a short stint in 1950 working for transportation consultants in Chicago. While there, he tackled a railroad assignment to study the handling of LCL freight. He visited the Chicago Great Western and the New Haven to observe their physical operations. He talked to the early intermodalists about the constraints. He talked to his old friends and customers in the trucking fraternity. The intermodal bug had bit. Ryan quit the consulting firm and formed his own company in 1951.

He quickly began looking for allies. Pullman Inc. gave him a consulting retainer, and this was enough to enable him to open an office.

Ryan's fascination with piggyback was the forerunner of an unending push to apply new technology and management techniques to this emerging phenomenon. He quickly recognized the fragmentation that had existed in the early efforts, and understood that loading one trailer on a flatcar was a money-losing proposition. Also, he was very aware of the fact that some railroads were reluctant to spend money on what they considered a "flash in the pan" called piggyback.

It was not long before Ryan came upon an idea that he deemed to be an opportunity of a lifetime. It was the establishment of a company that would have the ability to solve one or maybe even all of the railroad's previous problems with piggyback. As a result he started the Rail-Trailer Company in 1952, and set out to conquer the world of piggyback.

His early attempts at improving piggyback had found a great deal of sympathy among several old GM colleagues. An early supporter was Nelson Dezendorff,

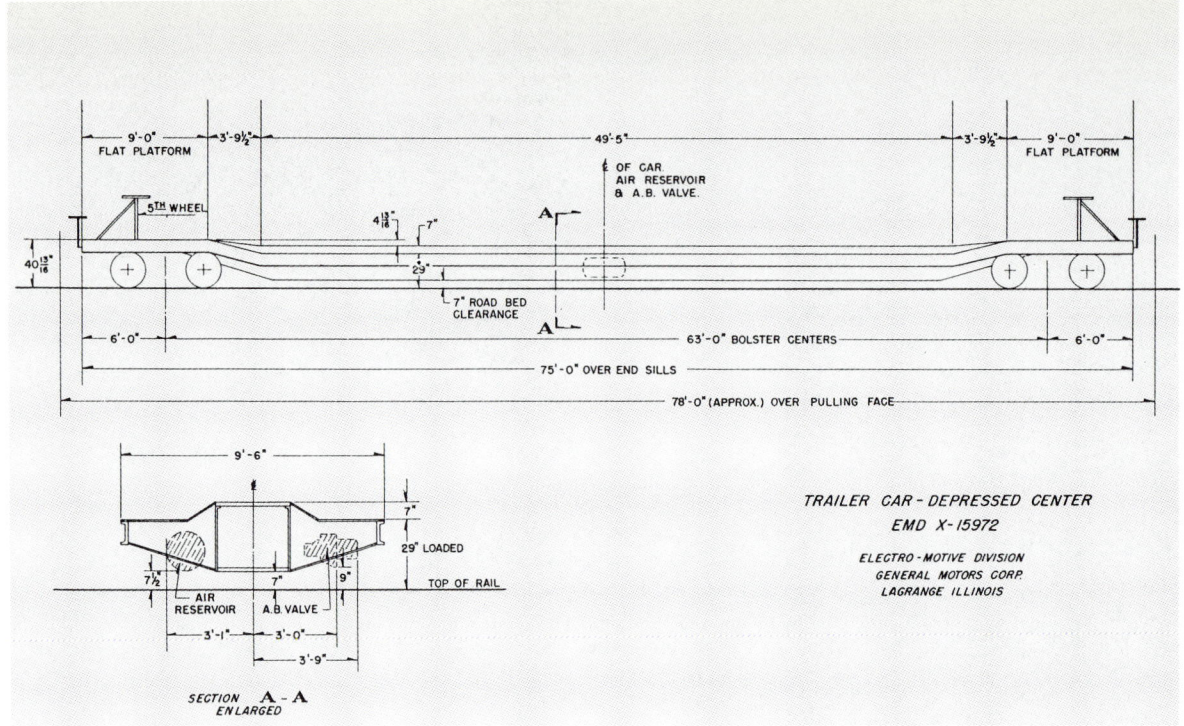

a former GM Group vice president, who later became a board member of Rail Trailer.

Other supporters were Cy Osborn and Paul Turner of GM's Electro-Motive Division. Osborn was EMD's general manager and Turner was the general sales manager. This was during the halcyon days of the conversion from steam to diesel, and EMD was the major advocate and beneficiary of this trend. What could be more natural than for GM to throw its technological weight behind the latest in railcar as well as locomotive technology?

The EMD engineers pursued their work with great enthusiasm. The program was dubbed the "Rail Highway Coordination Program." According to a later EMD brochure, "It is designed to overcome the disadvantages basic in present services where only one standard size highway semi-trailer can be carried per car." In addition it saw problems "...where trailer-carrying cars are handled in main classification yards as part of the regular freight service and end-loaded circus' fashion...Time schedules of these services discourage their wide usage by motor carriers."

The answer as designed by EMD was the Trailer Transport car hauled on Trailer Transport trains. GM was assigned the task of solving the engineering problems. However, as the EMD engineers saw it three problems still needed to be addressed.

The first problem was to design a car that could load two 35-foot highway semi-trailers while still meeting uniform clearances of the railroads. Since this was in the days prior to multi-level car usage, this, indeed, was a tall order.

Plans from a Electro-Motive pamphlet show concept drawings for General Motors/Ryan piggyback car. — GORDON C. MILLER COLLECTION

Radical 75-foot car, the X15972, built by General Motors Electro-Motive Division in 1953, sits in the snow on a yard track. The car is equipped with non-rotating roller bearings, fixed stanchion end-of-car trailer hitches and raised center section. Note the "disaster chains" mid-car that were required to be attached to the rear of the trailer. —GORDON C. MILLER COLLECTION

(LEFT) "Here's trouble!" Gene Ryan explains fine points to Al Perlman, new president of the New York Central System. Ryan's Star Service contract was signed with Bill White as president of the NYC. After a spirited and successful proxy fight by Robert R. Young, Perlman became NYC's prexy. Perlman canceled Ryan's contract. (ABOVE) Gene Ryan points out the single-point tie-down hitch on EMD X-15972 to a pair of railroad worthies after signing contract with the NYC to initiate Star Service. — BOTH GORDON C. MILLER COLLECTION

Secondly, a device was required which would speed up the loading process by eliminating circus loading (and its attendant costly and time-consuming switching). The third and last problem they felt was the development of special terminals which would not only increase piggyback efficiency, but it would result in getting piggybacking out of carload freight yards.

By May of 1953 GM had the prototype railcar "in iron" in the form of EMD X-15972. The car was a depressed center flatcar (with a deck height 29 inches above the top of the rail) with fixed stanchions mounted at each end of the car. The stanchions were equipped with rubber shock absorbers which allowed up to four and one-half inches of travel, and it appears to have been the first cushioned trailer hitch. The lightweight car was 75 feet long and had a weight of 74,600 pounds. It had a sloping raised center section to prevent trailer movement and, as an acknowledgement to past railroad "belt and suspenders" practice, a pair of hydraulic tie-downs which came up to the sides of each trailer.

Loading of the car was provided by a large, yard-type forklift dubbed a Trailoader built by Clark Equipment Company. The Trailoader had a front end with the forks modified to meet at a point in front of the lift truck. On the merged forks a pin had been welded in place to fit in a hole drilled 18 inches in front of the kingpin in the towing plate of the trailer. The forks had a five-inch lateral movement to allow seating of the kingpin in the stanchion.

As we will see much of what evolved later was in actuality embodied in this early EMD system.

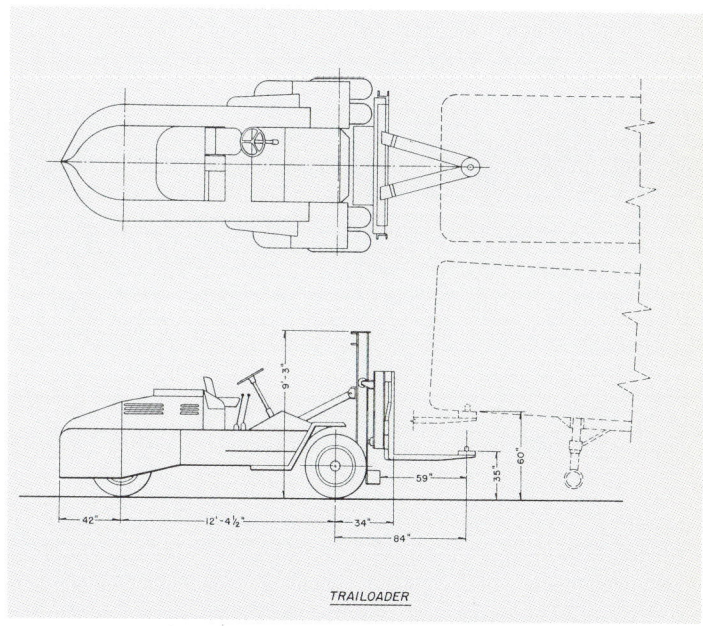

Drawing from an EMD brochure of the Trailoader - later built by Clark equipment for loading and unloading trailers on the EMD car. — GORDON C. MILLER COLLECTION

29

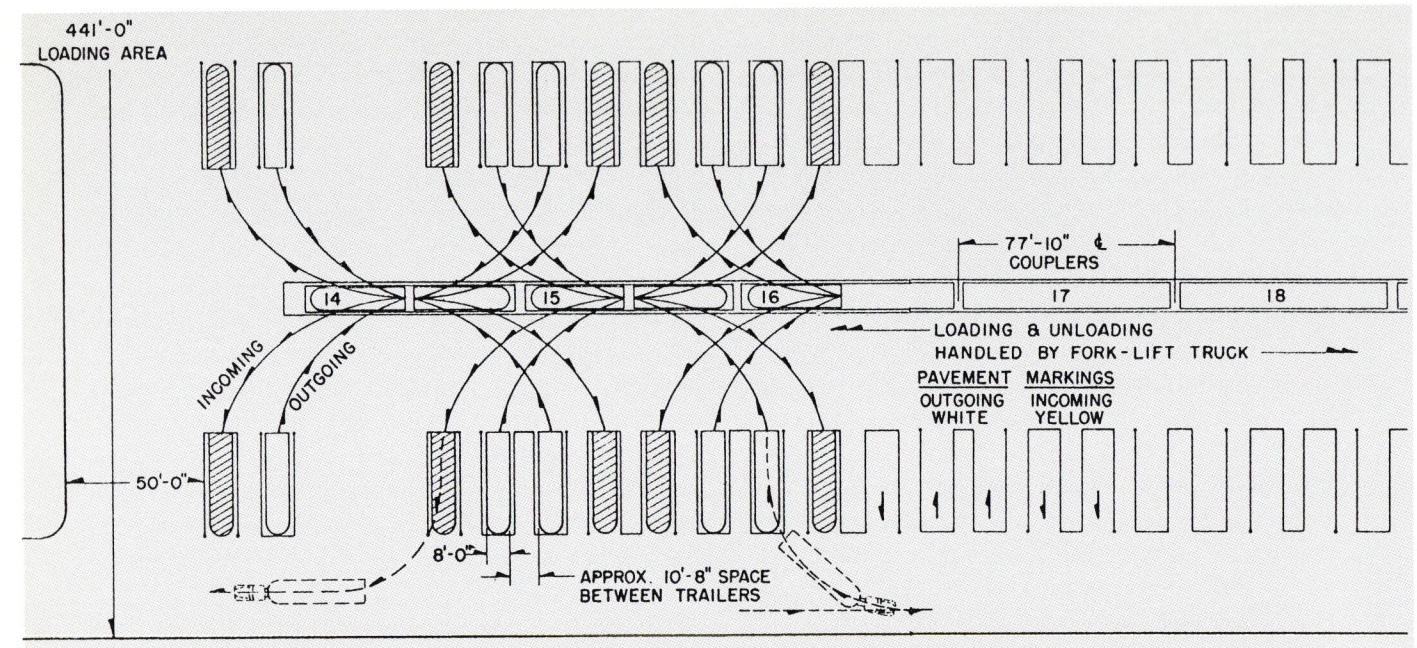

General Motor engineers also designed terminals for use with their cars. Note simple track arrangement with adjacent parking which is far more efficient than remote lots that soon developed with circus-style unloading. — GM RAIL-HIGHWAY COORDINATION BOOKLET

Unfortunately, this system required the use of a Trailer Transport Terminal to make it work. The terminal required that load-out ramp areas adjacent to the cars be the same level as the deck height of the cars. While this appealed to the engineers, in that it allowed for the simultaneous loading of cars, it also required a large capital outlay wherever the cars were to be used.

One of the terminal designs even showed a through track setup to minimize switching. As GM said "...no attempt has been made to discuss the economics to railroads and motor carriers inherent in Rail Highway Coordination. Rather, emphasis has been devoted entirely to solutions, as General Motors sees them, to the mechanical problems incident to successful operation of such a service." Unfortunately, it flew in the face of what was then the current railroad plans and implementation policies for piggyback.

The EMD car was shown at the 1952 Railroad Mechanical Officers Convention. In this early period, if railroads were getting into piggyback at all (and many were not), they were joining with great reluctance. Operating departments were loath to spend any capital money on piggyback. Ramps were generally stuck into the corner of a declining operation in the middle of a city. This usually meant a former passenger coach yard here, an under-utilized engine roundhouse area there or sometimes just next to the local depot.

Traffic departments had an even worse relationship with the emerging technology. Like a schizoid personality they saw piggyback as a threat to boxcar revenues, but in the next instance they viewed it as a way to get lost LCL and merchandise traffic back from the highway. Eventually, it proved to be more difficult to oppose piggyback since it was considered "a modern trend" in an old industry. To be against it, according to popular opinion, was regarded as anti-progressive.

Ryan plunged ahead with the Trailer Transport car. When attempting to sell his concept it was only natural to court the "GM roads," i.e., those roads who did heavy business with General Motors. One such road was the New York Central.

His approach to the New York Central was from the top — Chairman William White. Ryan's idea was simple. Let Rail-Trailer not only run the operation, but also build the terminals for the Central. Rail-Trailer would act as their agent to the truckers that Central had hoped to attract. Ryan felt that this would not be difficult since he knew many of them from his old GM Truck Division days. The truckers would be required to supply their own trailers, and Rail-Trailer would join with the Central and any other connecting road that cared to join in setting up a company to operate a pool of flatcars for the service.

White liked the plan. The old Alfred Smith desire to get LCL costs under control still simmered within the breasts of the New York Central men. In addition rumors abounded that the Wall Street maverick Robert R. Young was about to take a run at the Central. If that happened the somewhat stuffy Central could use any modern system that Rail-Trailer and Ryan might bring to the party. The fact that GM was involved didn't hurt either.

In 1953 the Central men and Ryan worked out a program that was dubbed Star Service. Ryan would build and finance the terminals, and his reimbursement would be figured on a per trailer basis much like a sidetrack agreement. As a subsidiary of Rail-Trailer Ryan established Van-Car for the purpose of purchasing the GM flatcars (initially slated at 200). He also inked the deal with the Central to establish a flatcar pool.

Then, Robert R. Young struck with a vengeance. The Central was at one time one of the bluest of the blue chip corporations in America, but it had fallen on extremely hard times. Battered by postwar inflation, labor demands, rate regulations and truck and air competition, the Central was not prepared for a Robert R. Young takeover and was slow to react. Basically, it was considered a genteel giant (a Vanderbilt still sat on the board of directors), but unfortunately it was in a time of immense change.

For Young this was merely grist for his mill. In April of 1954 he launched a proxy fight for control of the Central. The stakes were high. Young employed the services of Thomas J. Degan, a fiery public relations man, and White, chairman of the New York Central, countered with James A. Farley, former postmaster general under Franklin Roosevelt. The fight lasted two months and it was a real humdinger. Both sides received massive press coverage. In the end, on June 14, 1954, Young was the winner.

Robert R. Young then proceeded to hire Alfred E. Perlman, the young operating general manager from the Denver & Rio Grande Western as president. Ryan, not easily dissuaded, attempted to sell Perlman on the same concept he had originally presented to the New York Central. Unfortunately for Ryan, Perlman considered him tainted by the White regime, and Ryan was soon an early victim of the "new broom." Perlman, desperately short on cash, nixed the Rail-Trailer deal and, instead, substituted speeded up manifest boxcar train schedules. Ryan, in spite of what had transpired earlier, was not about to give up on his new fledgling, as we shall shortly see.

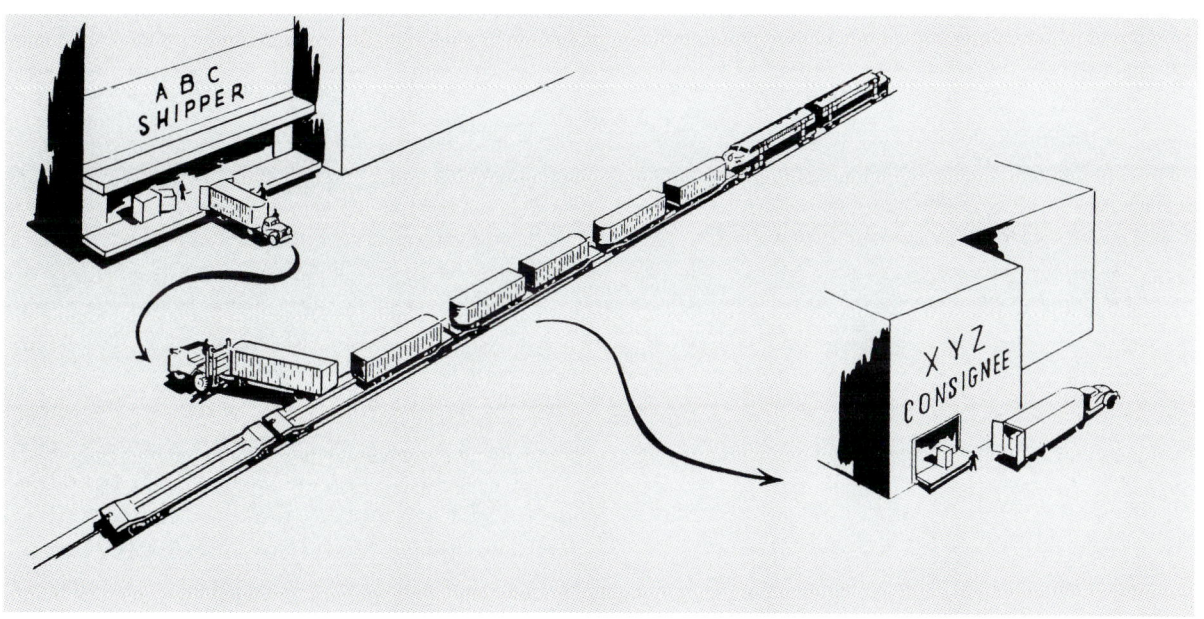

The system components as envisioned by General Motors engineers. Unfortunately, the terminals required expensive depressed tracks or built-up ramps parallel to the car to allow loading/unloading. This fact led to the demise of the concept. — GM RAIL-HIGHWAY COORDINATION BOOKLET

Commercial dealing proceeded at a low key on piggyback in the 1950's. That is until Donald J. Russell's Southern Pacific threw down the gauntlet and established SP piggyback service which was not available to truckers. Here an SP pig train rolls past a brand new '55 Ford (next to the pickup) on San Fernando Road on a clear day in Los Angeles. And how about that Studebaker convertible three cars back. — SOUTHERN PACIFIC

Chapter 4

Commercial Implications

Up until now we have been mainly concentrating on the physical and operating side of the business. However, the major impact on intermodal's growth and development actually came from the commercial side.

The various early attempts by railroads to control LCL costs have also been reviewed. A side effect of this effort was the railroad's urging that freight forwarders and brokers (third parties) be established to handle the retail operation (i.e., the direct relationship with the shipper or beneficial owner of the freight) in lieu of the railroad's historic traffic and agency functions. This produced a proprietary feeling on the part of the third parties that the freight being handled was ''their'' freight. The relationship between the railroads and the third parties was much more straightforward when the LCL movements were by boxcar, a time when all movements were cross-docked in the forwarders' facilities. Often the railroads leased these terminals to third parties at a bargain rate in order to help cement relations. Since the cross-dock terminal was generally served only by the leasing carrier, the association was mutually beneficial — and clearly so. In fact the largest forwarder, U.S. Freight, was owned for a time by New York Central.

When third parties expanded into areas beyond those served by the rail carriers with whom they had originally worked, this enabled them to play one rail carrier against another. This was the onset of the first natural tension between carriers and third parties.

The earliest rail carrier in intermodal (the Chicago Great Western) set up a program with truckers that provided basic terminal and line-haul service. The trucker provided the trailer, the cross-dock operation (if needed) and the basic retail connection with the shipper. As the service grew the tensions between the trucker and the third parties increased due to the fact that each was a customer of the railroad. One in trailers and one in boxcars. They were both actually competing for the same freight. Their only recourse was to come back at the underlying rail carrier in an attempt to gain a rate advantage over their competition. If one of them used volume as an argument for a rate reduction, then the other would rely on its long-standing relationships.

The tension that evolved within the railways themselves was not so obvious. They were able to use truckers or third parties to do the retail work, and thus cut out the traditional Traffic Department's job of calling directly on the shipper. Since the agency's job generally took place in the operating area and would involve the customer at the local level, it also had a negative impact on the Operating Department. The tension on all sides grew very acute when further complications occurred as the traffic and operating functions of the railroad continued to interface with the shipper when he originated carload shipments, but not for his LCL or piggyback.

Traffic Departments tended to make calls on their "new" customers — the third parties and the truckers. In general the kinship that developed with the third parties was easier since many of the founding and active third-party people were former railroaders. Often relationships with the truckers were initiated by non-railroaders such as Golden at the Chicago Great Western and later Ryan at Rail-Trailer. When traffic increased under the Ryan Plan (later Plan I), so did the opposition from the third parties and those within the railroad traffic and operating organizations. They disliked this growing opposition mode (and the outside facilitators), feeling that the railroads should "control their own destiny," and that the railroads should "do it ourselves and not waste the profits."

As was pointed out earlier, there was substantial sentiment in the operating departments against *all* lightweight freight. A segment of the operating department, however, actually felt some sympathy for the trucker. At least the trucker supplied his own trailers and, thereby, shared some of the basic commercial risk with the railroads. Later, this would become a key point of tension with the third parties.

Complicating matters on the commercial side was the ICC's stifling of the railroad's early endeavors to get LCL costs under control. The previous unsuccessful efforts of the Central and Pennsy to establish FAK rates (Freight-All-Kinds), in lieu of commodity rates for movement of this freight, was a factor which led directly to the Chicago Great Western's attempt to utilize the joint rate approach with its regional truckers.

After World War II inflation rapidly drove costs upward for both the railroads and truckers. Labor costs, the biggest component of the truckers' total operating expense, was their greatest concern. Any competitive edge that could be gained by using rail, at least for a part of the line haul, was certainly worth a try. Truckers pressed for meetings with railroads — those that offered piggyback and those that did not. This tended to stir debate within the railroad industry, focusing attention on the piggyback concept. A number of railroader's Operating Departments were annoyed by the service that the truckers required them to give in order to be competitive with their highway brethren. Many Traffic Departments were also irritated with the idea of being cut off from their customers, invasion of their territory and of the overall effect that the new service (and control of pricing by the trucker) would have on their carload rate structures.

The issue of territorial invasion that had been fought most vigorously happened between 1880 and 1920 when the rail barons laid track into each other's territory, upsetting established competitive balance and pricing relationships. This, for some railroads, led to price rebating, hard times and financial ruin. Ultimately, it resulted in the establishment of the Interstate Commerce Commission in an effort to combat some of the symptoms of excessive competition, including "invasion of territory."

The Traffic Departments also tried to do their part by starting rate bureaus which operated with highly structured procedures. This was effective, and helped to slow the pricing process down to a crawl. It subjected prospective rate-cutters to immense peer pressure and to a long series of procedural hurdles. One should not conclude that rate cutting was dead, but it certainly was under control better than it had ever been in the history of the railroads. Anything that could possibly upset this carefully crafted equilibrium was not to be taken lightly.

"If the trucker originated freight in some other railroad's territory," went the argument, "wasn't this as bad as a railroad building track there?" "Well, the trucker has the freight now anyway," went the response, "so why don't we get a piece back for the railroad?" "Well, what about helping the enemy?"

Railway Age, in 1952, sagely observed:

> For the reason [lack of mutual affection], as much as many others, [piggybacking] has been and is opposed on many railroads which ought to be able to generate a large traffic in the movement of trucker's trailers. It might profitably be recalled that not all alliances of mutual advantage are contracted for reasons of affection — there are also what the French call marriages of convenience!'

And so, the debate continued.

However, as the decade of the 1950's rolled around two groups began to force the issue. In that era the railroads and what they did or did not do were big news for the American public. A railroad president's pronouncements normally received major news coverage as did the statements of labor, political and economic leaders who voiced their views about the railroads. Piggyback, the new kid on the block, really tickled their fancy. Even the name itself was evocative. Maybe just the suggestion of it would help to get some of those darned trucks off the highway. Basically, it was felt that the real problem centered with what they considered to be a group of old stick-in-the-mud traffic types, and if in fact this was the case, then somebody ought to do something about it.

Which leads us to the second group, the railroad presidents. Although public comments by this group about piggyback were admittedly small in number, some of the railroad presidents were listening to the public clamor about this "natural combination of functions." Also, the question arose, what about the serious financial drain of the remaining LCL traffic, and the potential for capturing some of it back from the highway? Not to be overlooked, what about the fact that equipment utilization for piggyback on the roads that had already tried it seemed to be a whole lot better — and terminal costs were a whole lot cheaper? It certainly made the railroad look bad to the public, government and stockholders (not necessarily in that order) to be so negative about such a modern idea.

In 1953 the Missouri-Kansas-Texas Railroad's President Donald V. Fraser said that he thought that this piggyback idea made good sense and it had possibilities of showing some real growth for the railroads. Remember that in the 1950's there were about 100 Class I (i.e., large) railroads. That meant there were 100 Chief Executive Officers, 100 Vice Presidents of Operations and numerous others who opined on the problems of the day. However, if a small road's president appeared to be more progressive it provided the needle that would cause the larger road's Chief Executive Officer to react immediately. The statements which were credited to a large road's president definitely carried a lot of authority with members of the board of directors on small roads. While the word of a small midwestern railroad president may have caused some stir, imagine the effect of a November 1955 *Newsweek* feature that stated, "Piggyback is a double-barreled approach to the truck problem: It develops new business while proving that railroaders can serve truck shippers, too. One of its big boosters, President James M. Symes of the Pennsylvania, expects to have 500 extra-long, trailer-carrying flatcars on his railroad at the end of the year. Said one Pennsy offical, "Piggyback would seem to have an annual gross revenue potential for us of $100 million in five years."

With this kind of support from the top piggyback would grow. But, needless to say, not before there was a great deal of harassment from all levels of the "regulars" of the railroad. Intermodal jobs might be interesting, but they also were usually uncomfortable.

The matter of tampering with the rate structure was far more complex. When a piggyback rate was set for a trucker it was on a per-trailer basis. It had to be put low enough to attract the trucker, but high enough (under value of service pricing) to cover the most expensive freight in the trailer so that as a result of this charge other similar high-value freight would not be drawn out of the boxcars. The rates often ran afoul of the FAK rates (Freight-All-Kind) published for the freight forwarders who were using boxcars, and helping to relieve the railroads of some of their LCL cost.

The Chicago Great Western service in 1936 had been established to serve trucking customers exclusively. For the next year the New Haven built on that concept for the bulk of its traffic. Dan Sundel also felt that it was important for the New Haven to maintain direct contact with some of its most important customers such as Sears. That particular practice planted the regulatory seed. Years before the Commission had turned thumbs down on the New York Central and the Pennsylvania Railroad when they tampered with the class rate scales.

Initially, the commercial piggyback system of the late 1930's tended to rock along without upsetting anyone. However, bear in mind that at that time only a few scattered railroads were participating. Non-trucker piggyback was miniscule, and World War II intervened, diverting attention away from the fledgling service. After the recovery years of the late 1940's and as business increased, more and more rail carriers began to show an interest in the new traffic.

Then, in May of 1953 the Southern Pacific dipped its toe into the proverbial piggyback pool. Its toe proved to be so big and the splash so severe with its entrance that piggyback's commercial wraps were immediately off.

D.J. Russell of the Southern Pacific embarked in the piggyback game in a very provocative fashion. It was in that period when the Southern Pacific was a force to be reckoned with on a national basis. In the case of the piggyback situation SP decided three things. First and foremost was the decision to try this new concept. Secondly, it planned to try it on an intrastate basis between Los Angeles and San Francisco so it would not be subject to ICC regulations. The third determination was that it had absolutely no intention of cooperating with or assisting competitive truckers. The Southern Pacific would buy and furnish the trailers to its customers and publish the commodity rates. It would extend interstate service to Phoenix on a substitute service basis through Pacific Motor Transport, its wholly-owned trucking subsidiary.

In terms of the commercial tension that had built up between players, this action served to fuel the fires and produce a lot of very unhappy campers. Many truckers felt betrayed. A group of truckers immediately challenged the Southern Pacific's action by going through the regulatory process, but as an intrastate matter they were powerless to act.

Before the Southern Pacific action took place, the New Haven had already developed a number of ideas for its new piggyback services. Nevertheless, they still had to confront a lot of unresolved regulatory questions.

Southern Pacific Embarks in the Piggyback Game

In the above view, four groundmen from Southern Pacific's Pacific Motor Trucking subsidiary secure an SP trailer to an early flatcar in San Francisco in the 1950's. (UPPER RIGHT) A PMT driver backs a van up the ramp at the Oakland circus-style terminal in 1954. — BOTH SOUTHERN PACIFIC

A trainmaster supervises the switching operation while making up the CME (California Merchandise Express) at San Francisco in 1955. The SP was still using a considerable number of steam switchers at the time. — WILLIAM D. MIDDLETON

In the scene below, with the head end power now on the point of the train and the air pumped up, the CME begins its run to the "City of the Angels" from San Francisco's terminal. — WILLIAM D. MIDDLETON

Complete with specially lettered white caboose, Southern Pacific's pig train prepares to leave Los Angeles for San Francisco. — SOUTHERN PACIFIC

SP brochure from the 1950's. Even with the "largest fleet of piggyback equipment," SP couldn't resist placing a boxcar in the advertisement. — DONALD DUKE COLLECTION

All saddled up and ready to go, two side-door Southern Pacific trailers wait for the conductor's highball at Taylor Yard (Los Angeles). Note that the trailers are painted silver, not the regular Daylight colors of red and orange as most Pacific Motor Trucking trailers were at the time. — SOUTHERN PACIFIC

While this was an annoyance and bothered them somewhat, it probably would never have come out in the open and just remained internal to the New Haven's Law Department, surfacing only as a theoretical luncheon discussion, had the Southern Pacific not made their move. With that move, however, the New Haven lawyers now felt that they were open to regulatory censure — perhaps even on the plans that were already in operation. So, on September 15, 1953, the New Haven filed the famous 20 Questions Case (Movement of Trailers by Rail, 293ICC93) with the Interstate Commerce Commission. The answers that would be returned from 12th and Constitution Avenue in Washington, D.C. would determine whether or not there was a future for this most fragile service.

In a late 1953 reaction to the case (which no doubt reflected the deep-seated feelings of the chief traffic officers of its two major members, the PRR and the NYC), E.V. Hill, chairman of the powerful TEA Eastern Railroad Rate Bureau, noted four problems with piggyback. First, it was his belief that this service benefited the truckers more than the railroads. Second, he estimated the terminal capital costs for each railroad would be from one to two million dollars, and that truckers were not obligated in any way. Consequently, there was nothing to prevent them from merely walking away. Third, that piggyback itself would certainly upset the rail rate structures. Finally, that piggyback trains created too much capacity for the good of the railroads, and not enough service for the truckers.

These were all very serious issues for the traffic fraternity and the commerce lawyers of their Law Departments. The New Haven went to the Commission and asked for a declaratory order that would resolve the questions they had originally posed. It also should include those issues which had been raised by some of the enraged truckers, reacting to the Southern Pacific's move.

These questions could generally be classified as an attempt by the truckers to eliminate piggyback service altogether, by requiring that the railroads have a motor carrier certificate for each move (a very difficult, expensive and time-consuming process which was often unsuccessful) or an attempt to ban any moves that were not truck-rail joint rate moves. These would include moves for forwarders and shippers. Some of the railroads and freight forwarders were unsure as to just how the ICC viewed the appropriate roles of each of the parties involved. Those who wanted to proceed with the movement of railroad, shipper or forwarder trailers were stymied, pending the outcome of the case.

After a procedural set-to the Commission resolved the problem by reframing the original 20 questions to only 12, and then asked for participation by the interested parties. This invitation succeeded in bringing them to the meeting by the truckload. In addition to the presence of the Eastern and Western railroads there were shippers, freight forwarders and truckers of every stripe, including long-haul truckers, private truckers, contract truckers, cartage operators and yes, also Gene Ryan. Needless to say, the Commission got an earful.

Some of them argued that it was against the law and intent of Congress for the railroads to operate motor vehicles (i.e., trailers) door-to-door without holding a valid motor carrier certificate from the ICC.

Having examined this basic question, the Commission responded by citing many instances of the movement of freight loaded in vehicles of one mode on another mode. They included canal boats on flatcars, and the inevitable reference to the Long Island Rail Road's ''Farmer's Trains.'' It then mentioned the successful movements on the North Shore, the Chicago Great Western and the New Haven for both joint truck-rail service and through ''open'' tariffs.

The discussion then went to the issue of the 12 questions, starting with question one — May a railroad transport its own freight (i.e., freight tendered it by shippers for movement by railroad on railroad bills of lading and at railroad rates) in its own trailers on flatcars without holding any authority under Part II [the trucking section] of the act?

The motor carriers were placing most of their chips on the table on this one issue (since it would still not interfere with the movement of trucker's trailers by piggyback using trucker's tariff authority). They cited the Interstate Commerce Act that ''no common carrier by motor vehicle subject to Part II of the act shall engage in any interstate or foreign operation on any public highway unless it holds a certificate of public convenience and necessity.''

In addition the truckers argued that such a service would be a door-to-door ''single-vehicle trucking service.'' They argued that the Motor Carrier Act preserved that inherent advantage to the trucks. It was their contention that rail piggyback was usurping the advantage.

The railroads countered with the argument that the truckers needed to make a case which would prove to all concerned that the operation of flatcars over a private right-of-way actually constituted movement on a public highway (since movement on a private highway had been ruled not subject to Part II). The Commission agreed, and ruled that movement by rail was not the same as travel over a public highway. The end result was that the railroads did not need a trucking certificate to operate their own service. Thus, the New Haven fledgling moves for shippers, and the overt intent of the Southern Pacific to do the same thing were given official Commission sanction. The possibility of commercial tension between the intermodal players was now formally locked in place.

As a result of the first question, question two now became basically insignificant. Could the rail carriers do motor carrier pickup and delivery under the partial exemption for terminals? The answer was yes.

The third question, however, was of great importance to the shippers. Could railroads transport the trailers of private carriers (i.e., those working exclusively for a shipper)? The answer to this was based on a 1936 Commission decision when the Chicago Great Western had filed an open tariff that they had approved. This ruling was also available to private carriers and, therefore, was still okay. The fact that at the time the Commission had suggested that the Chicago Great Western refile a joint truck/rail tariff (which it did and upon which all of the Chicago Great Western traffic moved) was apparently of no consequence. Ah, the regulatory mind!

When it came to question four it was another throwaway. May a railroad haul trailers for a motor common carrier and must the railroad police the motor carriers certificate as to territory and commodities? Under the open tariff theory, and because of the lack of a through-route, the service was okayed for the inbound in the absence of "knowingly joining with the motor carrier on a violation of the law."

The fifth question read as follows: May a railroad and motor common carrier establish joint rates and routes? That issue was well settled — both by law (Section 216 (c)) and by regulation. An obvious yes.

They next ruled on question six. May a railroad make joint rates with some common carriers and refuse similar arrangements with others? The commission's decision was affirmative. Joint rates are permissive not mandatory.

Question seven was a technical tariff question.

The question which was of key interest to the railroads and to the forwarders was number eight. Could a railroad without Part II authority handle freight forwarder trailers? The answer was academic once question one had been decided. Freight forwarders are shippers, and under an open tariff. . .The stage was now set for additional customers and, ultimately, additional tension between the parties of intermodal.

The balance of the questions were largely procedural. The die was now cast, and the participants and potential participants reacted. Piggyback literally exploded. The 20 Questions Case quickly led to the establishment of a formalized series of plans for intermodal.

Plan I was the original "Ryan Plan." The motor carrier solicited, rated and billed the freight, and provided the trailer and dray at either end. The railroad simply did ramp-to-ramp service. This meant that the railroad had no direct customer contact (the truckers, not the shipper, became their customer). They had no knowledge of what was in the trailer (and whether it was diverted from boxcars or was truly "from the highway"), and the pricing was generally on a "one way" basis (which the trucker often used to balance his loads on a peak or seasonal basis). When truckers and railroads actually formed a true working partnership, Plan I worked very well, but when one or the other tried to take advantage it worked badly. Unfortunately, the Commission rules did not make the distinction of a player who was "pure of heart" from one who was not.

Plan II was a fully run railroad retail service. It was rated, billed and operated door-to-door in railroad equipment. Rates were made for individual commodities, and they tailored them to compete for highway freight and often with boxcar commodities. While Plan II offered the greatest competitive flexibility to intermodalists, it was not without its problems.

First, it required a large investment on the part of the carriers, and allowed for no risk assumption (or long term commitment) on the part of the customer. Second, drayage was often provided by the railroad trucking subsidiaries, and as such was extremely expensive due to union contracts. Rail management usually required intermodalists to use these subsidiaries without being able to get outside bids. This practice led to more than one rail trucking subsidiary "cooking" its intermodal books. The trucking company for example could use labor and equipment charged to intermodal for its cross-dock or over-the-highway operations, leading to large losses for intermodal "account high drayage cost." Plan II was also carefully watched by boxcar people. "Mixing rules" were required where a trailer had to contain at least two different commodities with no more than 60 percent of its being of one commodity.

Plan III was designed as "the shippers plan." The rates were FAK (Freight-All-Kind). This meant that the railroad charged a flat fee to move the shippers trailer ramp-to-ramp regardless of what the trailer contained. Some commodities that were dangerous as well as those that were valuable, such as automobiles, were excluded. Plan III appeared to many railroaders as being quite fair. However, it often had problems with drayage. While many shippers used their own labor to move the trailer from their plant to the piggyback ramp, the delivery point was also their responsibility. This end is where the problem evolved in that the shipper did

Intermodal Tariff Plans

PLAN No. 1 — Shipper deals directly with the motor carrier, using their container or trailer. The trailer or container is then shipped by rail - ramp-to-ramp. Pickup and delivery is handled by the motor carrier.

PLAN No. 2 — Shipper deals directly with the railroad. Trailer or container equipment is provided by the railroad. Pickup and delivery service is handled by the railroad.

PLAN No. 2½ — Shipper deals directly with the railroad using their trailers or containers. It becomes the responsibility of the shipper for pickup and delivery of trailers or containers. Plan No. 2¼ or Plan No. 2¾ provides Plan No. 2 service for pickup or delivery.

PLAN No. 3 — Shipper deals directly with the railroad for ramp-to-ramp service. The shipper provides his own trailer or container, and also handles his own pickup and delivery service.

PLAN No. 4 — Shipper deals directly with a third party, such as an association or forwarder. The forwarder provides the trailer or container, arranges the loading and unloading, the ramp to ramp rail car lease and handles pickup and delivery service. The railroad handles only the trailer or container ramp-to-ramp.

PLAN No. 5 — Shipper deals with the trucker or railroad for service. Either party provides the trailer or container to the shipper. The shipper then loads or unloads the cargo. The railroad or trucker handles the pickup and delivery. The ramp-to-ramp service of the trailer or container is handled by the railroad.

An early 1957 unloading operation during a spring rain in downtown Chicago on the Illinois Central Traffic types might be suspect that the freight in the trailers had come out of sisters of the boxcars behind. — WILLIAM D. MIDDLETON

not want to be bothered with arranging and managing destination drays.

Plan IV was designed for the third parties — freight forwarders and agents. As participants in early intermodal they had often used both their intermodal and LCL boxcar volume in order to hammer rates to their lowest level. Plan IV was originally designed to place most of the investment with the forwarder, including the trailer, flatcar, drayage and ramp service. As a result he would also be responsible for traffic balance. The railroad (went the theory) would only offer "hook and haul" service. Unfortunately, a major forwarder was to browbeat a major railroad into one-way trip leasing of flatcars and per-lift ramp charges which left the bottom line theory of forwarder investment and commitment moot.

Plan V was developed as a joint truck/rail plan. Unlike Plan I, the railroad was involved in the retail transaction for rates and selling and often providing the trailer. Also, the trucking partners under this plan were often regional truckers who used the railroad to offer a service between themselves in a Trucker A-Railroad-Trucker B fashion. Some truckers went so far as to obtain a regional authority at both ends of the railroad which allowed them to offer a Trucker A-Railroad-Trucker A service.

This system of formal plans appears to have been stilted and arcane in the light of the current era of dealing directly with customers in the marketplace. However, while it was imperfect it did serve as a structural framework for intermodal growth for almost three decades. The accompanying chart illustrates the details of each plan.

After the 20 Question Case was settled at the Interstate Commerce Commission, Railroads announced piggyback startups on almost a weekly basis. In this scene, a Baltimore & Ohio pig train passed over the venerable Thomas Viaduct located near Baltimore, Maryland. These were the first modern trailers, 40-footers no less, on the B&O's new TOFEE service. — GORDON VOLKERS COLLECTION

Chapter 5

"Load 'Em Up"

In addition to the initial half-dozen piggyback pioneers operating in 1954, an additional even dozen Class I railroads introduced piggyback services of some kind that year. Included were the Santa Fe, Baltimore & Ohio, Chicago & North Western, Delaware, Lackawanna & Western, Erie, Great Northern, Kansas City Southern, Lehigh Valley, Missouri-Kansas-Texas, Nickel Plate, Pennsy and Wabash. With their involvement, this brought piggyback service to the East, Midwest and West Coast. Only the Southwest still had not entered the piggyback race, although, in 1955, the mid-south started with service on the Louisville & Nashville and Illinois Central.

Major problems developed when the commercial side of the business began to outstrip the operating sides minuscule infrastructure and technology. The initial problems began to occur as carriers attempted to interline business. When a shipper's business went beyond the parochial boundries of the individual railroads, the move became interline. In 1955 there were about 30 carriers operating piggyback, and each railroad had a mechanical officer with a very fixed idea as to what was safe and proper for his own railroad. Unfortunately, the cars and their tie-down mechanisms were the sole domain of the mechanical officer. There was no uniformity for this strange new service — piggybacking.

Some of the railroads ran cars that were long enough to load two trailers. However, there were others who felt that cars longer than 53 feet were unproven, and as a result refused to operate them. Of greater concern to the people who worked the ramps was the plethora of tie-down systems. While everyone used a basic version of the Chicago Great Western screw jack/chain and binder system, each one was just a little different. On average each car had 40 pieces of tie-down equipment.

When they would circus load, cars with through trailers either had to be switched out or unloaded and then reloaded to an outbound "home car" cut. Because of the service pressure of piggyback, the latter most often occurred. This meant a problem in matching up foreign, i.e., offline trailers with flatcars of the same ownership. This situation prompted the need for *somebody* to do *something* about standardization.

Along with the explosion in service came the demand from shippers for a piggyback ramp to serve their plants. While many railroad traffic departments disliked and resisted piggyback service, the siren call of shippers (or patrons as they were often called in those days) was difficult to resist. Thus, in addition to the big hub ramps

You can bet that the two fellows with hats are senior railroad officials and that they're checking on this newfangled piggyback service to make certain the chains will stay in place. With all of the chains and binders, front and rear, and screw jacks, the load was almost bombproof. Many years later the Norfolk Southern would acquire the company who owned the trailer in this photograph. — GORDON C. MILLER COLLECTION

Operating a piggyback ramp in the 1950's was easy. First, build a tie pile to a stub or use a portable ramp as is shown in this photo of a Chicago & North Western ramp. Next, find some driver who can back a trailer in a straight line for about 700 feet. — WILLIAM D. MIDDLETON

in the major metropolitan areas, now, in the hamlets of the nation, small ramps began to blossom like the flowers of Spring. As we shall see these small ramps produced a delayed reaction problem of their own making.

Ryan, meanwhile, had not been sitting on his hands as the storm clouds brewed at the New York Central. With the difficulties involved in trying to launch a fledgling company, he had decided to hedge his bet by looking around for another sponsor just in case the Central deal collapsed.

In the marketplace, the fact that the Central was interested in piggybacking was well-known. And if they were interested, could the Pennsy be far behind?

Jim Symes, Pennsylvania Railroad's chairman, had been watching from the sidelines with great interest, thus, began the development of the Rail-Trailer-Pennsy liaison. So, too, had Jim Newell, his progressive vice president of operation, become interested. Newell had been keeping an eye on several railroads experimenting with trailers, but the double trailer on a flatcar idea struck a real chord with him. The Pennsylvania Railroad had begun a small Plan II operation, using single trailer cars in mixed trains in 1954. To Newell and Symes the Rail-Trailer approach looked like a whole different ballgame. Besides, the Central began to focus its attention on the Robert R. Young takeover. In the meantime the Pennsylvania Railroad quietly moved in.

Fred Carpi, the crusty old Pennsylvania vice president of traffic, was not crazy about piggyback in any way, shape or form. He suspected that piggyback traffic would only come from one place — at the expense of the boxcar. Newell was not enthusiastic about the GM car, and the capital that would be required at the terminals. Pennsy Vice President of Finance David Bevan wanted nothing to do with anything that would cause a capital expense. His balance sheet was already weak. The Rail-Trailer idea of outside financing of terminals and cars was music to his ear. Bevan also took into consideration the fact that he viewed Newell as his chief rival to succeed Symes as president. Supporting Newell's idea, he might be able to benefit in more ways than one.

Negotiations to establish service on the Pennsylvania Railroad moved quickly, but the GM car was still a major sticking point. Ryan conceded the point and, instead, ordered 100 75-foot long flush-deck piggyback cars from Bethlehem Steel — a key PRR freight account. The PRR signed a long term lease, and Ryan had to go to the financial markets to get them funded.

He concentrated his efforts on New York Life Insurance Company, but it proved to be far from simple since people who manage money are inherently cautious. As such, they generally ask a lot of questions before parting with their money — especially for untested concepts.

The New York Life people wanted to know several things about the proposed operations and, basically, Ryan handled most of their questions with ease. One, however, allowed him to play his proposal to the hilt and, consequently, clinch the deal. The question which was of most importance to them was what would happen if the Teamsters Union decided to fight this new innovation?

Ryan responded that he would bring in an expert who would specifically answer this question to their satisfaction. At the next meeting the "expert" produced was Jimmy Hoffa — new president of the IBT. Ryan had previously convinced Teamster President Dave Beck to set up a committee for the purpose of studying the effect of piggyback on the Teamsters Union, and Hoffa headed the committee. Earlier staff work by Ryan's people showed that the Teamsters jobs would increase. Ryan then submitted to them the following assurances: (1) New terminal employees in Rail-Trailer operations would be IBT members; (2) Teamster city delivery jobs would increase; and 3) the truckers with whom he contracted would not lay off line-haul drivers due to a move of freight from highway to rail intermodal.

At the luncheon meeting held with the New York Life committee, Hoffa presented the Teamsters position and his information carried the day. New York Life financed the cars.

Ryan hired a bright young man as his equipment manager named Les Robinson. Robinson had his start with Consolidated Freightways and then moved to PIE and Eastern Express. Robinson hated the chain tie-downs and screw jacks in use at the time, primarily because they were expensive to buy and costly to maintain. Also, they had proven to be large consumers of manpower when it came to installation and removal. And very often they got lost.

Ryan, impulsively and with little forethought, set the charge paid by the Pennsy to Rail-Trailer at $4.00 for loading or unloading. Consequently, unless Robinson could come up with a new mechanical device to handle the volume of trailers, it would, from the beginning, put Rail-Trailer in the hole on their terminal operation.

Robinson had talked to Joe Gruca, the Chicago regional man from Fruehauf, about areas of the trailer that were both uniform and strong enough to take the tie-down abuse of operating on the railroad. He even went so far as to buy a new trailer kingpin to experiment with. Rail-Trailer's time was rapidly running out before

Another Les Robinson invention - drawn on a napkin at lunch. The collapsible screw hitch is being raised in place by a power wrench (watch your hands). When fully raised it will engage the trailer kingpin (seen just beyond the hitch head) and the power wrench will then be used (where his left hand rests) to lock the jaws of the hitch head in place. No more screw jacks or chains and binders or associated labor costs. The boards on the floor on either side of the hitch allow equipment to pass over a recessed hitch. —GORDON C. MILLER COLLECTION

Gene Ryan hired many talented people. Among them was Les Robinson, his operations manager. A talented inventor, Les cobbled together this "Kingpin grabber" to ease the labor burden on Rail Trailer's contract with the Pennsylvania Railroad. Chains hooked directly to the grabber so no eyes needed to be welded on the trailer. Note the trailer rub rails on this car - looks like 110-pound rail. — GORDON C. MILLER COLLECTION

In the late 1950's shippers wanted a piggyback ramp in every hamlet. Here a Wabash Railroad drayman carefully backs a trailer up a portable steel ramp to the waiting car.
— R. B. SHORT COLLECTION

Next, make sure all the bridge plates are down so the trailer doesn't fall between the cars. Also, be sure the hitches are down or, as in this early pre-hitch photograph, that the screw jacks and chains are out of the way. This really gets to be fun in the rain and snow. — TRAILER TRAIN COLLECTION

This backing move is *only* 300 feet, but that single-axle trailer load of early 1960's Nash *Ramblers* can do strange things. — TRAILER TRAIN COLLECTION

they initiated service.

The short-range solution to their problem was a "Kingpin Grabber," an eight-foot steel beam that locked onto the trailers kingpin and had pockets to receive the screw jacks and hooks to receive the chains. Robinson developed the "Kingpin Grabber" as a last gasp effort after having looked at the side rails and the bottom of the trailer as potential areas to "latch onto." It was ready just in time for the departure of the first TrucTrain-1 and TrucTrain-2. Robinson and Pennsylvania Railroad's 47th Street Terminal Manager Larry Keoughan could finally breathe a sigh of relief.

The "Kingpin Grabber" was a great idea, but it still required chains and binders — just no screw jacks. What was *really* needed was some kind of trailer hitch that would get out of the way so that cars could be circus loaded similar to a chain and binder car, but still be labor saving due to elimination of the chains.

It was in 1954 while at lunch at the coffee shop in the Builders Building on North La Salle Street in Chicago that Les Robinson began doodling on a napkin and talking about the hitch problem. His doodling turned into a sketch of what turned out to be the first collapsible trailer hitch. Would it work? Ryan felt so, and took Robinson to American Car & Foundry to try to put the concept "in iron." Robinson stayed and worked with the people at their plant in Berwick, Pennsylvania, including Al Johnson and Fred Mueller. They succeeded in developing the hitch, but it still had to be sold to the Pennsylvania Railroad. Robinson who had previously worked with Max Seel, assistant chief mechanical officer, convinced him to take a look at this new concept.

The next step was to try and persuade Mechanical Engineer C.K. Steins. Steins listened patiently to Robinson's presentation and, occasionally, would nod his head. At the end of the dialogue, his only question was, "Where do you put the chains?" "We don't use chains, sir." said Robinson. "The damned thing won't operate without chains, binders, and wheel chocks on my railroad," said Steins. Robinson patiently explained that the lack of chains and binders was the whole point of the hitch and that the move would reduce loadout crews from two drivers and eight groundmen to two drivers and one groundman per cut of cars. "Over my dead body," said Steins. At that point Robinson felt like taking him up on his remark, but quickly thought better of it. He then decided that his next best move was to go through his friend Max Seel in order to make contact with the Vice President of Operations Jim Newell who he knew was a piggyback booster.

Newell arranged with Howard Kohout, who was to head up the PRR's piggyback function, to test the hitch

If you were a groundman at the ramp (LEFT PHOTO) this is the business end of collapsible screw hitch in the recessed position. Plug your power wrench into the bottom fixture. It will rise up and engage the kingpin protruding below the "27" of the chalked 127175. Put your wrench in the top fixture and the jaws will lock around the kingpin. Neat! This is a container on a chassis as a TOFC move on a railcar. A container "on its belly" can be seen on the adjoining track. (RIGHT PHOTO) Improvements in hitch technology came rapidly. From the 1955 invention of the collapsible screw hitch, to the automatic hitch by General American in 1959. In this scene, a ramp trailer with a hook attachment pulls up a hitch. Later, hitches would automatically lock in place as they were loaded on the car by side lifts or overhead cranes. — BOTH TRAILER TRAIN COLLECTION

(ABOVE-LEFT) This ground perspective will give you some idea of the consequences of not backing straight down the cut of cars You also get an idea of how far it might be to the end hitch. (UPPER-RIGHT) The tricky backing technique. Luckily the bridge plates were in place. (LEFT) In this scene, groundmen attach safety chains to allow the railroad's Chief Mechanical Officer to sleep well at night.
— ALL WILLIAM D. MIDDLETON

at Berwick and to be the judge of its performance. The most critical tests were the impact tests which were to be done in steps up to five m.p.h. Everything went well, and the final test was completed at five m.p.h. The hitch had passed with flying colors. Robinson and the engineers could now relax.

However, after the test was fully completed, the ACF's test engineer asked, "Any questions?" Howard Kohout spoke up. "Run it up to ten," he said. Once again the loaded hopper car was "hoisted," and it took a run at the hitch car. With what was described as "a helluva bang," the cars hit at ten m.p.h. When the dust settled, the trailer was found to be intact on the hitch, but the hitch itself had suffered some minor damage. "That's it," said Kohout, apparently satisfied. By early 1955 ACF had refined the idea and the collapsible screw hitch was born.

Through the years Robinson's inventive genius continued. He recognized early on that the rail environment affected trailers differently than the highway environment did. He developed the plymetal door which became a piggyback standard, is credited with the two-position cast steel tandem and contributed to the design of the piggyback upper coupler.

Robinson, having originally signed a standard company patent agreement, assigned his rights to Rail-Trailer. In turn, Ryan, as a sign of his faith in piggyback, signed the rights over to American Car & Foundry for a reported $7,500.

Things were now moving at the Pennsy. Symes had given Newell the go ahead to develop something with Ryan. Ryan agreed to build and operate terminals at Kearny, New Jersey, and 47th Street, Chicago. And to commit through the Van Car subsidiary the 200 75-foot cars, each capable of handling two 35-foot trailers.

Ryan's commercial idea was simple. First, he would organize the truckers in a given lane, whose confidence he had gained in his GM truck sales days, into a group. Then take their combined traffic to the railroad and offer them good service for a fixed amount of new highway traffic at a reasonable rate. Under the then current ICC rules, the rate was technically a division of a through rate and was not subject to rate restrictions. This in essence meant that rate control and traffic solicitation was removed from the railroad and given to the truckers who controlled the traffic. Operating control remained with the railroad. The concept was first known as the Ryan Plan. Later, due to objections, it was changed to "Plan I." For Ryan and Newell it appeared to be a marriage made in Heaven. Nonetheless, it contained the seeds of Ryan's destruction since Fred Carpi and the PRR's boxcar-oriented traffic department did not take the challenge to their kingdom lightly.

The fixed-rail line-haul rates, with Ryan and Newell controlling the service and Ryan and the truckers controlling customer contact and price, left Carpi without any weapons to fight a war with the intermodal upstart. He did not give up, but instead bided his time.

Notwithstanding the potential minefields, on March 3, 1955, Pennsylvania Railroad and Rail-Trailer launched TrucTrain. At 11:00 P.M. train TT-2 (for TrucTrain) departed 47th Street with three units and 12 of Ryan's 75-foot cars loaded with 23 trailers. With this departure the Pennsy was now officially in the piggyback business.

At this point the art of ramp loading was technically well developed. The screw hitch quickly replaced the chain and binder as well as the short-lived "Kingpin Grabber." Loading tracks were generally of a size from one to eight car lengths long. Switching crews placed empty cars at the ramp to begin a shift which could involve one or a series of side-by-side tracks.

Next, ramp crews would go along the cars and unlock bridge plates (on the left side of each car). This would form a steel "drawbridge" between each railcar to allow the trailers to be backed aboard. In addition all screw hitches would be placed in the recessed position with power wrenches.

When the cut of cars had been prepared, the first trailer was backed up the ramp with the yard hostler tractor. Then, successive trailers were backed down to reach the end. A ground crew lowered the trailer landing legs and uncoupled the yard tractor which then drove forward off the cut to get another trailer.

The ground crew next attached the power wrench to the trailer hitch on the deck of the car and raised it into position under the trailer, engaging the trailer kingpin. The power wrench was then used to lock the jaws of the hitch head to the kingpin. Trailer legs were cranked up and the crew would go on to the next trailer being backed down to the cut of cars.

Later hitch improvements would see the development of "knock down" hitches. This would eliminate the need for power wrenches to lower the automatic heads which locked the kingpin on contact and the wrench for locking the kingpin to the head. The automatic hitch was raised by driving the yard tractor over it and pulling it into position with a hook.

What Newell saw of the Pennsy operation, he liked. The trains were operated on a tight schedule and with two trailers per car. Naysayers, however, had latched onto arguments against piggyback. As one "anti" put it, "For thirty years truckers have been taking away our business, but now they are where we used to be.

An early day night shot of Pennsylvania Railroad's 47th Street Terminal in Chicago. Note the first six tracks (from the right) have bridge plates deployed and tracks No. 2, 5 and 6 have received trailers. — GORDON C. MILLER COLLECTION

A Rail Trailer terminal tractor backs the first load of Pennsy's first TT-2 Truc Train up the ramp at the 47th Street Terminal in Chicago March 3, 1955. — GORDON C. MILLER COLLECTION

They're stuck with labor troubles, their wage bills are soaring and there isn't a thing they can do about it; they are paying more for fuel and at last their taxes are going up to pay for the highway they use. Now that they are on the ropes, they come to us asking us to haul their trailers.''

This was an opinion that was widely held by many traffic and operating officers of the time. It demonstrated a total focus on cost — both of rail and truck, and totally ignored what was most relevant — the customer. The fact that customers were responding to truck service — its smaller shipment size, its quality in terms of speed, reliability and freedom from damage to lading, did not occur to the piggyback ''antis.''

As a paranthetical note there were about three-quarters of a million boxcars in 1957 when the quote was made. As this is being written there are fewer than 200,000 and their number is falling rapidly. The marketplace teaches a severe lesson to those who focus on anything other than customer needs.

Pennsylvania Railroad's first Truc Train No. TT-2 departed Chicago's 47 Street Terminal for New York at 11:00 P.M., March 3, 1955, right on the dot. Seen here, somewhere in the midwest, it is interesting to see how few of the 1950's truckers have survived today. — GORDON C. MILLER COLLECTION

49

The Western Pacific Railroad inaugurated piggyback operation in 1954, but only in conjunction with the Great Northern and the Santa Fe via the Inside Gateway. The start was a slow one, and generally only one trailer per car which enabled the WP to gather experience in the handling of trailers. On March 17, 1959, piggyback service was inaugurated between Salt Lake City and the San Francisco Bay area for the handling of truck trailers of Pacific Intermountain Express, Interstate Motor Lines and Garrett Freight Lines. In this scene the piggyback train rolls through Spring Garden, near Portola, California. — DONALD DUKE COLLECTION

Chapter 6
Technology
Never Weres, WannaBes, and Sorta Weres

Through the years, railroaders, terminal operators, carbuilders and other suppliers created new intermodal technology. Some of the technology reflected engineers' perceptions of intermodal needs. Other efforts were key solutions to real intermodal needs. All were very well intended, but costly. Some worked and some didn't. But in the late 1950's a sudden burst of creativity in car design occurred.

Initially, in 1953, we saw the Gene Ryan/EMD Trailer Transport System effort. It required expensive terminal investment, and the system never got past the test car X-15972 and the demonstration terminal built by EMD.

Shortly after the EMD car was built, Pullman-Standard came up with a two-trailer car of its own. This car was a side loader and required terminal pads built up to the height of the car's side sill. If GM had engineered a side loader, who was P-S to argue? The car was fitted with two turntables to hold the trailer running gear, thus, allowing an "easy on and off" movement. In 1954, as it became obvious that the advocates of end loading were not easily swayed, the car was fitted with collapsible hitches and was offered in a dual side load/end load version. The turntables were converted to "elevator platforms" in order to reduce the clearance profile. By 1958 the side load feature, the "elevators" and turntables were abandoned altogether.

At this point a visionary from Romania, almost the equal of Gene Ryan, burst upon the scene. Deodat Clejan, a young engineer in his early thirties, brought his considerable engineering and organizational talents to bear on the new U.S. intermodal phenomenon. Clejan tackled the problems of tie-downs and clearances. He was able to combine it with the work he had previously accomplished on improving net to tare ratios for freight cars while with the French National Railways. Teaming up with General American Transportation Corporation, he initiated his concepts for intermodal in the United States.

The basic idea for the car was a parallel box girder center sill arrangement. This allowed the trailer wheels, by straddling the center sill, to rest a foot lower than on full deck cars. The construction technique without the solid decking, substantially reduced the car weight and, consequently, saved fuel. The use of a pair of skates bolted to either side of the trailer axle eliminated the chains and binder tie-down system. These skates rolled along the box girder as the trailer was end loaded.

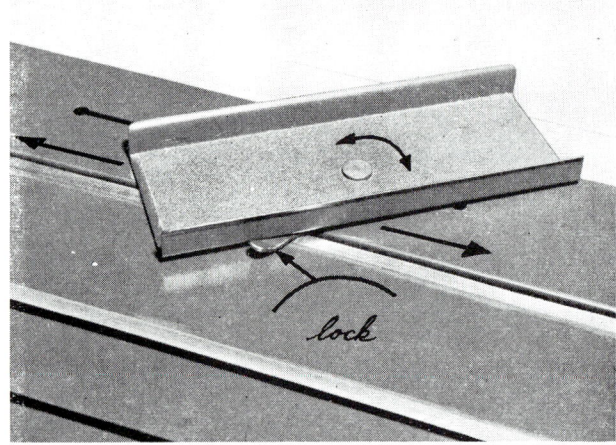

Pullman-Standard, the largest car builder at the time, felt threatened by Bethlehem's efforts for the Pennsylvania Railroad and by EMD's designed car for Rail Trailer. Here is the early Pullman-Standard response - complete with turntables. (LEFT) The turntable pivots are in position for guidance in spotting and to ease strain on trailer tires. (LOWER LEFT) Truck trailers would also be used in side loading. Note how hold-down equipment accommodated varying trailer heights and lengths. (BELOW) The rear stand was adjustable in the same degree as the 5th wheel stand. It could be slid in the floor track to any position on the car or could be removed entirely. — RAILWAY AGE - MAY 31, 1954

A Pacific Motor Trucking (SP) auto carrier with a load of new 1959 Chevies aboard a Clejan car. Note the dolly that guides the trailer along the center sill. This dolly contained a kingpin that fit into the trailer. Another dolly fit onto the trailer axle to guide the rear of the trailer. — SOUTHERN PACIFIC

A 35-foot reefer van, owned by SP subsidiary Pacific Motor Transport, aboard a SP built Clejan car in 1958. SP became a early member of the General American flatcar pool along with Kansas City Southern, the New Haven and the Erie. Note the lack of a kingpin - a feature, specified by PMT, that would later cause piggyback interchange problems for parent SP. — SOUTHERN PACIFIC

An early version Clejan car designed by Frenchman Deodat Clejan and built by General American. The cars were lighter with less decking and both containers and trailers rode lower. Look closely under the word "Fruehauf" on the lower right door and you will spot the cable attachment used to wrench the container onto earlier cars. The railing used to help groundmen stay on the car in rain or snow and is a sure giveaway in spotting Clejan cars. — TRAILER TRAIN COLLECTION

The trailer was loaded aboard the car through the use of a hostler tractor mounted with large rollers that also used the center sill as a guidance system. Once aboard, the trailer axle skate was locked to the center sill, eliminating the tie-down system and saving a substanital amount of terminal labor.

The system was developed and sold with missionary zeal by the young Frenchman. The New Haven and Southern Pacific were early converts. The Southern Pacific initially built a 79 1/2-foot prototype car in its own shop and then ordered 150 more from General American. The cars carried three 24-foot or two 35-foot trailers. New Haven ordered 200 of the cars for its New York-Boston service. With two of the three biggest piggyback operators in the country in his camp, Clejan was off to the races.

He next established Piggyback Inc., an operating company that managed piggyback terminals and leased terminal equipment — especially Clejan equipment. General American then started a pool for leasing the Clejan car in competition to the Trailer Train car pool. In addition to Southern Pacific and the New Haven, pool members also included Erie and Kansas City Southern.

The GATX pool members operated a virtual closed system, so the initial use of Clejan cars caused little problem. However, truckers, a large part of New Haven's piggyback business base, did not like the "extra jewelry" of the dolly skate for their trailers. It also tended to produce some problems operating in ice and snow and in the more rugged rail environment. Carmen and groundmen found the footing on the center sill to be dangerous. Ice, snow or bent parts made loading difficult.

As trailers began to be interchanged, the Clejan car produced some real problems. In initial terminal designs you often found that a separate track was provided for loading or unloading Clejan cars. This proved to be a switching nightmare up until 1959 when General American invented the G-85 car.

The car was 85 feet long, and had automatic retractable hitches that could be deployed by a terminal hostler tractor instead of with a power wrench like the ACF hitch. It was capable of loading either standard trailers or those equipped for the Clejan system. The car also provided the capability to belly-load containers from the infant seagoing system.

While the G-85 car solved the compatibility problem of the Clejan car, it also added car weight (counter to one of the principal early Clejan features), and was probably the biggest factor in sounding the death knell for the Clejan system. It was much easier for the General American pool roads to use Standard trailers in their own systems, and one by one the GATX roads joined the Trailer Train pool. The biggest crossover occurred in 1960 when the Southern Pacific joined with Trailer Train, taking over the G-85 fleet.

RAILVAN

While still at the Chesapeake & Ohio, Robert R. Young established a research department in an attempt to bring "new thinking" to the railroad industry. To head up the effort he hired a solidly built, crew-cut young man named Ken Browne from the airframe industry. He also engaged an energetic, young, tall and lean engineer named Alan Cripe to assist him. Browne had some fresh ideas of his own about this new piggyback service, and he and Dick Wade immediately went to work, tackling the technical side. Coming from the budding aerospace business, Browne was highly conscious of net to tare ratios. This meant how much dead iron you haul around in the line-haul vehicle to carry a "live" payload. The less the vehicle weight, compared to the payload, the more efficient is the vehicle — all things being equal.

The only necessity Browne could see, in order to make a highway trailer run on the railroad, was to add a coupler and some flanged wheels. Eliminating the flatcar was the ultimate in the attempt to increase net to tare.

Browne solved the coupler problem by using a lead adapter unit. All trailing units were coupled through the use of a fixed tongue attached to the center sill at the front of the trailer. It mated with a receptacle built into the rear trailer bolster and engaged both the coupler and air line on impact. The underframe had a tubular center sill and was made of Cor-Ten steel. The body was aluminum. The rail wheels were single axle and were raised and lowered by a screw mechanism operated by an air motor.

The initial units were demonstrated in 1956 at a Chesapeake & Ohio annual stockholder's meeting. After a period of debugging they were placed in limited passenger service. Initially, they were used between Detroit and Grand Rapids, Michigan, hauling storage mail for the Post Office on the rear of C&O passenger trains over the old Pere Marquette line.

In the meantime the C&O waited to enter the piggyback fray. Technical bugs, including evidence that the lightweight Railvan units were derailing and then rerailing themselves, made the Operating Department nervous about fully adopting the technology.

By 1959 the C&O decided to order flatcars and get into the trailer business. It would go to the more modern technology later on if it was warranted. Young, the driving force in moving to the new technology, had left the C&O for the New York Central five years earlier.

Close-up of the effort of the Chesapeake & Ohio's research department to eliminate car tare weight in intermodal equipment. Arms supported the highway wheels and the railroad wheels were attached to springs. — RAILWAY AGE - MAY 14, 1956

Air motor deploys rail wheels for the rail move and then retracts for the move over the highway. The air motor also raises and lowers the body to give equal coupler heights for rail movement, regardless of weight of lading. — RAILWAY AGE - MAY 14, 1956

The Railvans were quietly retired to serve as parts storage at various Chessie piggyback ramps. This was not, however, the last we would hear of Browne and Cripe or of their technology.

HOSTLER TRACTOR

Hostler yard tractors of the mid-1950's were a sight to behold. Backing trailers up a ramp and onto a cut of up to a dozen flatcars was a real challenge. Large railroads, of which the Pennsylvania Railroad was perhaps the best example, developed a collection of Rube Goldberg units. Pennsy's examples of this included one called "The Monster" with a cab and a steering wheel mounted facing the fifth wheel. They also had a nameless unit that had a conventional steering wheel, seat in the cab, a reverse-facing steering wheel and a seat mounted on the left front fender. If the wheel wasn't sheared off in a "close encounter," it almost certainly did not survive the first month of winter weather.

Ryan had hired Sy Aramian to work for Les Robinson at TOFC Inc. Aramian had managed a ramp for the Chicago Great Western. He met Canzoniero on his visit from the New Haven in 1937. Aramian succeeded Robinson and ran the ramp under contract for the Chicago & North Western at 40th Street in Chicago. In 1959 he took delivery of a yard tractor from Ottawa, a tractor manufacturer.

Never a bashful sort, Aramian complained to the Ottawa salesman about the cab (there was none), the engine, the transmission and the fifth wheel. About the only thing he didn't complain about was the color. The noise did, however, attract the Ottawa engineering staff, who spent long hours and many visits learning about this new piggyback business.

In time the unit evolved a high-lift fifth wheel. This allowed the tractor driver to back under a trailer and

Chesapeake & Ohio's Railvan was a 26-foot unit used to haul mail on passenger trains. Note the "rail" equipment, including ladders and brackets to allow the display of kerosene marker lamps. This was to be the forerunner of RoadRailer. — RAILWAY AGE - NOVEMBER 17, 1956

automatically lift the unit from inside the cab. The trailer would then be moved around the terminal or onto the cars without raising or lowering the dolly legs. This single feature has saved countless man-hours of terminal labor throughout the years.

From the work done by Sy Aramian at Ryan's TOFC Inc. terminal subsidiary has evolved the hundreds of hostler yard tractors that have been used in intermodal facilities over the years.

TRAILERS

In the beginning trailers hauled in intermodal service were standard highway trailers. The only exception was the rings used to tie chains and binders to the railcar. As time went on, the need to beef up the trailers to withstand the rigors of the rail environment became

A ramp manager's nemesis — the meat trailer. This Missouri Pacific unit with beef swinging on meat hooks from meat rails. The meat hooks that were lost had to be replaced which often meant a loss on this class of traffic. — ROBERT KREHMEYER COLLECTION

apparent. Stronger doors and extra hinges (five per door became the TOFC standard) helped prevent blown doors — a condition in which the freight in a trailer decides to try to escape through the doors due to train slack action or an errant switch move.

If the trailer was facing the opposite direction on a flatcar when a shock was delivered, the result could be a damaged trailer nose. In severe cases freight could actually cause a "blown" trailer nose, i.e., freight would break totally through the front of the trailer. The specs for a TOFC trailer were changed to reflect the needs of a rail operating environment.

The means for changes in trailer specs was the Intermodal Steering Committee — a subcommittee of the Operating-Transportation Committee (the vice presidents of operations of the major railroads) of the Association of American Railroads. In conjunction with the Mechanical Committee of the AAR, standards were set for the interchange of trailers.

As terminal mechanization became more common, damage to the bottom rail (the lower frame) of the trailers was more frequent. Trailer specs for TOFC were upgraded to require bottom lift pads along the lower rail where the lift shoes of side-lift machines or overhead cranes attached to the trailer.

Trailers were developed for use in all types of business. Besides dry vans, manufacturers produced reefer units that could carry meat and other products. The meat trailers handled "swinging meat," i.e., carcasses on meat hooks, suspended from meat rails on the roof of the trailer. The meat hooks themselves were routinely thrown away by the receivers rather than being put back in the trailers as they should have been.

This practice caused ramp managers to have to spend a portion of their budgets to replace them.

Similarly, some dry trailers were equipped with D-F (for damage free) aluminum bars. This device was used in conjunction with plywood in order to keep the freight in place. Like the meat hooks, the D-F bars were regularly discarded by dock workers, necessitating replacement by the ramp manager out of their skimpy budgets.

Tank trailers, flatbed trailers, bulk trailers, open top trailers, insulated trailers, refrigerated trailers, compressed gas trailers and almost any other kind of trailer that was required were developed and placed in service.

THE CONTAINER

In the middle of the 1950's an all encompassing technological concept developed that would wash across all modes. Rarely in a work career does one experience such an innovation. An obvious example of this for railroaders was the coming of the diesel locomotive and for the airline industry the jet engine. But for intermodal nothing compares to the idea hatched by a North Carolina trucker in the early 1950's. His concept was to simply separate the wheels from the box. This would allow movement of freight by highway, rail and sea without ever unloading or reloading at the piers or at cross-dock facilities. His name was Malcolm McLean.

McLean took his idea to all of the big, established steamship companies on the East Coast, such as U.S. Lines, Moore McCormack and AEIL. Those who bothered to listen at all declared that the idea was half-baked. Besides, what did this trucker know about the sea, ships, tradition and marine engineering? The upstart landlubber was shown the door.

Unable to sell the containerization concept to any existing steamship line, McLean considered entering the business on his own. The idea was, of course, preposterous. A new boy, and a low capitalized trucker at that, entering an old boy, highly capitalized industry. Not likely. But as time would show, the world had seldom seen the likes of Malcolm McLean.

Rivers of the United States were filled with mothballed ships unused since World War II, but established steamship operators were not worried about any competition from these derelicts. Ship technology had improved dramatically since World War II, along with increased ship speed and size. There was no reason to believe that any new boy with old ship technology could muscle in on their action. Especially not a trucker with a crazy idea.

As a trucker McLean understood something that the steamship people did not. He realized that the rapid turn-around time which the container idea allowed the ships in port would in turn make the rapid line-haul speed by break bulk carriers irrelevant. Thus, when McLean bought old T-2 and C-2 bottoms to convert to container handling vessels, the scene was set for the most significant transportation innovation of the second half of the twentieth century.

McLean originally planned to combine McLean Trucking with the coastwise shipping rights of the Pan Atlantic Steamship Co. However, regulators would not permit the combination, so McLean sold the trucking company and, in January 1955, bought Pan Atlantic. Four months later he purchased its parent, Waterman Steamship Co. This, now, set the stage for the grand experiment.

McLean labored for ten months to convert the old T-2 tanker into a "seagoing tractor." Then, on April 26, 1956, the *Ideal X* set out from New York with 58 containers bound for Houston, Texas, and the transportation world would never again be the same.

The Matson Navigation Company was the next to follow on August 31, 1958, with its inaugural sailing of the *Hawaiian Merchant* from San Francisco to Honolulu. It was a converted C-3, also from World War II, with 20 containers on deck. Thus, Pacific containerization was launched.

While it was not long before containers began to move by rail, there were only a few rail carriers who tried containers in preference to trailers. At first containers started to move inland mostly on chassis as TOFC, and since it was owned by a carrier regulated by the Federal Maritime Commission (FMC), the steamship companies maintained a unique position in relation to the railroads. Truckers, who were also carriers using the railroads, were regulated like the railroad by the Interstate Commerce Commission (ICC). This started a major feeling out process.

First, the ICC and FMC disagreed about the jurisdiction over various parts of the intermodal move. This brought about a hesitation by the railroads and steamship companies in dealing with each other.

Second, the two industries needed to establish an interchange agreement that would allow steamship containers and chassis to be accepted by the railroads. The steamship companies established the Steamship Operations Intermodal Committee (SOIC) to deal with truckers on these issues. Gordon Volkers, head of Chessie's Intermodal Department, took on the early job of melding the railroad and steamship company interchange interests. By doing this, they would both benefit from the rail movement of containers.

In the mid-1950's intermodal technology was in a turmoil. Everyone had his own idea about the "right"

Malcom McLean's *Ideal X* set sail from New York to Houston, Texas, with 58 containers on board. From that day forward transportation around the world would never again be the same. — SEA-LAND

Matson Navigation Company's *Hawaiian Merchant* was their first container vessel. It is being unloaded here at San Francisco in 1958. — MATSON LINES

technological equipment for intermodal. Some rail carriers were attracted to the container.

Like Matson and Sea-Land (successor to Waterman/Pan Atlantic), each of the rail container systems started out as being quite unique, operating in a closed environment. On the rail side the first carrier to adopt container technology for domestic traffic was the Missouri Pacific. To a no-nonsense, expense-conscious, operating man's railroad, the idea of a "cut-out-the-wheels" system was inherently appealing.

MISSOURI PACIFIC GONDOLA SYSTEM

Initially, the Missouri Pacific began hauling containers from its Gulf ports for Seatrain Lines who offered a containership operation between the Gulf and the East Coast. MOP established a committee, headed by research director P.P. Wagner, to look at the options for carrying highway freight. Their recommendation was for a container system. The containers that were used had angled braces with lifting eyelets. While it

Early Missouri Pacific reefer container being loaded into a gondola by an early rail-mounted crane. MOP operating officers liked the idea of leaving the wheels behind and of using non-specialized cars for intermodal. — TRAILER TRAIN COLLECTION

did require overhead cranes to pick up the containers, there were two features which attracted the cost-conscious MOP officers.

P.J. Neff, Missouri Pacific's chief executive officer, explained, "This new and unusual operation may be the answer to motor carrier competition and in our opinion is superior to the so-called 'piggyback' method in that it does not require the use of any special type of railroad equipment for train movement." The "special equipment" referred to was a "messed up flatcar" as it was described by one operating type. MOP would load the container on plain vanilla flat-bottom gondolas, using the tie-downs carried on the containers. As a side benefit, Neff noted that the system, "also eliminates carriage of dead weight in the form of chassis and wheels, which is necessary in conventional piggybacking." In August 1956 Missouri Pacific initiated service between Kansas City and St. Louis.

The Baltimore & Ohio also initiated container service, but with more standard flatcars. The system was named TOFCE Service and was operated both as TOFC (on chassis) and COFC (on their bellies). Both the B&O and the MOP operated an odd "side squeeze" system of loading/unloading which added to the woes of early manufacturers of mechanized terminal equipment.

ACF ROAD-RAIL SYSTEM

American Car & Foundry Company, a major carbuilder whose offices, Technical Center and one plant were just outside St. Louis, was an early and enthusiastic supporter of intermodal. Since the Missouri Pacific general offices were also located in St. Louis, it was only natural that ACF engineers watched MOP's gondola and container experiment with great interest.

In February 1954 John Furrer proposed a system that would substitute trailers for the MOP containers, but still retain the gondola. This system used a "standard" drop-end gondola with end bridge plates (for the highway trailer wheels) between car ends and a top chord extender (for the metal trailer wheels). The trailer was to have had special metal wheels attached to the trailer frame at each corner so that when deployed, it would guide the trailer along the top chord of the gondola. These wheels would also serve as a tie-down device, eliminating the screw jacks, chains and binders of the then current trailer system.

The system was designed to replace the Chicago Great Western tie-down system. It was also a reaction against the EMD Trailer Transport System. In the proposed system Furrer goes through a long discussion of "End Loading vs. Side Loading — Today's Solution." It concludes that the side-loading systems would not bear fruit due to the "...vast square footages of elevated platforms running beside the tracks or else thousands of feet of track laid in excavated pits to bring the height of the car floors down to ground level."

As to the arguments of random load/unload and more rapid loading and unloading, the conclusion was that a "sensibly planned" end-loading operation would always have the trailers in the right place. Too bad that Furrer was not allowed the pleasure of operating a "sensibly planned" multiple arrival and departure from a Chicago intermodal terminal in a snowstorm with several wrong-way cars, wrong car sizes or types, a

St Louis based American Car & Foundry designed the Road-Rail system as a trailer and gondola system. Note the large rollers attached to the front and rear trailer frames of this model to guide the trailer along the top cord of the gondola.

third of the hostlers out with flu and a hot UPS schedule up next.

Despite the lack of practicality of the Road-Rail system, the proposal clearly indicated an important grasp of the moneymaking potential of small system pieces for manufacturers. In order to create a larger market for gondola cars, the goal was to produce additional trailer hardware, bridge plates and chord extenders required by the system. The "jewelry" associated with intermodal could, indeed, be profitable, and American Car & Foundry would find a major market there in the coming years. But not through the Road-Rail system which never got beyond the planning and design stage.

ACF ADAPTO SYSTEM

The second container service to be initiated in 1956 was designed by American Car & Foundry at their Berwich shops, calling it the Adapto System. Adapto was designed as a 35-foot lightweight car with single-axle trucks and an air-cushion suspension system. This took about one-third of the car weight out of the conventional car. The ACF project engineer was Boris Terlecky. The car carried two 17-foot containers.

Initial orders for the system included 50 cars for the Rock Island and 1,000 cars for Trailer Train. Rock Island initiated Convert-A-Frate service in November 1956, using the Adapto System. Reaction from railroad mechanical department forces against the two-axle trucks caused Trailer Train to cancel their orders. Two-axle trucks were standard fare on European railways, due to the fact that there they operated in a shock-free environment. The weight of American trains and the train action caused trouble for Adapto. Within three years all of the Adapto cars had disappeared and only a few of the 17-foot boxes remained.

RAILINER/STEADMAN SYSTEM

Two similar systems came into existence in the 1950's, one was U.S. based and the other was from a Canadian manufacturer. Both were container systems that operated off "loader chassis." The U.S. system, built by the Southern Car & Manufacturing Company, was dubbed Railiner. The Canadian company produced the Steadman System.

Both systems produced chassis and railcar fittings that operated on a side-slip principle. First, a road chassis

American Car Foundry designed *Adapto* a lightweight single-axle car at its Berwick Shops. Designed to handle either trailer or containers, it was ordered and operated only by the Chicago, Rock Island & Pacific Railroad. — RAILWAY AGE - JULY 2, 1956

Two side loader systems were designed for low volume operations and saw more early success. The Railiner System was designed to be used in "wide spots in the road" like the pastoral southern scene shown here. The unit closest to the flatcar had a roller system to transfer the box to or from the chassis. A chassis jack system helped to adjust height for uneven surfaces. — TRAILER TRAIN COLLECTION

The Stedman System was used in Canada by Canadian National and was examined by many U.S roads. A similar system was used by Railway Express in its later days. The system also used a side slip loading scheme similar to Railiner. — TRAILER TRAIN COLLECTION

would pull alongside a transfer chassis which had been pre-positioned alongside a railcar. (In Canada, with very light density of traffic, the transfer chassis also operated over the road.) Transfer arms would be connected between the road chassis and the transfer chassis, and the box was then pulled to the transfer chassis. At this point hydraulics on the transfer chassis could be used to raise or lower the box to align with the height of the flatcar. The box was then transferred to the flatcar where it would be secured.

The systems had extendable front and rear legs, allowing a unit to be dropped while the chassis was returned for additional loads. This was commonly referred to in Europe as "swap bodies."

Railiner added an additional twist to their system with a telescoping chassis. It was designed to handle any container from 20- to 40-foot lengths, presaging the common use of extendable chassis by 30 years.

The Steadman System saw some acceptance in Canada by the Canadian National, but was later phased out. In the United States the Railway Express Agency attempted to use the system in combination with a rolling wire-mesh cage unit in a service they called Unit-Pak. The units were designed to be loaded by the customer rather than using high-priced REA labor. At REA terminals the cages could be transferred between containers with a minimum of labor.

This setup allowed REA to propose dramatically slashed rates which, in turn, brought about major complaints from truckers, forwarders and the American Trucking Association. In those dark pre-deregulation days competition and efficiency was good, that is if no one elses ox was gored in the process. In this case the REA's ox was allowed to expire instead. Once again the regulatory mind relegated the potential efficiency to a "what might have been" footnote in a history of intermodal.

PORTAGER

Late in the 1950's General Motors once again took a shot at intermodal. This time it was the GM Diesel of Canada. Perceiving a need to get into a growth market after dieselization, GMD moved engineering resources in to take a look at intermodal. At the time it found a willing partner in the Canadian Pacific. CP was interested in whether a car could be built that would have the best of both worlds, that of the TOFC and COFC. CP owned Smith Transport, a major Canadian trucking company, and it had watched several U.S. roads experiment with containers. It liked what it saw, regarding the idea of the weight and fuel savings (CP was *always* a frugal road), but at the same time it wanted to be able to use its Smith Transport trailers. This raised

Carload of Railway Express containers filled with express freight. The boxes were loaded at an REA terminal, shifted to its legs in an adjoining REA storage area by a yard hostler and picked up by a line-haul unit for movement with three other units to the piggyback terminal. — TRAILER TRAIN COLLECTION

General Motors was an early supporter of intermodal. GMD, a Canadian subsidiary, came up with a single-axle lightweight car called *Portager*. It was used only in commercial service on the Canadian Pacific. The single-axle car would reemerge in intermodal's third generation. — TRAILER TRAIN COLLECTION

Open top Fruehauf trailer rides single-axle, single-trailer Adapto car designed by ACF. Trailer Train initially ordered 1,000 cars. Harsh reaction from railroad mechanical officers caused Trailer Train to cancel its production orders. Rock Island continued using their 50 cars in its Convert-A-Frate program. — TRAILER TRAIN COLLECTION

the question, what about a car that was capable of carrying a Smith trailer with the sliding tandems "slid out" entirely?

There were six initial criteria. First, the car had to carry a 35-foot or a 40-foot box. Second, it had to be able to operate in conventional trains. Third, it should be able to run at a speed of 75 m.p.h. without problems. Fourth, it would have no steel decking. Fifth, it should exhibit inexpensive maintenance. Sixth, it should be no more expensive to buy per slot of capacity than the existing two-hitch cars. The obvious benefits would be its light weight which would translate directly into performance, fuel and locomotive savings (an interesting goal, considering GMD's primary business). General Motors Diesel set to work.

It developed a car that consisted of a center sill, two body bolsters, draft gears and couplers, a fifth wheel, two single-axle trucks and little else. The Smith trailer minus its bogie — or looking at it another way, a Smith container, including kingpin, landing legs, but minus bogies that fit onto that car.

In the spring of 1959 GMD rolled out a 26,000 tare weight prototype T-40 (later No. GMDX 401). In recognition of its Canadian heritage the car was named *Portager*, for the French-Canadian voyageurs who carried their canoes on their backs over land and around dangerous rapids and falls. As the car was rolled out for extensive testing on the CPR, Yale & Towne was contacted to develop a loader. Yale came up with an articulated unit that could fit under the car on a paved track. This eliminated the need for heavy counterbalancing, and thus, a heavy "footprint." However, it added the track paving requirement which placed a heavy strike against the system.

As the CP began to test the unit, GMD looked south to the U.S. for potential customers. It had to have the sponsorship of a U.S. carbuilder who was strictly interested in intermodal, and did not have a pet project of its own. North American Car fit the bill.

Both GMD and North American agreed that the U.S. roads that were already into containerization would probably be their best potential. These included New York Central, Missouri Pacific, Southern and Baltimore & Ohio. Tests were run on all of these roads and the Central's Cleveland Labs had a car to test in March of 1961. These container roads were actually a very small part of the U.S. rail system, however, and, therefore, it soon became obvious that a parallel effort would be needed to truly test the U.S. marketplace. It was concluded that a trailer-carrying version would be what was needed in order to have any chance with those roads.

GMD rolled out two more prototypes, Nos. GMDX

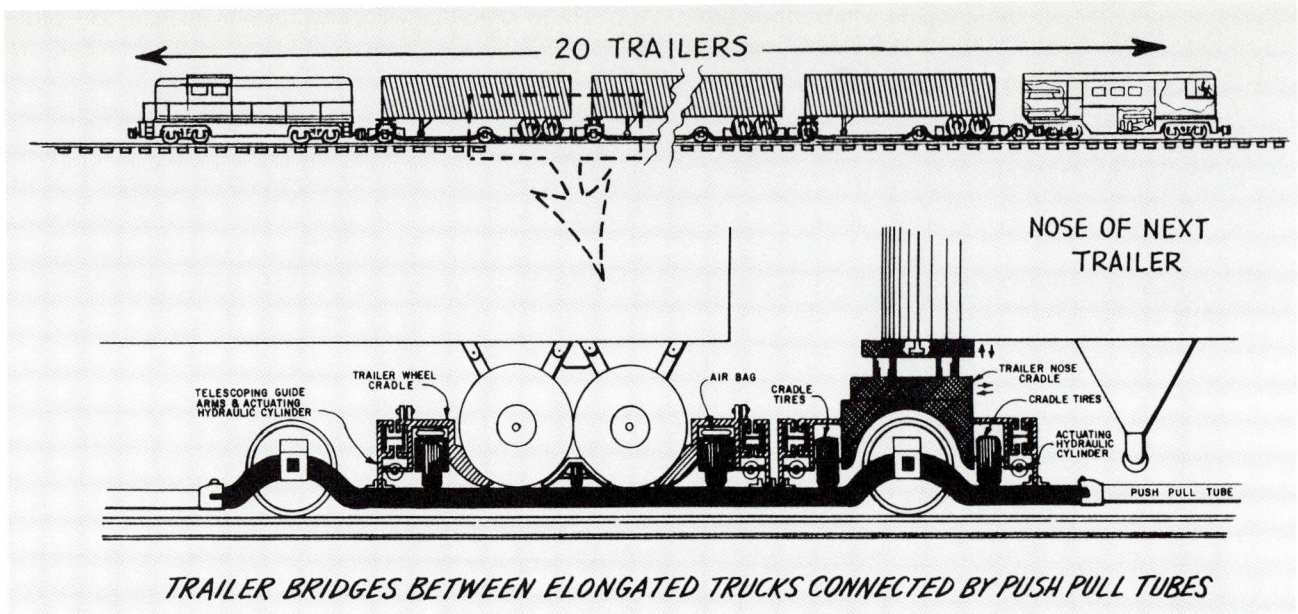

A concept developed by A.T. Kearney in the late 1950's, the *Minipiggi*, anticipated the move to articulated equipment by two decades. A stacked container concept was also worked on by Kearney in this same time frame. — THE MINIPIGGI TRAIN - A.T. KEARNEY & COMPANY (1968)

405 and 406, with landing pads for the trailer running gear. This complicated the problem for Yale & Towne since, unlike the container, the only uniform thing about the underside of a trailer is its lack of uniformity. If it's not a spare tire, a tire chain hook, a belly-mounted reefer unit or a unique cross bracing, it could be any one of a dozen other items. All of this implied the necessity of a major expense of having an overhead crane (side-lift machines had yet to be invented).

While it is difficult to realize the problems of any new non-circus loading system from today's perspective, consider the fact that all of the side and overhead lift machines built in the last 30 years would not have mechanized all the big ramps that existed in the early to mid-1960's. In addition to the loading problem, many railroad chief mechanical officers went apoplectic at the mention of two-axle cars. These two problems, plus the rise of the ubiquitous two trailers on 89-foot flatcars, killed any chance of the Portager car in the U.S. by the end of 1961.

On the Canadian Pacific the end came when Smith Transport returned to the highway once the new Queens Highway was opened between Montreal and Toronto. GM engineering had again been ahead of its time. Later on the *Portager* spector would rise in the form of third-generation technology.

THE A.T. KEARNEY CARS

In the 1950's and 1960's A.T. Kearney's Frank Macomber and Les Kloss were more involved with intermodal concepts and intermodal technology than any other consultant. They worked with most of the leading intermodal innovators of that era.

It would be impossible to say just who should be credited with the real innovative genius behind this technological concept. So, perhaps the identification of the synthesizer of the ideas is enough, and what else but a synthesizer of ideas is the role of a good consultant? Macomber and Kloss were clearly good consultants.

In their work with various groups over a 15 year period, two concepts emerged. The first was a stacked container car designed to haul either containers (up to six 20-footers) or trailers. While their car idea appears to be the forerunner of the stack cars of the 1980's, they are, in fact, actually very different in both construction technique and cost. Ryan's depressed-center flat was essentially a single casting that would have been both heavy and expensive. It would have cut into the relative capital and operating economics of the third-generation design.

The second Kearney synthesis was a trailer car they called the Minipiggi. The car was developed in conjunction with an assignment for Westinghouse Electric. The idea was a trailer-hauling vehicle that self unloaded and operated in smaller origin to destination units.

The use of small line-haul units, some of which self unload, has been the kernel of the ideas behind Minipiggi and later the Pogey Bogie, the Banner Bogie and the Iron Highway. The concept of packing the highest possible density on the train and increasing the net to tare ratio of rail equipment is what, ultimately, led to the double stack. Many things would need to move into place, however, before the technology could be effectively utilized.

FLEXI VAN

New York Central had originally signed with the Ryan/EMD Trailer Transport system, but then after a change in management they cancelled. Upon his arrival in 1954, Al Perlman, the new president, found that the Central was desperately short of cash. Ryan's ideas clearly required capital, but the company had none. In lieu of intermodal, Perlman sped up his manifest schedules. He was forced to spend the Central's scarce capital to convert the four-track passenger railroad to a modern, CTC, high-speed freight railroad.

Even with all the modernization he still had clearance problems on key eastern main lines. Neither the line into New York nor the Boston & Albany line into Boston would clear standard TOFC moves. If Perlman were to get into the intermodal business it would probably be through the use of innovative technology.

Three years after the original rejection the EMD Trailer Transport System was still available, but the problem was that it required expensive terminals. The solution was to get a low profile car for main line clearances that could be loaded and unloaded in an inexpensive terminal.

The systems that were examined included C&O's Rail Van and the Steadman side loader. Also checked out was the new container system developed by Malcolm McLean. The one that was finally decided upon was Flexi Van. Strick Division of Fruehauf developed an experimental car in 1957. They delivered an old 42-foot flatcar with a new single, hydraulically-operated turntable powered by a motor-driven pump. Power was supplied by the terminal tractor units.

The experimental car worked as designed. The Strick van backed at right angles to the flatcar until its bottom rails lined up with the car's turntable mechanism. The driver then unlocked a pin in the demountable bogies, and backed the van off the wheels and into slots on the turntable. When the van was fully engaged on the turntable, a pin locked it in place. Using a push rod mounted on the Commando hostler unit, the driver engaged the van, pushed it 90 degrees until it paralleled the flatcar and locked into place on the car.

The production cars contained double turntables, capable of handling two 40-foot vans with or without nose-mounted reefer equipment. They were a skeltonized frame car. The lighter container (minus running gear) saved almost a quarter of the car and van tare weight of a standard pig flat with trailers. The lower center of gravity and reduced wind resistance, also paid dividends in the high-speed Flexi Van trains. In a joint test with Santa Fe in October 1966, it was found that,

A Flexi-Van container is being loaded onto a Flexi-Van Mark II Hydraulic car. The Van has already slid off the bogie. It will next be swung around to the center of the car and locked into place like the adjoining cars. — NEW YORK CENTRAL SYSTEM

This photograph shows the hostler tractor swinging the container on the turntable to the closed position on the car. The "Bazooka tube" on the front of the tractor provided an arm to grab onto the unlocked container in order to pull it around and position it over the bogies for unloading from the car. — JEFF MOREAU COLLECTION

An end view showing the prototype Flexi-Van with the turntable positioned to receive the special Flexi-Van container. The unit will be slid across the unlocked tandems (with the brakes set) and onto the turntable. — JEFF MOREAU COLLECTION

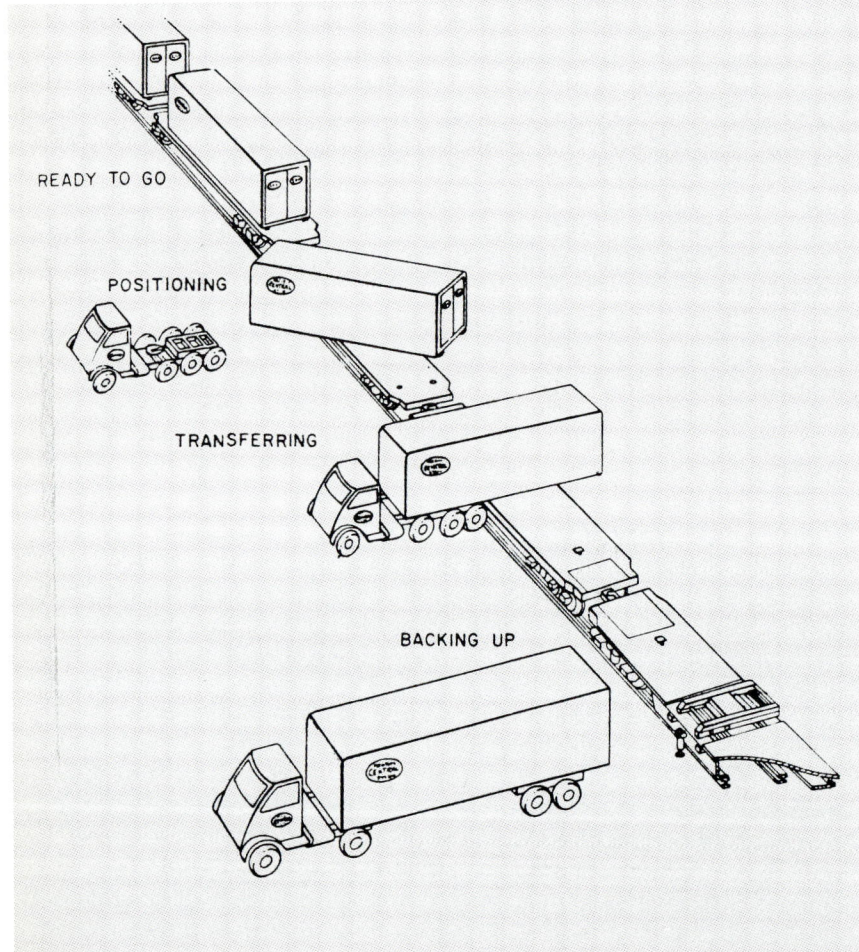

New York Central publicity photograph shows that deck cargo containers in low volumes were probably a whole lot better in theory than in practice if you had to rent a crane for each loading. — JEFF MOREAU COLLECTION

depending upon speed, the Flexi Vans produced a five to ten percent savings in rolling resistance. Unfortunately, this was in the days of ten cent per gallon diesel fuel.

Over a period of eight years the Central bought over 7,000 vans and 859 Flexi Van cars. This was enough to equip almost 50 daily high-speed solid Flexi Van trains. In addition it purchased 625 cars equipped with premium freight car trucks, steam and signal lines. This was done for the operation of most of the storage mail and express head-end business on the Central's extensive passenger fleet. Operating speeds of 85 m.p.h. were not uncommon for this fleet.

Maintenance expenses of both the fleet and the terminals were ultimately higher than originally expected. This was due to the rather exacting needs to match up the bottom rails of the van with the turntable. Snow and ice became a problem with both the sliding surface and the height misalignment in the terminals.

While a few railroads (including Illinois Central, Seaboard Air Line and Milwaukee Road) briefly flirted with the system, it was largely confined to the New York Central. The only interchange of Flexi Vans of any magnitude was in passenger service mail and express.

Two things are generally not recognized about the Central's intermodal experience. First, the captive nature of the Flexi Vans allowed the Central's commercial forces (many of whom were ex-truckers) to operate the system like a truck line. That is, selling price and equipment control were done on a lane specific basis and profits were carefully monitored. This was a major contrast in an era when piggyback was sold by most railroads for system volume or revenue goals, and trailers developed loads based upon who picked up the equipment.

Second, the Central began to get into TOFC (trailer-on-flatcar) before most people realized it. The need to interchange traffic with other carriers forced the issue. By the mid-1960's the New York area traffic was shifted from High Bridge in the Bronx to New Jersey where clearances for TOFC were sufficient. Additionally, the Massachusetts Turnpike extension opened up clearances which allowed the Central to operate TOFC to the outskirts of Boston. The New York Central, in 1964, joined Trailer Train in order to secure a source of piggyback cars. In 1966 the Central purchased the largest number of piggybackers ever built to that point. This was done so they could mechanize their major terminals to handle trailers. By the time of the merger with the Pennsy in 1968, the days of the Flexi Van had about drawn to a close.

STANDARDIZATION

As international container systems progressed and more carriers entered the picture, the need for international standards became evident. Ports were unable to maintain separate systems for the handling of each individual carrier's equipment.

Standardized corner fittings, spreaders, chassis and boxes, as well as widths and lengths, were adopted. The domestic counterpart container systems had no standardizing group similar to the International Standards Organization (ISO). Indeed, they had little cross-traffic flow to encourage the establishment of such a network that would require the standardization of system components.

The trailer was the vehicle of choice on virtually all of the early rail intermodal applications, starting with the Chicago Great Western onward. So, the trailer had history on its side (not an unimportant element in the railroad industry). In addition the institutional framework favored trailers. The rail intermodal leasing companies leased trailers. The Pennsylvania Railroad was the driving force in Trailer Train and it used trailers for TrucTrain service. Gene Ryan and Deodat Clejan, dominant figures in the decade of the 1950's, were dedicated trailer advocates.

Containers, to be cost effective on the railroad, needed to move on their bellies. This required the mechanization of terminals. Many of the carriers were not totally convinced that the large cash outlay required was warranted for a service that many railroaders were just not comfortable with.

So, the rail system stayed with trailers, and trailers achieved a critical mass. Each of the rail container systems became just another interesting hardware anachronism, discarded as trailer hardware systems standardized and spread.

Nevertheless, containers on railroads were not dead, they were merely dormant. Time was on their side, and later, if they were patient, they would be back in a rush. However, for now the world of intermodal belonged only to the trailer.

En route from Long Beach Harbor to the east coast, a string of Phoenix Container Line containers ride the rear end of a train as it surmounts the summit of Cajon Pass. —SANTA FE RAILWAY

Chapter 7

The Birth of Trailer Train

Newell and Ryan had hit on an idea that was just what the market wanted. As it became obvious that this would be a growth business, Pennsylvania Railroad ordered 300 more 75-foot cars to go with the original 200 Van Cars. At this point Bevan encouraged Ryan to establish a pool for these "oddball" cars. The PRR finance department clearly wanted no part of them on the Pennsy's balance sheet. The argument heard from many of the industry's mechanical and operating people was that these cars, like tank cars, were specialized, and as such, if the cars or the piggyback concept did not pan out, then the railroad should not be saddled with the risk of ownership.

Ryan, however, was in his element — new frontiers and untested territory. It would be a challenge, even to his sales ability.

Bill Johnson of the PRR law department, who was later sent to try and rescue the Railway Express Agency and still later became president and chief executive officer of the Illinois Central, helped incorporate the new Trailer Train Company on November 9, 1955. The Company issued 2,500 shares (at $100 each) to the Pennsylvania Railroad, 2,500 shares to Rail-Trailer and 1,000 shares to the Norfolk & Western Railway.

Prior to the establishment of Trailer Train, in negotiations with Newell, Carpi and Bevan, Ryan had to agree to a provision which would require him to resell his Trailer Train stock if his management contract was terminated. As we will see, this was an action that Ryan would live to regret.

On December 16, 1955 the new company held its first board of directors meeting. The Pennsylvania named Fred Carpi and Bevan to the Trailer Train board. The N&W selected Stuart Saunders, their vice president and general counsel. Rail-Trailer's representatives were Arthur Berry (later president of Pullman Leasing) and Rudy Smutny, managing partner of Solomon Brothers. At the board elections Newell was made president and Ryan vice president and general manager, and it was decided at this same time to buy the 500 75-foot cars used in TrucTrain service from the Pennsy and Rail-Trailer. Thus, was the Trailer Train Company born.

For economic and political reasons the Pennsylvania Railroad and Trailer Train became inextricably intertwined — both at its inception and over the next few decades. The PRR was eager to financially distance itself from this new creature called piggyback. The traffic department was openly hostile to the new company, but the rest of the company gave unstintingly of their time to launch and support it.

Newell maintained a dual role as operating vice

president of the PRR and president of the fledgling Trailer Train. Thus, he was able to use his powerful position in the PRR to assure that there would be compliance with the Symes policy to support the growth of TrucTrain on the railroad, and the establishment of Trailer Train as a national intermodal rail equipment pool. Ryan, with his sales and financial background, found Newell as the perfect counterpoint. Together they formed an unstoppable partnership.

The initial purposes and functions of Trailer Train have changed very little through the years. They were:

(1) To provide railroads with special flatcars for TOFC operations at minimum cost.
(2) To modernize and standardize flatcar and related equipment, and thus to promote the development of interchange as well as on-line traffic.
(3) To achieve the most efficient use of flatcars by the establishment of a car pool through which members can adjust their car supply to their actual needs.
(4) To provide a centralized agency for flatcar purchasing, financing, distribution and maintenance, and other activities related to the sound development of this field of transportation.

Among rail intermodalists Trailer Train has always played an interesting role. Beginning slowly, Trailer Train's staff and management was mostly part time and clearly dominated by the Pennsy. This fact set some other railroaders' teeth on edge.

The initial arrangement that Trailer Train made was a contract with Ryan's Van Car to run their operations out of Chicago. Trailer Train hired Ed Martin (formerly of the PRR) and moved him to Chicago. For the first few months Martin was the only full time Trailer Train employee. The executive offices remained in Philadelphia and were staffed by part-time employees from the Pennsy.

With Newell and Ryan working double duty on both Trailer Train and Pennsy's TrucTrain, each fed on the success of the other. TrucTrain grew rapidly and within three years it had grown to over 73,000 trailers. Trailer Train kept pace.

In its second year Trailer Train added six new member railroads, most of which were from outside the PRR sphere of traffic influence. The Company appeared to be on its way. By 1957, however, a major problem occurred for the first time since railroading had really focused on trucks as a source of revenue. Congress, in its consideration of highway legislation (in this case the Interstate Highway Act), increased trailer sizes from 35 feet to 40 feet.

Instantly, Newell's beloved 75-foot flatcars became obsolete. Bevan surely must have smiled to himself at having these financial dregs on the balance sheet of Trailer Train and not the Pennsy.

Trailer Train might have folded right then and there had it not been for three things. First, piggyback was still expanding and needed some kind of rail equipment to handle the business. Second, the 75-footers just wouldn't go away — even if they were financially obsolete for the moment. As this is being written the last three 75-foot cars are being retired from the fleet. Finally, there was Ryan and Newell and they were not about to let the Company go by the boards without a fight.

Trailer Train struck out in two directions. One, they got together with the car builders, Pullman-Standard, Bethlehem and American Car & Foundry, and two, Newell promoted a longer car, in this case an 85-footer, even with others urging a drop in size to a "safer" 50-footer.

Although the tare weight per trailer of the 50-footer was dramatically higher than for an 85-footer, and single cars could not produce adequate revenues, this seemed not to matter. In the design of freight cars many elements must be considered and trade offs made. They involved elements critical to transportation, mechanical, terminal operation and finance.

For example, the mechanical forces would have liked a car that lasted forever, and over its lifetime cost little or nothing to maintain. The fact that it weighed too much, cost too much or loaded with great difficulty was someone else's problem. The transportation people would have preferred an indestructible car with good tracking capability that weighed next to nothing and, most of all, was so cheap that it didn't have a major impact on their per diem budget.

The terminal operators only cared whether the car was easy to load and unload. If that perchance required expensive, hard to maintain cars, so be it. Finally, the finance people wanted a long-lived asset that was flexible (i.e., non-specialized) so that it could easily be sold to the bankers who needed to come up with the money to finance the equipment.

Within the structure of Trailer Train, the finance and mechanical functions are the only thing internal to Trailer Train. Trailer Train neither operates nor loads and unloads the cars. The natural bias, absent strong customers, i.e., railroad input, is to build an indestructible and cheap to maintain car. The customer input was mixed.

Trailer Train board members tended to be people from within the member roads who had backgrounds in finance, law or transportation. Intermodalists did serve on advisory committees, but internal railroad or

A 75-foot class F-39 double-hitch car in Trailer Train livery is like the cars built for the Pennsylvania Railroad and acquired by Trailer Train. This car has modern roller bearings, but has a tare weight of 41,100 pounds per trailer slot. — TRAILER TRAIN COLLECTION

Behold the "safe" car, a 50-foot single trailer car which weighs 58,800 pounds per trailer slot versus 42,000 pounds per trailer slot 85-foot car. This 40 percent penalty was bad enough even in the days of 10 cent per gallon diesel fuel. Extra maintenance cost put this car on the borderline of profitability. — TRAILER TRAIN COLLECTION

As highway trailers grew from 35 to 40 feet, the original 75-foot car became obsolete. Debate centered on whether "long cars" were safe. Jim Newell argued for the 85-foot car, while conservative Pennsylvania Railroad "Mechanical Department types" argued for the "safer" 50-footers. Shown is a trailer with nose mount reefer on the F-85 car being tied down by a groundman. — SANTA FE RAILWAY

Trailer Train politics usually blunted any effective representation. More often than not the railroad's Trailer Train board membership was appointed from among those with a "boxcar mentality." It was not until 1981 when Gordon Volkers, head of Chessie's Intermodal Department, was appointed by the road to the Trailer Train board that an intermodal officer moved to that position.

Through most of its history, this internal focus has been a strong driving force within Trailer Train. It is reflected in this very early key decision on the part of the conservative elements — most likely in the Pennsylvania Railroad mechanical department — to opt for the "safe," moderate 50-foot car for a part of the new car order in 1957, the first full year of operation for Trailer Train. The balance was 85-foot cars.

The change to the 85-foot car size helped to strengthen Trailer Train, as the risk of car ownership became more clearly focused for the railroads. As shown in the accompanying chart, the membership in Trailer Train grew rapidly. Initial active piggyback holdouts included the balance of the eastern roads and all of the far western roads. Most of the southeastern roads were late getting into piggyback.

MEMBERS JOINING TRAILER TRAIN IN FIRST TEN YEARS

1955 PRR, N&W, Rail-Trailer
1956 B&M, CB&Q, MKT, MP, SLSF, Wabash
1957 C&NW
1958 B&O, U.S. Freight
1959 Rail-Trailer Dropped, ACL, GM&O, IC, L&N, NYC&StL, SSW, SAL, WP
1960 AT&SF, C&O, CMSP&P, DT&I, GN, KCS, NP, RF&P, SP, SRS, T&P, TP&W, UP
1961 C of G, CGW, RDG
1962 None
1963 D&RGW, E-L, WM
1964 FEC, NYC, CRI&P

In 1958 an important breakthrough came with the addition of the Baltimore & Ohio to Trailer Train membership. It was the first major non-"PRR" family "Official Territory" road to break ranks and join Trailer Train. The fact was that the B&O was facing financial hard times and badly needed a source of car supply if it was to enter the piggyback game.

Significantly, the other member to join that year was U.S. Freight, a major freight forwarder — and by definition a major user of boxcars on the railroads. U.S. Freight's representative was Morris Forgash, an aggressive entrepreneur who was generally not reticent about letting people know exactly what he thought.

What was foremost in his mind was that long-haul truckers were his (and the railroads) mortal enemy. Anything or anyone who aided and abetted truckers was, at best, wrongheaded or, at worst, a traitor. That, of course, damned well included Gene Ryan. Fred Carpi had gained an ally on the board.

Forgash, however, had also become a passionate supporter of piggyback. For the life of him he could not figure out why the railroads would not cancel their Plan I traffic agreements with "unfriendly truckers" and deal only with the "friendly forwarders." With all the major boxcar traffic that he controlled and the growing piggyback traffic, Forgash's sentiments did, at least, gain him a hearing in very high places on most railroads.

On the positive side Forgash became a tireless salesman for Trailer Train and the concept of piggyback. He probably did as much as anyone to help blunt the attacks made by railroad traffic departments on piggyback.

As an interesting sidelight Trailer Train appointed Paul Turner, the director of sales of GM's Electro-Motive Division (diesel locomotives), to the board of directors on January 1, 1959. This unusual step of appointing a director from a non-stock owning company was accounted for in the organizational meeting held on January 16 where the office of chairman of the board was created, and Newell was named to the position effective April 1 of that year. Turner was appointed to fill the vacated presidency on the same effective date.

The thought was that Turner, who was on a first name basis with most railroad presidents, would be an effective spokesman to convince more railroads to become Trailer Train members. The General American Transportation Company pool, with some very powerful railroad members, was then viewed as a real competitive threat to Trailer Train.

Turner attended the March director's meeting still in his role as a board member. At the May and July meetings, after the appointments were effective, Newell presided as chairman, but Turner did not attend. On August 24, 1959 Paul Turner died in Florida, apparently without ever setting foot in Trailer Train offices after he became president. Jim Newell reassumed the presidential duties shortly thereafter.

By 1959 eight more Class I's joined Trailer Train. Member roads now accounted for 40 percent of the Class I mileage in the United States. Representation included most roads from the South, but, significantly, also from the West with the addition of the Western Pacific Railroad. A further crack in the "Official Territory" wall was made with the addition of the

A Nickel Plate belly-mounted reefer rests on a TTX flatcar. The Nickel Plate Road (the New York Chicago St. Louis Railway) was an important non-Pennsylvania Railroad eastern road addition to the Trailer Train pool. — DONALD DUKE

Chicago & North Western Railway trailers at Proviso Yard in Chicago. The North Western was an important early addition to Trailer Train. — DONALD DUKE COLLECTION

Nickel Plate.

More importantly, this was the time that the final act of the Gene Ryan — Trailer Train drama would be played out. The board terminated Ryan's contract. He was replaced by J.E. Wightman as general manager, and had his stock bought out under the hastily signed agreement of 1954. Internal Pennsy politics claimed their first Trailer Train victim.

Nevertheless, Trailer Train was definitely on a roll. In 1960 the General American transportation flatcar pool was disbanded, and most of the members joined Trailer Train. With 13 railroads joining that year, Class I mileage for TTX accounted for 74 percent of the U.S. total.

As the era of the first generation of intermodal drew to a close, many of its problems had been solved. The early chain and binder systems had been replaced, intermodal interchange between roads had been facilitated through the use of a more-or-less standard car fleet and most carriers offered some kind of intermodal service.

Piggyback terminals began to spring up everywhere as shippers demanded the new service. The terminals were generally a tie-pile ramp with an earth fill which allowed tractors to back the trailer up and onto the cut of flatcars.

Traffic grew rapidly. From the small beginning on the Chicago Great Western in 1936, traffic had reached 700,000 trailers by the end of 1959. But history had also set the stage for a love-hate relationship for intermodal during its crucial growth period in the 1950's, 1960's and 1970's. Operating people hated the critical service requirements and high horsepower per ton use of locomotives. Also with the use of trailers, intermodal was not "real railroading." Needless to say, even with all this, operating people loved the idea of getting rid of LCL costs. Traffic people hated having truckers and forwarders call on "their" customers and intensely disapproved of the boxcar diversion, but they could not deny their love of all the new traffic they were acquiring. Truckers hated to have the railroads offer intermodal service to forwarders, but they loved the cost savings. Forwarders hated to have the railroads deal with truckers for "their" traffic, but they, too, enjoyed the cost savings.

Yes, the next two decades would be full of — as the Chinese say — interesting times.

71

Bill Murray, General American Transportation Co. field engineer, trial tests a Fruehauf container on an experimental car. — DONALD DUKE COLLECTION

Chapter 8

Intermodal Gains A Voice

In the mid-1950's, as more and more Class I railroads initiated piggyback service, there were few places for the railroads' new intermodalists to meet and exchange ideas. With many of the new breed coming from trucking companies in the West, the Western Railroad Trunkline Association was established in Chicago. While it proved to be helpful, the organization in no way met the total needs of the new mode. Interchange traffic had become such an increasingly important part of the business that a nationwide organization appeared to be needed to deal with an exchange of ideas.

The Association of American Railroads, was a bit at sea over how to handle this new hybrid mode. An avalanche of railroads had moved into piggyback after the 1954 New Haven case. To deal with this the AAR's Operations and Maintenance Department, in 1955, organized the Committee on Motor Transportation, Freight Station Section. Their mission was "to study and report on subjects relating to highway motor vehicles operated by railroads. . . .in coordination with rail transportation."

Reflecting the LCL part of its heritage, the participants of the committee were almost equally split between the railroad trucking subsidiaries and station services. Interestingly, a representative was also appointed from the operating side of the Railway Express Agency.

In 1961 the group was reorganized as the Motor Transportation Advisory Committee, and was charged with serving as liaison to both motor transportation and rail piggyback. The committee remained heavily oriented toward stations, terminals and trucking. By 1966 the group was again reorganized, this time to the Steering Committee of the Motor and Piggyback Section. The committee received permanent staff support and called for rail officer membership on the committee with "responsibility for motor or piggyback transportation." It was as a result of this committee's version that the intermodal people started to join in great numbers.

Finally, in 1971 in recognition of the broader scope of the business, the committee became the Intermodal Steering Committee of the Intermodal Transportation Section.

The Association of American Railroads is made up of railroad members. It is organized with railroad board chairmen and presidents serving as the AAR board of directors. A committee structure covers transportation, mechanical, engineering, legal and public affairs. All areas are covered except for the commercial functions which were performed by the geographically organized rate bureaus.

The most powerful committee is the O-T (Operating Transportation) Committee. It is made up of the vice presidents of operations or vice presidents of transportation of AAR member railroads.

Back in the early 1960's intermodalists were looking for a broader scale organization in which they could exchange ideas. It was in 1963 when the Western Railroad Trunkline Association was holding a meeting in New Orleans that a small group, consisting of Charlie Groton of the Missouri Pacific, Dave Greer of the Pennsylvania Railroad and Ed Walters of the Kansas City Southern, met in Milwaukee Road's Laurin Cowling's room at the Monteleone Hotel. All in attendance agreed that a national organization of intermodal operating people and intermodal equipment manufacturers should meet on a regular basis. They could exchange ideas and try to solve mutual problems. There was, indeed, a great need to have someone to talk to since many of the early intermodalists were isolated on their own properties by the "real railroaders."

Intermodalists wanted to find someone in the fledgling industry with the stature to direct their effort. Ed Walters volunteered to try and enlist the help of Jim Newell at Trailer Train. Newell was enthusiastic about the project and offered to host a luncheon in Chicago the following month to discuss the matter. On the appointed day everyone involved appeared at the Chicago Knickerbocker Hotel. Newell agreed to spearhead the organization and to spread the word. The group elected Ed Walters as interim president of the new National Railroad Piggyback Association, but at the first meeting he became its first regularly elected president. Pat Crowe became administrative secretary, a position she held for the life of the organization.

The organization filled an obvious need and, consequently, it grew rapidly. It met, concurrently, with the AAR's Steering Committee. In those days two problems plagued the group. First, the high cost of going to the meetings had a tendency to discourage railroad attendance. This was due, in part, to the fact that many of the railroaders reported to the operating department and were on extremely tight budgets. The crux of the problem was that vendors and railroaders paid the same meeting fees. The second problem was that the National Railroad Piggyback Association was a huge success with the vendors of intermodal equipment. This led to some vendors trying to out-do their competition by setting up fancier hospitality rooms and entertaining during meeting times, impacting on the meeting's attendance.

These dissentions were solved in 1967 when the vendors restructured the organization. Among the changes to be made, the vendors would absorb virtually all of the meeting costs. This would reduce expenses for railroaders to a nominal amount in order to attract more carrier personnel. All hospitality rooms were canceled.

Another key element of the NRPA was introduced during the stewardship of Larry Keoughan of the Norfolk & Western - the Silver Kingpin Award. This presentation is an actual chrome-plated trailer kingpin mounted on a plaque and handed out by the Rail Board of this organization. It is the highest recognition of intermodal excellence. The recipients of the Silver Kingpin Award are listed in the appendix.

In 1976, with Chessie's Gordon Volkers as president of the Rail Section, the National Railroad Piggyback Association considered broadening its mandate beyond the consideration of trailers. Volkers had pioneered the relationship between the railroads and steamships in the negotiation of interchange agreements. Tom Fante of the Southern Pacific and Laurin Cowling of the Milwaukee Road gave active support to the idea. The National Railroad Piggyback Association then became the National Railroad Intermodal Association.

Two organizations were formed parallel with NRIA, the intermodal operating organization. These included the Intermodal Transportation Association and the National Association of Shipper Agents (later the Intermodal Marketing Association).

The Intermodal Transportation Association (ITA) had its earliest origins in a group set up in the American Trucking Association in the late 1950's. Called the Equipment Interchange Association (EIA), it was designed to facilitate the interchange of trailers among trucking companies in an era when most trucking companies were regional in nature. Ken Hauck, an employee of the Regular Common Carriers Conference of ATA was also Executive Secretary of the EIA.

In 1961 the EIA applied to the ICC for and received antitrust immunity. It was then set up as a separate nonprofit organization. As containerization began to prosper, the container steamship companies (many of whom were former truckers) also began to use the EIA for their container equipment interchange agreements with truckers. By 1973 this had evolved into the Uniform Intermodal Interchange Agreement (UIIA), an agreement generally limited to trucking and steamship companies.

Interchange agreements between railroads, railroads and steamship companies and railroads and truckers as a rule remained the standard AAR trailer interchange agreement. Some rail intermodalists such as Lauren Cowling of the Milwaukee Road and Jim Cunningham of PRR's Penn Truck Line supported both.

In 1979 in a bid to broaden the intermodal concept, Guy Cutler from Consolidated Freightways and EIA President appointed an ad hoc committee to examine the issues. The committee was chaired by Jim Cunningham of PTL and contained two representatives from each mode. In addition to Cunningham, Buddy Osborne from Southern Railway represented the railroads, Guy Cutler from C-F and James Farish of Overnite represented the truckers. From the leasing side came Robert Forbes, Rentco Division of Fruehauf, and Bernie Rosner of TransAmerica Realco. From the steamship companies came Robert Futrell of Sea-Land and Robert Goodwin of Kerr Steamship. Edwin Zimmerman of Seaboard World Airways and Jim Jackson of American Airlines rounded out air cargo.

In a final break with trucking, the ad hoc committee recommended that a broader intermodal organization be formed in addition to the EIA. In April of 1981 the first meeting of the Intermodal Transportation Association was held. The new organization also assumed the duties and staff that administered UIIA in 1985.

The organization was headed by Jim Cunningham of PTL with the staff led by Ken Hauck. In 1983 Al Mascaro became Executive Director where he served until his retirement in 1990.

After the 20 questions case had resolved the legitimacy of intermodal in the 1960's, regulatory questions continued to plague other groups - the shippers' associations and shippers' agents. These groups had emerged in the 1940's through an exemption to the Interstate Commerce Act. The exemption basically allowed the associations to act as freight forwarders, handling the freight of member shippers without getting authority from the ICC. Shippers' agents were likewise deregulated for the purposes of consolidation or distribution of freight, but not both. Most pre-1960 agents began by consolidating boxcar loads of supplier merchandise for retail stores. The growth of TOFC service in the early 1960's presented an opportunity for a new kind of shippers' agent to become dominant. These agents matched trailers in TOFC service under rail tariffs.

As piggyback grew, it is easy to see how trailer matching (most tariffs required a two-trailer tender) and load matching (to meet the 60-40 commodity mixing rule) became an important segment of business for both the shippers' associations and shippers' agents. As might be expected, the agents largely had backgrounds as truckers or forwarders, although a few, such as Phil Yeager of Hub, came from rail backgrounds.

By 1960 both truckers and freight forwarders began to challenge the legality of the agents and associations. Over 30 cases were filed, both in federal courts and at the ICC. The ICC cases were identified in the docket series MC-C-3192:

Both beleaguered groups felt a need to establish an umbrella trade association to defend themselves and to set overall standards. This led to the establishment of the American Institute for Shippers' Associations (AISA) in 1961.

While working their way through the cases, the shippers' agents became convinced that the agents had problems that were unique and needed to form their own trade association. With the blessing of the AISA, a group of agents got together in October of 1968 to form the National Association of Shippers' Agents (NASA).

Included in the new group were Keith Barrow and Dick Sanders of ITCO, Maury Sheer of Ft. Pitt Consolidators, Avery Eliscu and Don Middleton of GENEX, Duane Barnes of Shippers Traffic Service (two of whose sales people - R.C. Matney and Troy Stubbs would later form a larger shippers' agent, National Piggyback). Also in the founding group were Tony Sicilia of Expressways Terminals, Bob Marden of Trailer Train, Inc. (This shippers' agent is not to be confused with Trailer Train Company which changed its name to TTX in 1991), Milt Day of Dominion, Dominic Marino of Keystone Terminals and Frank Wayman of Delaware Valley.

Barnes served as the first NASA President and Marden as the first VP. Ron Cobert represented the trade association as General Counsel and served as Association Secretary.

As the cases began to be decided, it became clear that the agents were, in fact, deregulated and did not require a freight forwarders license. NASA then served to set standards of conduct for their members and to help the agents to understand how to deal with the railroads for this growing intermodal segment of business.

To that end, in 1974, NASA attracted Russ Talbot, a knowledgeable former rail traffic officer to act as Executive Director. Talbot had served most of his career as a traffic officer on the Pennsylvania Railroad and Penn Central, but had left to become Chairman of the Transcontinental Freight Bureau. After serving three years with the TCFB, Talbot became Executive Director of NASA. In this role he was particularly effective in bringing the agents and the railroads together in a joint effort to promote intermodal business. Talbot served until 1981 at which time John Murphy became Executive Director.

Murphy had a background in journalism and served until his death in 1988. At that point John McQuaid who had done Washington work for the National

An early Realco refrigeration unit. Even though the unit is loaded on a hitch, note the holdover practice of securing the rear of the trailer to the car with "disaster chains." — GORDON C. MILLER COLLECTION

Realco was a major leasing company formed by the Railway Express Agency. It had a definite leg up in the leasing business because of its repair depots that maintained its large existing truck fleet. Realco and others quickly established Mobile Service Units, such as the one seen here, to repair its leased trailer fleet at the intermodal ramps. — GORDON C. MILLER COLLECTION

Industrial Traffic League took over.

By 1987 the shippers' agents had expanded enormously and the role of freight forwarders had dropped off precipitously. The agents had become much more of a marketing arm for the railroads for intermodal moves. Discussions at the NASA convention that November of 1987, led the organization to change its name to the Intermodal Marketing Association in order to more accurately reflect the role of the shippers' agents who were also now being called intermodal marketing companies. In 1989, IMA changed its bylaws to allow railroads to become voting members of IMA, thus, reflecting once again the close ties between the shippers' agent industry and the railroad industry, and their joint desire to market intermodal service.

While the three organizations had some overlapping membership, they each found that many common issues caused convention programs of the three to overlap. Rail multiple membership also led to cries for a "single unified voice for intermodal."

In 1990 the three organizations began to explore the possibility of merging into a single organization representing all the needs of the intermodal service industries - rail, steamship, trucking, retail and the supply industry. By the end of 1991 it appeared that the three intermodal voices NRIA, ITA and IMA would blend into a single group - the Intermodal Association of North America.

The Intermodal Association of North America became a reality as each of the three organizations voted themselves out of existence at the end of 1991. In February 1992, the Intermodal Association of North America held its first meeting in Orlando, Florida, and elected a 15 member Board of Directors. Three directors were elected from each of the five divisions - railroad, steamship and stack train operators, truckers, marketing agents and suppliers. Don McInnes, Senior Vice President for Intermodal for the Santa Fe was elected Chairman. John McQuaid was hired by the board to be President and to head up the permanent staff of IANA. Connie Sheffield was hired as his deputy. Now, at long last, intermodal began to speak with one voice.

Chapter 9

Trailer Leasing

As intermodal progressed in the 1950's, many elements were in place that helped to encourage the use and growth of piggyback. Trailer Train made it easy for a railroad to obtain cars; a ramp made of a detrucked flatcar or a pile of ties and some dirt placed against a stub track could be put in very cheaply. If a railroad needed a "big" terminal, Rail-Trailer would build and operate it — all paid for in the lift charge. The trailers, if a railroad was required to supply them to the customer, posed the only potential capital problem. It was the trailer purchase where the diehard railroad boxcar types resisted, thus, throwing sand in the gears of the budding intermodal business.

Trailer leasing, even in the very early days of piggyback, was not unknown. As early as the 1940's Berhman Leasing, a Philadelphia leasing company, wrote month to month leases with the New Haven. The first hybrid lease, i.e., a trailer owned by a leasing company, but leased by a term lease and carrying railroad reporting marks so that it may be interchanged, was written in 1946 for the New Haven by the same group. In 1953 Jim Head at Trailmobile wrote a long term lease with the Chicago & North Western, covering 700 trailers.

By 1956 Gene Ryan had formed Van Pool for the express purpose of leasing trailers to his customers who, for the most part, were truckers. Ryan was totally committed to the Plan I concept of piggyback, and convinced his old friend Roy Fruehauf to build and finance the trailers for him. As a result of their dealings, Ryan got Fruehauf interested in intermodal. Ryan next hired Rocky Canzoniero from the New Haven and Palmer Bayer from a Chicago traffic bureau. While the business continued to grow, it was still basically limited to fairly straightforward leasing transactions.

Leasing helped the railroads, but only indirectly. What it really needed was one or more leasing entities that had a clear understanding of this new piggyback business, and would also supply trailers to the railroads.

In 1957 fate came upon the scene to fill this need. The New Haven, having leased 50 35-foot trailers from Gindy, were planning to send them back. As a consequence, Carl Tomm, who had originally leased the trailers as a way of getting them into the intermodal marketplace, decided that if they were returning them he might just as well set up a leasing company. And XTRA was born.

The three founders, Carl Tomm, Selwyn Kudick and Frank Ventre each put up $5,000 in initial capital to start the venture. Two of the founders had backgrounds with the Boston & Maine Railroad. It was to the B&M that XTRA leased their first trailers.

Gene Ryan convinced Roy Fruehauf to build trailers for leasing to intermodal customers. In this scene, a Fruehauf trailer leased to Rail Trailer and sub-leased to Interstate Truck Line System, is being switched at Proviso yard on the Chicago & North Western System. Note the names of various truck lines such as Briggs, Mueller, and Hallpin, that no longer exist today! — CHICAGO & NORTH WESTERN COLLECTION

A REALCO Trailer Leasing trailer, leased to C. Fiortio & Sons, rides aboard a pioneer intermodal flatcar together with a pioneer container with no identification markings on it. Apparently it was under test at the time? — DAVID DEBOER COLLECTION

Trailmobile wrote a long term lease with the Chicago & North Western, covering some 700 trailers. In this view, a Trailmobile trailer is being switched at Madison's Monona Yard. — WILLIAM D. MIDDLETON

XTRA leased their first trailers to the Boston & Maine Railroad. One of these trailers rides aboard a Nickel Plate Line converted flatcar, and was photographed crossing the Hudson River at Mechanicville, New York. Here the road had an interchange with the Delaware & Hudson and the New York Central. — JIM SHAUGHNESSY

The following year the company suffered a net loss of $2,733 on revenues of $6,684. Ten years later XTRA had revenues of $16 million with a net profit of $4.5 million. In the interim many things had transpired that were key to the growth of piggyback.

As the company was getting its start, trailers were being offered on a classic pool basis, i.e., participating railroads agreed to pay XTRA for trailers received in interchange, loaded or empty, for the time the trailers remained on the railroad.

Those railroads whose management supported piggyback and allowed the purchase or long-term lease of trailers used XTRA as a source of trailers for peak seasonal business. There were some railroads whose operating, traffic or finance departments did not permit the purchase or lease of trailers. For them the XTRA pool, and later Realco, meant the difference between being in business or quietly being strangled out of existence.

In 1963 XTRA introduced the idea of per diem relief to trailer leasing. Basically, this meant that railroads could take the trailers to one of several national relief points and once there, they could call time out on the daily lease payments. This concentration of relief points helped distribute trailers from carriers who were surplus to those who needed the equipment.

The ability to obtain pool trailers was the most critical factor in the early success of piggyback on many railroads. That initial success also nurtured the growth of XTRA as a company.

In addition to the railroads, one of the leasing customers for Van Pool was the almost moribund Railway Express Agency. The advent of express companies as an adjunct business started with stagecoach companies and the railroads. Wells Fargo and Adams Express were two of many. In some areas they were movers of bullion or bankers as well as being rapid movers of parcels. Many became very large companies, and competition between express companies for the express contracts with major railroads was especially fierce.

As railroads were consolidated in the late 1890's, the profit potential of these express companies did not escape the attention of the financial barons who were in the process of assembling their railroad empires. The result was the Railway Express Agency, a jointly-owned company whose profits were returned to the railroads.

However, through the years competition reared its ugly head in the form of freight forwarders, Parcel Post, United Parcel Service and express companies who also used other forms of transportation. REA, confronted on the revenue side with a plethora of competition, was faced on the cost side with outmoded facilities (albeit in every hamlet in America that had a railroad station) and with hidebound labor agreements. The result for the railroads was a large and growing deficit. No longer did the goose lay golden eggs for the railroads. It did, however, continue to eat an increasing daily ration of grain.

In an attempt to get the situation under control, the railroads elected Bill Johnson as president. This was the same Bill Johnson from the Pennsylvania Railroad Law Department who had drawn up the incorporation papers of Trailer Train.

Johnson entered the fray ready to go. Immediately initiating a study with Arthur D. Little to diversify REA, he appointed Warren Sarrenbetz to coordinate for REA.

Shortly after Johnson's arrival at REA, Canzonerio and Bayer called on him for Rail-Trailer's Van Pool. Their mission was twofold. They were extremely interested in increasing their leasing business with REA, and in addition to that, they were also aware that REA maintained a nationwide network of repair depots for their huge vehicle fleet. This, they hoped might help them because as the Van Pool fleet increased, their maintenance problems were growing even faster. Could Van Pool utilize REA as a contract repairman?

Johnson came up with what he felt was a better idea. Since the hard part (i.e., the repair facilities) was already in place, why couldn't REA go into the trailer leasing business? All it needed were some bright young guys to run it. He solved this need by hiring Palmer Bayer as vice president and general manager and Bob Budorick as director of sales. Once they were employed, he established Realco Trailer Leasing in December 1960. Four months later Canzoniero followed as New York regional manager. Les Robinson was hired as director of operations, Gordon Miller as Midwest sales, and with their acquisition, once again, Ryan's Rail-Trailer group was the supplier of the core group of a major intermodal function.

In April 1961 Realco, by assuming the Fruehauf leases, bought the 450 used trailers from Van Pool. Ryan's leasing business had fallen on hard times due to the loss of the Pennsy contract, and its trailers were not making money.

The Realco board was initially made up of representatives from six railroads and four Realco managers. The initial concept was simple. Provide the railroads with a tiered leasing system. One system was a standard, fixed-term finance lease and the other was a home-pool lease with railroad marks. Railroads were offered incentives to join the pool by having Realco buy out any existing straight trailer leases the railroads might have signed.

The idea grew rapidly, and in two years the fleet had

increased to 2,100 trailers and a rail membership of 43 participating carriers. The home-pool points were agreed to between REA and the railroads and were points on the leasee's railroad rather than common-pool points. The idea of relief from lease payments during slack demand periods was extremely attractive to the railroads.

As successful as the Realco segment was, it was not enough to overcome the loss sustained by REA's main express business. Bill Johnson and his new people did yeoman service in trying to turn REA around, but a combination of bad labor agreements and years of accumulating dry rot were too much. Railway Express as a company was shut down over a period of time and in 1968 Realco was sold to the Transamerica Corporation. Budorick, Canzoniero and Sarrenbetz left to found Interpool, and Bill Johnson was elected chief executive officer of the Illinois Central Railroad.

Rail Trailer operated a trailer pool to facilitate truckers use of piggyback. The design of this modern Ottawa hostler tractor was largely shaped by Sy Aramian who worked for Rail Trailer. Look closely below the rear wheel of the tractor on the tie-ramp structure. It's a leftover set of chains - and below a screw jack. — GORDON C. MILLER COLLECTION

Paceco got an early start in intermodal mechanization. In 1961 they placed a unit in Pennsylvania Railroad's major east coast facility at Kearny, New Jersey. This unit, located at the Baltimore Ohio's Chicago Forest Hill facility, joined units at PRR's 48th Street, Chicago facility and Western Pacific's Oakland, California Terminal. Paceco decided to concentrate on maritime cranes and left the intermodal market to others. — GORDON C. MILLER COLLECTION

Chapter 10

Terminal Mechanization

The year following Ryan's demise at Trailer Train, Pullman-Standard brought the industry into the "Second Generation" of intermodal cars. They produced a prototype 89-foot double hitch car in 1960. With slight modifications, this car would serve the railroad industry for the next 20 years.

Problems, such as varying tie-down equipment or totally different systems (such as Flexi Van or Clejan) that hampered one-car intermodal interchange, were over. No longer would ramp managers (and their terminal superintendents) be required to switch out their trains, and no longer would ramp personnel need to scramble to match trailers to cars — at least for a time. The attention of intermodalists would now turn to terminal, management and service improvements.

Now that the car problem was eased substantially, the sixties would see a burst of creativity. There would be the testing of new concepts in non-car areas. Some would succeed while others would not and some would sow the seeds of the future.

Intermodal terminals in the 1960's had proliferated to an estimated 2,100 locations. Shippers had pressured railroads for these facilities in order to gain a service edge or advantage. This in turn caused small vest-pocket ramps to spring up at old engine houses, nearby depots or in some forsaken corner of a freight yard. Many of these ramps provided only seasonal, low-level or imbalanced traffic. Some provided a combination of all three.

During the mid-1970's it had become very apparent that the overbuilding of piggyback ramps was causing a severe profit problem for intermodal. Small ramps led to poor service. This meant that a road freight train was required to stop for numerous pickups and set-outs while on a terminal to terminal run. This caused poor car and hitch utilization since most of the time only one trailer was loaded aboard a two-hitch car. Also, if the terminal crews happened to be unionized, the crews worked two hours in preparing the load and the actual loading, but were paid for an eight hour day. If a train's schedule happened to call for an early morning arrival and late afternoon departure, the loading and unloading could not be accomplished with a single crew. This often required two crews clocking eight hours when they were actually only providing minimal labor. Indeed, a tough way to make money.

Intermodal operating people saw the handwriting on the wall and immediately began to cut back on the number of small ramps in the 1970's. The concept was dubbed "hubbing," i.e., the gathering of trailers and containers by highway tractors rather than stopping a road freight train every 50 to 100 miles.

Pullman-Standard, in 1960, brought out the 89-foot, double-hitch car. Important changes would evolve from this basic car, but radical new car designs would end for the next 20 years. This Trailer Train car was built by Bethlehem Steel in 1966. — TRAILER TRAIN COLLECTION

At its peak in the 1960's I have estimated that 2,100 intermodal ramps existed in the United States. As the hubbing concept picked up steam two things happened: small ramps were closed and medium to large size ramps flourished and became mechanized. That meant these terminals were equipped with large machines that could lift trailers on and off the cars.

EXHIBIT I
Class I Intermodal Terminals

Year	Total	Percent of Reduction
1965	2,100	--
1975	1,500	29
1985	420	80
1990	231	89

Ramp reductions had a dramatic effect on car utilization. For example in 1975 the Trailer Train fleet ran 153 miles per serviceable car day. By 1990 that usage had increased by 57 percent. Car days spent at small terminals were often excessive due to traffic imbalance and extreme day-of-the-week traffic variation.

In addition the rapid mechanization of intermodal facilities put in place a capability that would be critical to the fostering of a later revolution — double-stack containers.

A perfect illustration of the "tie-pile" ramp. This example of a cheap ramp is why intermodal terminals grew in number to nearly 2,100 at the highwater mark. This great burst in the number of terminals led to compromises in service from the original intermodal trainload service to reduced mixed train service. — ROBERT KREHMEYER COLLECTION

EXHIBIT II
Class I Mechanized Intermodal Terminals

Year	Total	No. Mechanized	Percent Mechanized
1965	2,100	63	3
1975	1,500	110	7
1985	420	150	36
1990	231	196	85

Early lift devices were used largely to handle containers or heavy objects. Here a crane designed to handle lumber on and off flatcars (and to straighten shifted loads) is fitted with a special spreader to handle the Baltimore & Ohio container shown in this scene. Later on Missouri Pacific containers had similar lift-latching devices. — TRAILER TRAIN COLLECTION

Think you've seen everything in lift equipment? Obviously testing a trailer lift sling from Broderick & Bascom Rope Co., this Wabash "Big Hook" (used to cleanup derailments) tests the concept. — TRAILER TRAIN COLLECTION

With the long car and the collapsible hitch in place in the 1960's, piggyback started to grow and became more efficient with the terminal consolidations of the 1970's. In the early 1960's the only recorded mechanized intermodal handling consisted of a rubber-tired forklift machine built by Pettibone. It was built for the Alaska Railroad in order to handle 20-foot containers equipped with fork pockets.

The Pennsylvania Railroad, a pioneer, big-volume road, sought ways to improve terminal efficiency. The early overhead machines used by the Missouri Pacific attracted the attention of Pennsy officials. Unlike the drive-on circus-style loading and unloading, the overhead machines solved the "wrong-way car" problem. Trailers, heading in a different direction to the loading or unloading position, did not have to be placed in the right direction to be deramped or to have the flatcar turned around. The overhead machine allowed for selective unloading or "cherry picking."

The Drott Company attracted the attention of the Missouri Pacific early on and they placed test units at their disposal. Gene Johnson, a salesman from Paceco Crane, made early inroads in overhead crane sales at the Pennsy.

On the West Coast during the early 1930's and 1940's, Paceco's cranes had gained a good reputation for sound engineering and heavy fabrication. In 1958 the Matson Navigation Company had contracted with Paceco to build a dockside crane for its pioneering West Coast containership operation. Paceco also developed

Rail worthies watch as a Missouri Pacific container is loaded by an early Travelift. A simple spreader on the crane was used on Missouri Pacific containers only (unless an occasional B&O unit dropped in). — TRAILER TRAIN COLLECTION

Conceived on the dining room table of Southern Railway's Bill Brosman and laid out on the dirt floor of the Charlotte Roadway shops, the Southern began with stationary home-built cranes. They quickly evolved to these rail-mounted bottom-lift versions. The Southern Railway began its intermodal service as a fully mechanized carrier. — SOUTHERN RAILWAY

"Transtainer" span cranes for lifting boxes within the steamship terminal. The firm installed its first railroad piggyback bottom-only lift crane at Pennsylvania Railroad's Kearny, New Jersey, facility in 1961.

This was followed by another unit for Pennsy's 48th Street, Chicago, Illinois, facility in 1964. In 1965 Paceco placed two cantilever units (the only ones ever built) in the Western Pacific's Oakland, California, terminal. Two more Transtainer units were placed in the Chesapeake & Ohio's Forest Hill terminal in 1967. Paceco appeared to be a real player in intermodal's future.

Roy Fruehauf, the giant trailer manufacturer who had visions of positioning his company in the forefront of intermodal's growth, was attracted to Paceco cranes. He believed that Paceco would be the terminal entry of that strategy. In 1968 he bought Paceco and made it a part of his trailer-building empire. Unfortunately, Paceco continued to concentrate on marine cranes, building very few for rail intermodal facitilites. In the late 1980's Fruehauf sold the division.

A lot of money was spent on intermodal facilities in the late 1950's in order to increase efficiency. The Southern Pacific's Los Angeles Transportation Center (LATC), for example, put in concrete circus ramps that extended nine-tracks wide. This was later increased to 17 tracks. While this was a marked improvement over less permanent ramps, the concrete ramp still caused problems.

First, there were delays caused from having to wait for inbound trains to be broken up and switched onto ramp tracks. And since there was much pressure put upon the superintendents to attend to carload customers first, this often caused a real problem. Secondly, even if the ramp was busy enough to justify a captive switch engine, the switching out of cars consumed time. Thirdly, even when the switching had been accomplished, "hot" loads such as priority mail or refrigerated cargo like meat could be buried eight cars deep at the end of a cut of cars. The hostler crews were thus required to deramp (pull off) as many as 15 trailers (also drop 15 hitches) in order to reach the desired "hot" loads.

The Southern Pacific's intermodal operations in 1953 was the responsibility of the Freight Protection, Merchandise and Stations Department (known around the SP as the "Broken Bottles Department"). Although it was headed by Phil Chamoff, manager of specialized operations, most of the intermodal duties fell to a young assistant manager by the name of Tom Fante. His right-hand man was Jack Sherbourne, the Supervisor of Flatcar Service.

With Southern Pacific's piggyback traffic growing by leaps and bounds in 1964, Tom Fante assigned Sherbourne to the task of finding a better way to load and unload trailers. Sherbourne had recollections of

Here are examples of Southern Railway's aluminum containers. On this CTTX Trailer Train all-container car is a 40-foot container, two 5-footers, a 10-footer and a 20-footer. On an adjacent car is an open top container on a chassis. — SOUTHERN RAILWAY

having watched a brawny machine load large logs onto flatcars in the Oregon woods. Called the "Lumberjack," it was basically a large forklift truck outfitted with oversized tires. The front end was uniquely designed to lift logs, and it had been beefed up to withstand the rugged lumbering environment. Sherbourne remembered the log-loading experience and wondered — "Why not use something like this to unload trailers from flatcars?" Why not, indeed!

Sherbourne also recalled seeing the machine at a time when he had met Dave Coulson, an early intermodalist from the Pacific Northwest. Coulson was working at outfitting logging trucks, and is credited with the invention of the folding arms which helped to increase log loads. He was also the developer of a sliding Coulson Bolster for use in securing containers on flatcars. The Coulson Bolster was capable of being used for both 20-foot or 40-foot marine containers.

Upon making a quick phone call to Coulson, he revealed to Sherbourne that the company that had modified the log-lift truck had the foresight to place a company decal, Nelson Equipment Company, on the machine. The company, located in Portland, Oregon, was the sales agent for Wagner Tractor Company and it was headed up by a tall, young go-getter named Scott Corbett.

Corbett had originally developed large, rugged machines for all phases of log handling. Initially, he had worked with L.G. LeTourneau developing diesel-electric log skidders and stackers. It was there that he met Chico Clark, but more on Clark later. Corbett decided to switch companies so he could distribute and sell Wagner Tractor hydraulic machines, primarily, because of the moisture problems which affected the electrical components of diesel-electric equipment.

Corbett, a good friend of Coulson, also hit it off with Sherbourne. Could Corbett modify his machine to do Southern Pacific's job? The question arose as to how

Although Missouri Pacific was an early user of containers, Intermodal General Manager Charlie Groton immediately decided he "didn't trust" mechanical terminal handling equipment. The result was probably the most expensive and extensive circus ramp system in the U.S. Although this ramp is asphalt, many were concrete. Note that the ramp is T-shaped with railcar work tracks going off each side. — ROBERT KREHMEYER COLLECTION

Drott bought the rights for Travelift from a manufacturer of marine boat lifts. At the left, assembled by Pullman-Standard, the earliest rail designed machine was placed at Santa Fe's Corwith yard in Chicago. Note the all-weather cab and the operator out in "all-weather." (RIGHT) Drott quickly broke in on other intermodal carriers placing this unit in Pennsylvania Railroad's Kearny, New Jersey, facility in New York Harbor. — BOTH TRAILER TRAIN COLLECTION

much a trailer weighed and was it uniform in weight? With preliminary answers to his questions, Corbett went to work. He began his efforts working with Wagner Tractor. Wagner's chief engineer was of the opinion that the whole idea of lifting trailers and loading them on flatcars was crazy and he would not get involved with such a scheme. Corbett's next thought was to handle the trailers with forks. Further study and field research at SP's Brooklyn Yard at Portland quickly disabused him of that idea. He found that trailers clearly required more support when being bottom lifted.

Corbett sketched out some ideas and asked Nelson Equipment Company to build the front-end modifications to a forklift. Nelson Equipment went to work. The result was a short forklift that fit under the near side of the trailer. It had a moveable bale mechanism that closed over the top, the far side and a small part of the trailer's bottom rails. Approximately five months after their first meeting, the original modified log-stacker "Piggypacker" was sent to SP's Los Angeles Transportation Center for testing. After some fine tuning the key to piggyback growth clicked into place.

Terminal mechanization has often been credited with cutting circus ramp costs. However, nothing could be further from the truth when it came to small facilities. From a capital investment standpoint, what could be cheaper than moving some dirt and opening a stub-track, circus-style ramp. While this approach had problems already discussed, it definitely was cheaper. Unfortunately, as volume grew terminal operating costs at a circus ramp escalated rapidly. At this point mechanization was the only thing that would keep terminal unit costs in line.

At Chicago, Lauring Cowling, another innovative intermodalist with the Milwaukee Road, watched Southern Pacific's experiment with interest. He bought Scott Corbett's first production "Piggypacker" and during October of 1966 installed it at the road's Bensenville terminal in Chicago. Because of its location, Bensenville literally became an intermodal terminal demonstration laboratory.

Chico Clark watched the inroads that were being made by the early hydraulic machines. As a consequence of his interest he joined with Corbett and Nelson Equipment, offering them more ideas. Clark proved to have a good feel for the mechanical side of the business, and was invaluable in terminal design concepts. He promoted the use of the side-lift "Piggypacker" equipment. Not a bashful man, he was a tailormade counterpoint to Corbett. Together they made a dynamite team.

Meanwhile, the New York Central was running into problems interlining the Flexi Van system. Planning to expand into trailers in anticipation of the Penn Central merger, Bill Kirk kept a close watch on this trailer terminal mechanization equipment. He liked what he saw and bought 14 "Piggypackers." Ray Tippet, manager of the Central's Chicago terminal, was also a big contributor to many mechanical improvements. By 1966 terminal mechanization for piggyback operations was clearly on its way.

Although containers were only a minuscule part of piggyback (less than five percent) in those days, there was talk of improving the efficiency of piggyback by "leaving the wheels behind." The early container experiments conducted by Bill Brosnan's Southern Railway and Al Perlman's New York Central encouraged a continuing discussion of container handling. Except for the Central and Southern operations, most containers were handled by mounting it on a truck chassis and either circus loading or bottom picking them up on the flatcar as a trailer.

In order to lift containers on and off ships, marine technology used "spreaders" mounted on large cranes that engaged the tops of containers. Spreader technology improvements, as used by the steamship industry, had railroaders clamoring for a top-pick machine. This was a machine where a spreader head either hooked into the side opening of a top corner casting by using a "side latch" into the side openings or by using twist locks into the top opening of the same top corner casting. Early B&O and MOP container systems used a totally different "side squeeze" fitting on the top side of the container.

One of the early problems of containerization was that container owners wanted to use their own "in-house" latching systems. Each one had a different idea. As an example, it was necessary to change the corner lifting devices if one was handling a Matson vs Sea-Land container.

Corbett believed that Ropco Corporation (RPC) had the best concept, one that was similar to those in marine terminals, a combined top/bottom pickup lift machne. Their first machine was developed in 1968 and delivered to the Union Pacific for service in Seattle. After eight machines were built by Wagner-Corbett-Ropco, Wagner decided to commit to an intermodal program, taking over all manufacturing and development. At this time Wagner Tractor was purchased by Raygo and became Raygo-Wagner.

The Southern Railway arrived on the intermodal scene late in the game. Piggyback had taken off on both coasts in the mid-1950's, but the South was far behind. The South was just beginning to extricate itself from the capital deprivation of the post Civil War times. The traditional financial centers in the East and Midwest were reluctant to provide the necessary capital to build a New South. Following World War II, however, the boom of the postwar era changed all that. With cheap labor in the South and labor trouble in the North, suddenly capital began to flow into the New South. A strong financial center was established in Atlanta.

Railroads of the South were slow to react to new things and financial opportunities, preferring instead to let things proceed apace. While the South was certainly genteel, its progress languished, including piggyback. One notable exception to the rule was Southern Railway's strong operating personality, Bill Brosnan, who initiated their entry into intermodal. He was once described as "A bigger than life package containing brains, leadership, terrorism, and charm — in about equal amounts." Brosnan relished meeting problems head on, and shaking them by the neck until the problem was solved. He had come up through the ranks of the Southern Railway's operating department.

In 1960 Brosnan was promoted from vice president of operations to executive vice president. As VP-O, Brosnan had continually stimulated his people to modernize, upgrade and innovate. As he said, "To do things like that you must have highly motivated people. You do need a top man pushing, one who's cognizant of costs, and thinking ahead as to how the system can be improved. Planning is the key. Painting the outlines with a big brush and assigning the details to others, but continuing to look over their shoulders to be sure they're carrying out the plan."

One of those "highly motivated people" was Stan Crane, a young engineer in the Test Department. He carried out numerous programs for Brosnan, both from the Test Department and then later from the Engineering Department. Crane and Brosnan provided much of the stimulus for mechanizing the maintenance-of-way function on America's railroads.

Brosnan used his new position to extend his unorthodox thinking to broader corporate matters. It was very apparent that he had been closely watching piggyback developments in other regions of the country for some time. It was shortly after his promotion that he got the Southern on board the piggyback movement. But not just on board — out front.

Like other forceful operating men, such as Al Perlman at the Central and Malcolm McLean at Sea-Land, Brosnan, too, was not convinced that it made sense to carry around the "excess baggage" such as the wheels that came with highway trailers. However, doing away with this "excess baggage" meant that the boxes could not be circus loaded, necessitating some type of mechanized terminal equipment.

Brosnan contacted Drott Crane Company for a proposal. Drott's salesman made a call on Brosnan early in July and reported that six cranes would cost $250,000 each and the first crane could be delivered by the following January. Brosnan wanted cranes in September. During this time regular luncheon meetings were being held with what Brosnan called his "bright young folks" at the old Ambassador Hotel. At one of these luncheons Brosnan put his problem to Stan Crane.

Another early Drott machine at work on the Baltimore & Ohio. Note the container being loaded "on the belly" or COFC (container on flatcar) on the same car as an adjoining unit loaded on a chassis as a trailer or TOFC (trailer on flatcar). — TRAILER TRAIN COLLECTION

Crane's response was, "Mr. Brosnan, we're going to have to build our own cranes. I've been up to Pennyslvania Railroad's Kearny Yard and looked at the Drott unit, and I think we can do it." As a result of Crane's remark Brosnan called a meeting for that Sunday at his home.

At his dining room table, Brosnan related his thoughts to Stan Crane, the two Fox brothers, Herb and Bob, Master Mechanic Dick Franklin and Joe Moore of the Mechanical Department. He wanted detailed concept drawings by Monday.

The drawings were ready Monday morning. Needless to say, when Bill Brosnan wanted something on the Southern Railway, he usually got it. O.K'ing the drawings, he said he wanted to see the first machine in 30 days. Brosnan had laid out the approximate dimensions in the dirt floor of the Charlotte Roadway Shops. The Shop Superintendent cordoned off the area until the machine was finished. Within 30 days Brosnan inspected the first crane at the Shops. It had been constructed by using material that was found "just lying around" — so it was cheap to build. The prototype was a stationary crane that allowed cuts of cars handled by a locomotive to move under it. Brosnan gave his blessing to the project and two other cranes were built and located in Jacksonville and Birmingham. Brosnan also bought Fruehauf aluminum vans in 40-, 20-, 10- and 5-foot lengths, original "standard" container lengths. The shorter length vans were designed to handle LCL (Less-Than-Carload) traffic. (Does this sound familiar?) The vans were built of aluminum since, coincidently, Reynolds Aluminum happened to be a good customer of the Southern Railway.

The stationery crane idea proved impractical, and by 1961 they had been mounted on rails and were self-propelled. Apparently, the maintenance-of-way people had "free" surplus rails and steel wheels, but not "free" tires. The Southern Railway was a rare intermodal exception. It began intermodal life as a fully mechanized carrier.

Soon other railroads started to flirt with containerization. The Missouri Pacific began with containers that had large diagonal braces tied into the top and bottom of the container rails, and each container had an eye at the top for lifting. Later, like the B&O, MOP containers were converted to the side-squeeze method. The cranes used to lift these containers were seagoing Drott units, but a few were old lumber and machinery stationary overhead cranes that had been used to unload flatcars in the 1920's and 1930's. When loaded, the boxes were tied down inside gondola cars. To the Missouri Pacific this system looked ideal; no wheels to haul around; existing cranes for lift-on or lift-off were used; and if the damned thing didn't work, one could use the gondolas for "honest" freight. A true operating man's system all the way.

Unfortunately, due to their advanced age the Missouri Pacific cranes were slow and prone to breakdowns. This led Charley Groton, general manager of piggyback and vice president of Missouri Pacific Trucklines, to opt for trailer loading by the circus method. Later on the MP would build some very modern, efficient and costly concrete circus-ramp facilities. While circus ramps became a burden as volume increased at the large ramps, they did improve the efficiency at medium-sized facilities. Groton, however, just "didn't trust" the new cranes and side-lift machines. Most of Missouri Pacific's operations remained non-mechanized for a long period of time.

The four early proponents of containerization, the

Missouri Pacific, the New York Central, the Southern Railway and the Baltimore & Ohio, all eventually threw in the towel. They had failed to convince interline carriers to adopt their form of containerization. Most of the railroads had pretty well standardized piggyback trailers and were satisfied with the system. Les Robinson's invention of the screw hitch solved the car interchange problem and did away with the myriad of chain and binder systems. Trailer Train provided a cheap and steady supply of cars and the trailer leasing companies provided the trailers.

Drott Crane Company had previously purchased a line of marine boat lifters from the Travelift & Engineering Company of Sturgeon Bay, Wisconsin, and teamed with Pullman-Standard, the major United States car builder, to fabricate the early trailer lift units. In 1956 the Missouri Pacific had taken one of the old marine machines to handle its expanding container business.

A young Chicago born lad named Jack Lanigan joined Drott Crane in 1961. As a youngster he had dreamed of owning a Lionel electric train which, unfortunately, his family could ill afford. As a result of Lanigan's interest in trains he was drawn to this new railroad innovation called piggyback. Lanigan was of the opinion that the machines had good potential for the handling of trailers and containers and of course Drott agreed as it was striving to broaden its business base. The converted marine travel lifts were tried on several railroads, including the Baltimore & Ohio, the New York Central and the Pennsylvania Railroad, in order to gain experience.

During this particular time the railroad supply industry had a floating group of entrepreneurs, acting as manufacturer's representatives for a number of small suppliers who were unable to afford their own sales force. They generally specialized in the needs of three or four railroad carriers and became knowledgeable as to their likes and dislikes.

One such representative was Jim Head who brought news to Lanigan that the Santa Fe had some people who appeared to be interested in Drott's new concept of intermodal terminal mechanization. The interested parties were a young terminal manager, Ed Frey and a mid-level operating man, Larry Cena. Lanigan called upon the Santa Fe to get a better understanding of their needs, and Drott put everything it had learned into a new design. It resulted in the development of Unit No. 1 for the Santa Fe's Corwith intermodal facility at Chicago. Like the Milwaukee Road's Bensonville facility, Corwith soon became an intermodal test-bed and industry laboratory.

The unique feature of the new crane was a stablizing bar. This bar prevented the swaying problems encountered by earlier cranes. The unit arrived at Corwith in 1963. After a break-in period as Lanigan puts it, "The unit handled the astounding total of 125 trailers in a day."

Drott Crane was clearly on a roll and expanding out from the marine travel lift. The placement of the second unit at Santa Fe's Hobart yard in Los Angeles occurred two year later. It was at this point that the Drott team learned that intermodal car deck heights varied dramatically. The first-generation car fleet was hardly uniform — particularly as railroads began to interchange intermodal cars. Not to worry, Drott would adjust.

The Santa Fe was moving into marine containers in a serious way. Matson, American President Lines and Sea-Land became important customers for Santa Fe, producing a need for top-lift capability.

Unfortunately, the lack of uniformity of corner castings required multiple changeouts on the top-pick spreaders. After a few years of non-uniform castings the maritime industry, through the International Standards Organization (an international standards group), finally mandated a uniform corner casting standard. In the interim Lanigan developed a side-latch device which hooked into the side hole of the corner casting. That part of the casting had originally been made uniform. It allowed a sling with grappling hooks to lift deck-loaded containers from ships, using ports that were not pier-crane equipped.

Although the intermodal crane sales to railroads had amounted to only two cranes in two and one-half years, Lanigan remained bullish on intermodal as a major customer. In his employment agreement with Drott Crane, the company had agreed to a condition whereby they would set Lanigan up with a Drott dealership if he could establish a meaningful rail business. Having fulfilled the condition, he set up Mi-Jack as his dealership. With low volume sales, it was difficult to keep Drott interested in developing new machines. Drott required Lanigan's dealership to book orders for an entire year before any rail orders were built. This kept the pressure on.

In 1970 Drott was purchased by the J.I. Case Company. For a time the pressure was off Lanigan while the larger company was learning its way around the Drott crane line. But with a recession looming, it did not take them long to reach the same conclusion as Drott previously had. The intermodal business had great difficulty supporting the three key industry builders of lift equipment, Drott, Le Tourneau and Raygo-Wagner. In addition to their low volume of business, there was always a new boy on the block who was willing to challenge the three existing manufacturers. Through the years, Paceco, Ropco, Clark Equipment, Silent Hoist, Hyster, Harnischfeger, Belotti, Kalmar, Caterpillar, Taylor Machine and others all made runs at the market. In the area of lift equipment this situation has tended to discourage all but the stoutest of intermodal believers.

As intermodal projects and studies were developing at the Federal Railroad Administration, I often saw people who were looking for support for their own intermodal projects. In the dark year of 1975 Jack Lanigan showed up with J.I. Case people, hoping to reassure them that, at least in the long term, there was a future for intermodal and intermodal suppliers. A review of some of the in-process work on the Intermodal Network Study seemed to help. Shortly, thereafter, I made a trip to Memphis to make a similar presentation to Bill Winter of Le Tourneau.

The relationship between Mi-Jack and Drott, a struggling Chicago area dealer trying to keep Drott in business, was matched by Howard Cooper and Allen VanDyne who ran the Chicago area dealership for the Raygo-Wagner "Piggypacker." In 1979 Raygo decided to take over their own sales and sell directly from the factory. At that point Lanigan approached Howard Cooper with an eye to merging their dealerships and to once again take over the sales for Raygo in the Midwest. This seemed like the solution to their problem since only 10-12 machines per year were being sold by the combined dealerships.

In 1980 Case announced they were dropping the Drott Crane Company line. Lanigan then decided to move from being a dealer to becoming a manufacturer. He bought all of Drott's patents, drawings and parts. It was his intention to completely redesign the machine. This he felt could be done based on what he had learned while designing a hydraulic device to lift M-X missile silo housings for the Defense Department. He had built a prototype for the department and held a contract for 22 more units. Unfortunately, a change in administrations saw the program cancelled, but the lessons he had learned from that prototype greatly benefitted the new redesign. The eventual product for the rail environment became the Mi-Jack "Translift."

Mi-Jack, in 1985, added the side-lift machines to its "Translift" machines by buying Raygo-Wagner "Piggypacker" patents, prints and parts. Since for a number of years the "Packers" had been built by the Allied Company of Portland, Oregon, Mi-Jack continued the arrangement.

In 1989 Jack Lanigan, who could now afford to buy as many Lionel trains as he wanted, now went beyond those childhood dreams. Lionel had approached him for the purpose of allowing them to build a model of

Clark-Ross T-260 loading a Spector Trucking Co. Mobil-van. This forklift machine required tine tunnels to be built into the container, reducing internal space. The car is an original Pennsylvania Railroad 75-foot intermodal unit. — TRAILER TRAIN COLLECTION

A model No. 512 straddle carrier by Clark Equipment. Clark, an early intermodal equipment builder, withdrew from the intermodal marketplace. — CLARK EQUIPMENT COMPANY

The Letro-Jib was produced by Le Tourneau for industrial applications. It was a short jump from this machine to a side-lift intermodal unit. — JIM NIX COLLECTION

The Straddle Lift shown here was another Le Tourneau machine produced for the industrial market. It was a short move to the Strad-L-Port overhead lift machine. — JIM NIX COLLECTION

a Mi-Jack "Translift" to appear in their Christmas line. In the Christmas spirit, Lanigan was very receptive and swapped his royalties in lieu of Lionel doing a story on how intermodal began. The article was in that year's Lionel Christmas catalog. In a twist of fate Lionel trains were brought into the intermodal age by a Chicago kid from across the tracks.

By the early 1960's, R.G. Le Tourneau of Longview, Texas, was manufacturing both industrial and logging cranes and lifts, along with what an intermodalist would recognize as terminal overhead and side-lift equipment. A large yard machine, called the Letro-Jib, was the forerunner of what would later become the Letro Porter side-lift unit. The Straddle Lift industrial machines became the start of the Le Tourneau overhead lift series. With this seemingly unmatchable base from which to launch into the intermodal business, for some unknown reason Le Tourneau held back and dragged its feet.

Frank Quinn, the owner of Quinn Equipment of Chicago, was an area dealer who possessed a persuasive nature that Le Tourneau did not count on. Frank was very aware of the development and invasion of railroad intermodal by outsiders. He believed that these firms had no business beating out Le Tourneau who he felt had just what the railroad wanted. Quinn said to them, "We need to get in the business, and to do it fast." So, they quickly copied a P&H Crane Company design in order to meet a bid for the Chicago, Burlington & Quincy Railroad for an overhead crane. In the process Quinn also employed a young hotshot salesman named Chico Clark who he knew had developed a fondness for the railroad market.

Chicago was fast becoming a hotbed for intermodal dealers. They were grabbing their manufacturers and

Chicago & North Western's Tom Schwartzlander (center) takes delivery of a Letro-Porter side-lift machine built by Le Tourneau. Frank Quinn (left), Le Tourneau's Chicago dealer, moved the company into the intermodal business. Inveterate missionary salesman of terminal mechanization and efficiency, Chico Clark, is shown on the right. — JIM NIX COLLECTION

The first crane built by Le Tourneau for rail intermodal use was this unit delivered to the Chicago, Burlington & Quincy Railroad in January 1966. A 68-foot unit spanning up to four tracks in the "Q's" Cicero, Chicago facility. This beauty cost $89,000 to build and is still in service on successor Burlington Northern. — JIM NIX COLLECTION

forcing them to develop lift equipment for this new piggyback phenomenon. Quinn was determined that Le Tourneau would be in the forefront of that group.

The requirements for intermodal equipment at the Burlington had been laid down by Ken Schramm. The Burlington had been an early intermodal pioneer, but up until the mid-1950's had languished. However, by the early 1960's Schramm had put the "Q" back on the fast track of intermodal growth. The road's new president, the lanky, young Lou Menk, would tolerate nothing less. That meant terminal mechanization in the Burlington's burgeoning Cicero-Chicago terminal. Bids for the required crane closed in 1965. Quinn won.

The crane was a real humdinger, having a 68-foot span which could reach across five tracks and had a one and one-half minute cycle time, i.e., the time to complete the lift of one trailer. It was delivered January 5, 1966, and the invoice (including parts) was billed out at $89,000. As of the writing of this book, the crane is still in daily service on the Burlington Northern.

With the Burlington as a base, Le Tourneau was able to expand to the Chicago & Eastern Illinois, Chicago & North Western and others around Chicago. From there they went to the Southern Pacific's new Cotton Belt facility in Memphis. Le Tourneau also developed an articulated side-lift machine to compete with the "Piggypacker." The big difference between Le Tourneau machines and his competitors was in the power transmission. In Le Tourneau equipment it was electric, but in Drott, Raygo-Wagner and others it was hydraulic. The battle between electric vs hydraulic, between original and maintenance cost and between overhead cranes and side-lift machines has been fought over the past 25 years. It continues to this day.

Like the other manufacturers Le Tourneau has also been a reluctant builder through most of those 25 years, but determined dealers kept them in the business. Unlike the Raygo and Drott lines which were purchased by Mi-Jack, a determined dealer who turned himself into a manufacturer, Le Tourneau continues as an independent manufacturer to whom its intermodal lines are a minor business. For 25 years, however, the big three companies who stuck with intermodal through thick and thin have been Le Tourneau, Raygo-Wagner and Drott — the latter two now under the Mi-Jack banner.

One lift manufacturer who may have broken into the charmed circle of the "Big Three" is Taylor Machine Works. A manufacturer of material handling equipment, it was established in Louisville, Mississippi, in the late 1920's. Like Paceco, Taylor entered into the business on the maritime side. Unlike Paceco they did not develop the massive quayside cranes, but instead concentrated on intra-terminal equipment such as Stackers.

Southern Pacific's Jack Sherbourne felt that terminal mechanization was important to the road's intermodal business. Contacting Scott Corbett, sales agent for Wagner Tractor resulted in the Piggypacker prototype shown here and sold to SP. Built from a logging machine, it is still in service. — LAURIN COWLING COLLECTION

"Big Bill" Taylor, a genuine Mississippi gentleman and son of the founder, was the head of the company. It was his decision to enter into the rail scene slowly, using Taylor technology and design. His initial machines were International Standards Organization top pick only side-lift machines sold to both the Canadian National and the Santa Fe in the 1970's. Additional machines were built mostly for the Canadian National and the Canadian Pacific.

By 1970 Taylor had developed a spreader machine head that handled both containers (through top pick) and trailers (through bottom pick). That unit also went north to the CP. By the mid-1980's several units were sold to John Gray of Stevedoring Services of America (SS of A), a contractor for the Sea-Land double-stack facility at Tacoma. Five additional railroads bought "Big Reds" in the 1980's. A 20-year commitment to intermodal may have moved Taylor into the "Big Four."

No chapter on intermodal terminal mechanization would be complete without a comment on the "bear terminals," the most difficult of the era to operate. Over perhaps a ten year period I have tested intermodalists young and old with what I consider to be the nominees for the three toughest major intermodal terminals through the years. My nominees have gone

New York Central placed the largest order for lift equipment when it ordered Piggypackers for most of its system terminals to prepare for merger with the Pennsy. Here a P-70 lifts a 40-footer aboard. — JEFF MOREAU COLLECTION

unchallenged. As long as no one tries to rank the three in any particular order, I think we have a reasonable list.

In alphabetical order, the first terminal is Conrail's Kearny, New Jersey Yard (the Pennsylvania Railroad, Penn Central and now Conrail). It has an electrified rapid transit line splitting the facility. Some would claim the worst feature is that it is located in the Jersey Meadows. Credit for keeping this beast afloat through the years goes to Gene Ryan and his Rail-Trailer group and the Penn Truck Lines people. It is currently a Conrail problem, bridged around most imaginatively by a new Sea-Land, K-Line and American President Lines terminals, also in the Jersey Meadows.

The second terminal you may wish you never ran is Southern Pacific's Los Angeles Transportation Center (LATC). Called "the Shops" by oldtimers, it was an early steam engine repair area and SP passenger car marshalling facility for the Los Angeles Union Passenger Terminal. It is a stub-track facility with a U-shaped track at the bottom. Hemmed in by freeways and the Los Angeles River it was designed to be switched to death. It has been kept afloat by SP's Pacific Motor Trucking people and bridged by temporary facilities at Valla, Spring Street and the permanent Intermodal Container Transfer Facility located close to San Pedro Harbor.

The third facility is the Chicago & North Western's Wood Street Terminal, best characterized as a "10-pound problem in a 5-pound bag." From its inception this facility has been historically tied to Chico Clark as a contract operator. On December 15, 1986 the venerable Wood Street facility was blessedly replaced by the modern Global One facility.

As an honorable mention, in the category of terminals you are glad you never ran, is the Baltimore & Ohio's Philadelphia facility. It is probably the hands-down winner for the operation of the largest non-mechanized facility over the longest period of time. Gordon Volkers wrestled with this problem longer than anyone else. The facility was finally mechanized in 1985.

A final commentary on those who brought us intermodal terminal mechanization would be incomplete without noting the lasting contributions made by them in other areas. Those who were successful in selling lift equipment over the long term, generally, gained a valuable overview of intermodal operations. Most cared so deeply about improving the business that they went substantially beyond the normal manufacturer-customer relationship. They often became missionaries for improvements that were only indirectly related to their primary products.

Three mechanization pioneers come to mind. Mi-Jack's Jack Lanigan created what he calls the 2 for 1.

In the 1970's Taylor Machine Works introduced their side lift machine with a top-lift-only spreader for handling containers. Here a Taylor machine works in a Canadian National facility. — TAYLOR MACHINE

Before this concept became a standard consideration of terminal design, most lift units served one track and one trailer drop lane. In the early 1960's he went looking for someone who could build a crane spanning three lanes — two trailer drop lanes for one track. This would allow tracks to be pre-staged, i.e., trailers or containers placed for outbound loading prior to train arrival. With 2 for 1, inbound units on the train had another lane for unloading. The savings came from allowing inbound drivers to place units trackside rather than dropping them in a remote part of the terminal and hostling them trackside with terminal labor. Likewise, it allowed outbound truckers to pick up the load from trackside rather than from a remote point after removal by terminal hostlers. The inspiration has paid big dividends through the years.

Lanigan pressed several railroads to try the idea. He was rejected by many until he found two young engineers with the Reading Railroad in Philadelphia who were newcomers to intermodal. N.P. Haven, E.C. Lawson and their General Manager J.M. Patterson were intrigued by the concept. In 1972 it was put in place and over the head of Pat Sullivan, terminal manager of the Reading Railroad at Philadelphia. Sullivan, like many field managers, had day-to-day pressures to "load 'em up.' Consequently, if a new idea interferred with that necessity it was considered an unacceptable risk.

However, when Sullivan became convinced that the new idea could not be scared off, he decided to take a look at it with an open mind and hopefully make it work. And make it work, he did. The Reading facility was only nine acres, but Sullivan claimed that he could handle more loads and make up more time for late inbound trains with 2 for 1. Over time he became one of the best salesman for the concept.

The National Railroad Intermodal Association had an Eastern Seaboard meeting in Boston that year. Lanigan took Santa Fe's Ed Frey to see the handiwork. Frey was so impressed that he had a 2 for 1 built in Houston next to a relatively new conventional facility. And 2 for 1 was on its way.

Similarly, Chico Clark, "Piggypacker" salesman extraordinaire, pushed the concept of center row parking in the late 1960's. Early terminals had generally been set up to receive "outside drivers" through a gate and to direct them to a "remote outbound" lot. From there terminal hostler drivers would move the unit trackside to an assigned spot alongside the assigned car for loading. Having seen the value of 2 for 1 in terminal movement costs, Clark's idea was to move the remote area in between a pair of 2 for 1 tracks. This would allow trackside pickups by everybody, trackside delivery by those outside drivers who understand the terminal, but do a short move to a between-track parking area in lieu of moving it "remote."

Again, the idea was resisted by most railroads. The field people did not want any part of outside drivers in their terminal work area — particularly as gate cutoff time (the time at which trailers will no longer be accepted for loading on an outbound train) approached. Things do tend to get a little crazy at that point.

Clark, in his less than low key manner, continued to press anyone who would listen to him on the savings inherent in center row parking. An initial trial of his concept was made by Bob Ingram, a very bright, young intermodalist at the Central of New Jersey's Elizabethport facility.

Finally, with the growth of containers, terminal managers were presented the problem of managing the required chassis. The "chassis problem" has been largely controlled in most facilities through the use of common chassis pools; i.e., rent a chassis from the pool when you needed it rather than leaving your owner-marked chassis to plug up my terminal — or yours. However, there is an irreducible number of chassis needed to operate a facility. And land is, indeed, expensive.

With all of this in view, Scott Corbett, intrepid inventor of the "Piggypacker," came up with the idea of vertically storing the chassis in racks. This simple device freed up space in crowded terminals. In the case of terminals without neutral pools, it also allowed the terminal manager to sort chassis by both size and ownership for easy selection of a required chassis. This method eliminated the need for hostler drivers to initiate long searches through chassis lots for one to match a specific inbound container.

The idea was first designed to be used at Southern Pacific's LATC facility in Los Angeles, but Teamster resistance blunted the effort. The prototype rack can still be seen in a back lot.

The first successful use of the rack occurred at the Long Beach Container Terminal. The first railroad to use it was the Chicago & North Western's Chicago Wood Street Terminal (now known as Global One).

These three concepts, 2 for 1, center row parking and the chassis rack have all become institutionalized along with the overhead and side-lift machines that modernized the business and allowed it to grow efficiently. Without the persistence of these pioneers of the business, intermodal efficiency and developments would have been significantly delayed.

Designed by the inventor of the Piggypacker, these chassis are stored vertically in chassis racks, freeing up terminal space and organizing a formerly difficult task in container terminals — the storage and organization of chassis. —SCOTT CORBETT COLLECTION

Seaboard Air Line's early all-piggyback schedule TT-23, provided high-speed trailer service to the southeast. Successor Seaboard Coast Line Railroad furnished key intermodal service to United Parcel Service. — PROGRESSIVE RAILROADING MAGAZINE

Chapter 11
United Parcel Service
The Little Brown Package Car

The railroad is a service business which requires daily attention to detail in order to succeed. The restaurant business, also service oriented, has a saying that is apropos for railroads: "You are only as good as the last meal you served." This says it all!

In the railroad business "serving the meal" may involve the coordination of hundreds or even thousands of people in order to get the freight moved from shipper to receiver, along with getting it rated and billed correctly. It is very easy to allow something to slip these days what with budget cuts, labor misunderstandings and a thousand and one other negative things that happen on a railroad.

One cure for "railroad operating blahs" in the old days of railroading was the operation of passenger service. It was a point of pride in most railroad operating departments to "do it right." Competition in terms of scheduled speed often made for precision and heads-up operating procedures. This pride and can-do attitude produced by the passenger service often had a spillover effect on fast freight service — particularly on premium freight trains.

The gradual downgrading of passenger service following World War II, and the eventual conversion of all rail passenger service to Amtrak in 1971 removed this halo effect. The gap created by the decline of passenger service was clear.

In hindsight it is remarkable that the pioneering roads such as the Chicago Great Western and the New Haven were able to operate intermodal trains properly right from the beginning. But, in fact, they operated dedicated trains which produced highway competitive service.

Virtually every major intermodal study has pointed out this basic requirement. Yet, particularly in the 1960's and the 1970's, most railroads operated intermodal in mixed train service with declining operating discipline.

What type of service would concentrate the attention of the railroad operating departments as a replacement for the "halo effect" the railroads once carried for the passenger train. The answer was a most unlikely one — the United Parcel train.

United Parcel Service originated in Seattle, Washington, in 1907 as a delivery service for large retail stores. Prior to the early 1950's it grew to become the premier delivery service for the Atlantic and Pacific coast states and the Great Lakes area. UPS concentrated its service within the so-called city commercial zones (an area regulated by the Interstate Commerce Commission). Thus, the United Parcel brown delivery vehicle was as familiar a sight as the early vegetable wagon, bakery truck or milkman. UPS always called their vehicles package cars rather than trucks. They felt that package car drivers would handle their vehicles and their freight more gently than truck drivers. Attitude *is* important.

The parcel business saw continuous growth up until J.L. Hudson, a major UPS account in the Detroit region, introduced the shopping center concept. Soon this became the hottest idea in retailing. Shopping centers bloomed like spring flowers across the United States. The result of this phenomenon eliminated the necessity of going into the city to shop and, thus, having to send the packages you purchased home by way of the United Parcel brown package car.

Shopping centers soon changed the shopping habits of America, and it also affected the way in which purchases were handled. No longer did we ask the store to deliver, we just took it home ourselves. This began to take its toll on United Parcel Services' growth — a situation that clearly was not going to go away. About the only things that were being sent home via UPS were heavy appliances and furniture.

The man at UPS headquarters who was paid to worry about such long-term implications was Elmer Nesholm, vice president of sales and marketing. He assembled a project team for the express purpose of trying to ascertain just where UPS could compete in the package business. On this team was Dan McKnight, head of labor relations, Bob Maisch who was responsible for long distance transportation and Larry Breakiron, head of engineering. Breakiron was the only exception to the UPS policy of promotion from within. He, in the past, had done consulting assignments for UPS while at Peat-Marwick-Mitchell, and had so impressed the UPS staff that they hired him to head up their Industrial Engineering — a key position. Looking over these gentlemen's shoulder was UPS President and Chief Executive Officer George Smith.

In order to stay alive UPS had to find a new business. They felt that the first and most likely place to tackle was the venerable United States Post Office and its parcel post service. However, this posed a basic question, could the UPS make money handling odd-sized packages? At the time parcel post would deliver everything to anyone, even a car tire or heavy metal parts to Rural Free Delivery areas (RFD). The Post Office had a set scale for the delivery of parcels based on mileage of delivery and within zones. The Post Office was also sack oriented. Every parcel was jammed into a sack and, consequently, many packages were torn or broken apart before they reached their destination. A customer had no recourse for damages unless the parcel had been insured.

Having made the decision to make some kind of change, UPS' biggest problem was whether it was possible to move packages locally as well as statewide or nationally? Breakiron set to work trying to determine the cost of designing, building and running package sorting centers. Of one thing he was certain, they would be able to handle parcels more cheaply than the post office and deliver them in good shape. Maisch's job was to look at potential flows and over the road costs.

In the final analysis it would be a tight run, but based on Parcel Post rates, cost-conscious UPS could make money. It knew it had better employees and, thus, could provide better and quicker service.

So in 1952 UPS applied for and received authority to operate a parcel delivery service between Los Angeles and San Diego. With the excellent success of that venture there was a rapid expansion of a similar delivery scheme in the Great Lakes region.

By 1966 UPS planned its largest expansion and long distance program. Their idea was to link up the Northeast and the Midwest areas with six Southern states. In the process of his research it had become obvious to Maisch that this expansion would produce some real delivery headaches for UPS. Florida's package business was extremely imbalanced — as much as 15 to 1. No trucker could survive over such distances with such an imbalance.

Maisch began to watch the growth of piggyback on the railroads. Maybe this was the answer to his dilemma. George Smith and Breakiron tackled the Atlantic Coast Line's Jimmy Plant and found a willing ear. Meanwhile, McKnight was busy convincing the Teamsters to allow some of the over the road business to go by railroad. The logic was that many more additional Teamsters would be required to handle the sorting centers and package car jobs than would be used to handle the over the road delivery.

Everything seemed to drop into place, and United Parcel Service was able to put its over-balanced traffic on the railroad. As a final stroke of good luck, the Atlantic Coast Line merged with the Seaboard Air Line to form the Seaboard Coast Line (later part of CSX). This instantly opened up the entire state of Florida. The Jacksonville-Miami traffic movement, negotiated through Gene Tonsager and Ray Wyckoff, was run over the Florida East Coast Railway.

The criterion for a railroad handling UPS business was the same then as today. "Can you give us highway competitive service? If so, we'll get along fine." Unlike many rail customers, UPS has traditionally not pressured the rate structure. They wanted service. This meant that you had better deliver what you promise.

Seaboard Airline was the original carrier to serve United Parcel's intermodal business. SAL's Jimmy Plant (left) takes delivery of Realco's 10,000th trailer from Realco's President Palmer Bayer (center). — GORDON C. MILLER COLLECTION

And the Seaboard Coast Lines did. Thus was forged a critical link in the intermodal chain. For, unlike most rail intermodal customers, UPS was made up of professional operating transportration people who paid close attention to those daily details that are so critical. Bob Maisch was put in charge of the long distance transportation and the sort centers. Along with Pete Keenan (and later George Joyce) who dealt with service at headquarters, and Guy Shively in the Midwest who dealt with rates and billing, the UPS traffic became the replacement with the discipline function that the passenger trains had served over the years.

Everyone on the railroads from the top on down knew the "UPS trains" and the commitments that were attached to them. The fact that in some cases only ten percent of the traffic on a "UPS Train" was actual UPS traffic testifies to the drawing power of running a consistant, properly scheduled service.

The success of the Seaboard service in 1966-1967 period of time led to the next big step in the UPS-piggyback relationship. That was the tying together of the major Northeast UPS business with the Great Lakes area.

This time it was more than just a replay of the Florida service. Here the volumes were so large that the baseload business was also sent by rail. Negotiations were held between the UPS group and, initially, the Pennsylvania Railroad whose merger with the New York Central and the New Haven would form the new and ill-fated Penn Central. On the PRR side Hank Allyn from sales, Roy Hayes from intermodal and Fred Shafer from Penn Truck Lines arranged the deal between New Jersey and Chicago.

Connections were negotiated with Frank Sutherland on the Rock Island Line to Des Moines, Laurin Cowling over the Milwaukee Road to the Twin Cities and the Chicago & Eastern Illinois to St. Louis. The service was a resounding success. This led to a further expansion within the grain belt states, the deep South and the Southwest.

While McKnight kept the flexibility of the Teamsters intact, Maisch and his group negotiated with Joe Nash and Larry Cena on the Santa Fe to extend service

The Pennsylvania Railroad, and later Penn Central, were also key to early United Parcel Service use of rail intermodal. This early photograph shows trains No TT-1 and TT-2 passing at Pittsburgh. — PROGRESSIVE RAILROADING MAGAZINE

The Santa Fe Railway provided early service for United Parcel Service between Chicago and Kansas City and from Chicago to Oklahoma City. They would later become a major carrier of United Parcel traffic. — SANTA FE RAILWAY

Early Illinois Central piggyback terminal activity in the middle of downtown Chicago. The Illinois Central established service to a key United Parcel Service sort center in Jackson, Mississippi. — ILLINOIS CENTRAL

between Chicago-Kansas City and Chicago-Oklahoma City. On the Illinois Central Lines, a key sort center for the deep south was established at Jackson, Mississippi, through negotiations with Buddy Logan. The Chicago-Dallas service was established over the Missouri Pacific through Charlie Groton and the Chicago-Denver service over the Burlington Northern was arranged through Jim Nankivell.

Strong relationships developed between UPS and the rail intermodal people. Then disaster struck. On June 21, 1970, Penn Central, the lynchpin that handled 60 percent of the UPS intermodal business, entered into what at that time was the largest bankruptcy ever recorded in U.S. business history. Service, *the* key ingredient to UPS, went over the edge.

Maisch and his group scrambled to recover. The only alternative to the Penn Central between Chicago and New York was the Erie-Lackawanna. They entered into intense negotiations with Paul Johnston and Gene Wogan to fill in the Penn Central gap. Johnston, a tall, striking railroader came from an old Erie family, but had taken to piggyback as though he were born to it.

They agreed to highly competitive schedules between Croxton and Chicago. In addition they set up terminals in Port Jervis, New York, and Marion, Ohio. The former served Pennsylvania and New England traffic and the latter the mid-Ohio and Michigan areas. Traffic in these terminals was unique in that it was loaded and unloaded from the trains by UPS employees rather than Erie-Lackawanna rail employees.

The agreements hammered out were fairly stringent for a carrier described at the time as "financially marginal." Could the Erie-Lackawanna perform? As negotiations wound down, Greg Maxwell, the big, gruff ex-operating officer president of Erie-Lackawanna gave Maisch his personal guarantee that it would. "That's enough for me," said Maisch. And the deal was sealed.

The UPS-Erie-Lackawanna relationship was a good one. It lasted until the E-L was melded with the other Northeast bankrupt carriers into Conrail. At that point the traffic again shifted and a strong relationship was formed between the Maisch group, Dick Hasselman, Don Swanson of Conrail and Jim Cunningham of Penn Truck Line who operated the terminals.

After getting the Chicago-New York service back in shape through the Erie agreement, the next step taken by the Maisch group was to tackle the "Rocky Mountain Hole." In the early 1970's UPS operated generally east of Nebraska, the Plains States and on the West Coast. They now needed to bridge that gap by marrying existing railroad operating authority with existing UPS authority. This consisted of bridging the Southwest part of the country with the Santa Fe, the Mid-Continent with the Union Pacific and Southern Pacific and the Northern Rockies with the Burlington Northern.

UPS continued to successfully feed all East Coast shipments through these rail bridge rights clear up until it battled a 48-state operating rights authority through the ICC in 1975. Even after that, UPS continued to place its growth business on piggyback, and expanded its service by rail piggyback.

In 1979 UPS began an experiment to balance some of its West Coast business by operating some UPS business in reefer trailers westbound and perishables eastbound. The Martrax service was started with 700 units and steadily grew to over 2,000 units.

Through the years the influence of UPS on the success of intermodal has been almost unprecedented. Even beyond its importance as an intermodal customer (UPS revenues to the railroads in 1988 were $450 million), the support of UPS has been present on almost every major innovation attempted in intermodal, especially in the area of new service. By far the largest freight transportation company in the U.S., the UPS railroad relationship seems to have worked well for both parties.

The ubiquitous "Little Brown Package Car" of the United Parcel Service, serving the publisher of this book. UPS provided the operating discipline for early intermodal service and has proven to be a willing intermodal partner with railroads since the mid-1960's.
— LARRY ARNOLD

A Sea-Land container rides "on its belly" on an 89-foot Trailer Train "All-Purpose" car at the head end of a Southern Pacific eastbound piggyback and container train at Colton, California. The "All-Purpose" car carried either containers or trailers. — WILLIAM D. MIDDLETON

Chapter 12

Trailer Train and Gene Ryan

In the early 1960's the politics of naming a successor to Jim Symes at the Pennsylvania Railroad were drawing to a close in Philadelphia. The traditional path to the chairmanship had been through the Operating Department. Jim Newell had come "through the chairs" in the Pennsy Operating Department and held the loyalty and affection of those he led.

David Bevan had made a run at the chairmanship through his stronghold — the Finance Department. He reportedly used his New York banking contacts to promote contacts on the Pennsy board of directors. And he used his social contacts within Philadelphia's more preeminent society to the same end.

Symes was highly aware of the rumblings on his board and the talk emanating from the high society cocktail circuit. He also knew of the strong feelings of his operating people. His railroad had emerged from the wear and tear of World War II in a financially weakened condition. Since then key competitors had merged around Pennsy. He felt that the only salvation for the Pennsy was a merger of its own. To split the railroad by choosing either Newell or Bevan would be counterproductive. So Symes decided to go outside the railroad for a successor.

He reached into the Norfolk & Western Railway. The N&W was controlled by the Pennsylvania Railroad, and it had a president who was the lawyer that had successfully maneuvered a merger with the Virginian Railway through the ICC. Ironically, he was also a founding member of the Trailer Train board. Stuart Saunders became the 14th and final head of the Pennsylvania Railroad.

The future for Jim Newell was no longer at the Pennsylvania Railroad. It now lay with the growing Trailer Train. On October 1, 1963 Newell retired from the Pennsy and took the helm of Trailer Train on a full-time basis. Trailer Train continued to grow at an increasing rate. In 1960 virtually all TTX officers had been full-time PRR employees. Rail membership covered 81 percent of the total Class I mileage by 1963, and the TTX fleet contained 15,000 cars. In the following year the New York Central, a longtime holdout with its Flexi Van service, joined Trailer Train. That same year Trailer Train hired a Corporate Secretary, Manager of Purchases and Materials and a Manager of Research and Development — all men from the PRR. Frank Quinto was hired into the Purchasing Department in 1960, serving Trailer Train for the next 30 years and eventually, heading up that function. There were 5,600 cars added to the fleet that year.

Another 5,500 cars were on the roster by 1965, and the first TTAX prototype all-purpose container/trailer

As containers became a larger part of intermodal loadings, the switching of trailer and container cars at ramps became a real problem. The remedy was the all-purpose car. As shown here, the trailer hitches of this American Car & Foundry prototype are "on the deck" and the adjustable pockets are set to receive containers. The car could hold two trailers or two 40-foot or three 20-foot containers. — TRAILER TRAIN COLLECTION

Pullman-Standard's version of the all-purpose car is loaded with two 20-foot containers (a dry box and a tank container) and a 40-foot container on a chassis moving as a trailer. — TRAILER TRAIN COLLECTION

car was developed. In its tenth year, 1966, Trailer Train emerged from its tactical cocoon and began a nationwide advertising campaign. Except for a few previous supplier ads, this was the first example of a major promotion for intermodal. Included were: "Where did so many warehouses go that used to cost manufacturers so much money? They went out when piggyback came in." And: "Do you wish train tracks came right up to your loading platform? They do when you ship piggyback." Also that year, Morris Forgash died and G. Russell Moir, chairman of U.S. Freight, succeeded him on the board.

Trailer Train purchased the largest number of freight cars in the U.S. in 1967, more than nine percent. The passing of early era board members continued that year with the death of Fred Carpi. By the end of that year, however, anti-piggyback/pro-boxcar railroaders on the board caused Trailer Train to discontinue its successful ad campaign. Trailer Train was once again forced into a tactical role by its own rail board members.

Newell was playing out his final role at Trailer Train in 1969. For over 14 years he had guided the company with a steady, but enthusiastic hand. The fleet had grown from the original 300 Pennsylvania Railroad and 200 Rail-Trailer, 75-foot cars, to a total of 54,000 cars of which 29,000 were piggyback.

Stuart Saunders at the Pennsylvania Railroad had carried off the merger with the New York Central in 1968. As with any major merger, a large amount of maneuvering occurred as to who would be named to the top spots. One of the plums was at a subsidiary of the former New York Central — the Pittsburgh & Lake Erie. The P&LE's rails carried the Central deep into the heart of Pennsylvania Railroad's Keystone territory, and was a continuing thorn in their side. Prior to the merger John W. Barriger had placed his distinctive stamp on the "Little Giant." Upon his retirement in 1965, he was succeeded for a period of three years by Curtis D. Buford, son of the former Milwaukee Road president.

The Penn Central merger was consumated in 1968. An early order of business was to place the P&LE under the stewardship of a Pennsylvania Railroad man. So, on March 16, 1969, the affable Henry Allyn, Jr. was named president of the P&LE. Curtis D. Buford became the third president of Trailer Train (but the second to actually take command). Considered a sidetrack job by the cognoscenti of the Penn Central, subsequent events have probably given Buford cause to smile at the outcome.

Buford saw an immediate need to distance Trailer Train from Pennsy politics and subsequent Penn Central problems. One of his first moves toward Trailer Train independence was to hire a full-time general counsel for the firm. One can most assuredly assume with confidence that one job selection criterion was that candidates not be from the Penn Central (or predecessor PRR) Law Department.

So, the first non-PRR department head hired at Trailer Train was ex-Reading attorney Bob Williams. He ended up being one of the longest serving department chiefs in Trailer Train's history. Williams was not long in making his presence felt nor in decreasing the former Pennsylvania Railroad influence at Trailer Train.

Upon its formation Trailer Train acquired David Bevan, Pennsylvania Railroad finance vice president, as a board member. Williams had researched a potential conflict-of-interest problem and found that Bevan's position as both a director of Trailer Train and of Penn Central did indeed violate a prohibition of interlocking directorates.

After informal meetings with outside counsel David Bevan resigned his Trailer Train directorship in 1970. The Pennsy's grip on Trailer Train began to wane.

In 1971 Buford moved the Trailer Train headquarters office from Philadelphia to Chicago. At that time Chicago was headquarters for five major Trailer Train members. Chicago contained the major operations for most railroads. To many this signified the cutting of the PRR umbilical cord and the establishment of Trailer Train as a truly independent company.

Gene Ryan and Rail-Trailer were badly hurt with the loss of the Pennsylvania Railroad contract. The forfeiture of his Trailer Train position and stock, plus losing several of his key people to Realco, hit hard on the man who helped to create the mode. He had run the course of the New York Central and the Pennsy in the East. Where was he to go? The Chesapeake & Ohio was a conservative coal hauler that briefly flirted with the Railvan carless technology, but the C&O did not serve New York where Gene Ryan had many major contacts. The Baltimore & Ohio did serve New York, but only through a circuitous series of connections. That left the Erie Railroad.

The Erie Railroad was almost custom made for intermodal. It was a reasonably fast, direct route between Gotham and Chicago. Being historically the last major eastern route into Chicago, it had little intermediate on-line industry (and therefore not much to worry about from a carload traffic diversion standpoint). So, it was to the Erie that Ryan next turned his efforts.

Since Jay Gould had thoroughly watered the Erie stock in the 1870's, the Erie had gone through trying financial times. Thus, for the Erie to find a source of new traffic from someone like Ryan, who would also fund construction capital for the terminals and finance the lease of trailers, was a real plus.

Early in 1961 Ryan and Paul Johnston of the Erie entered into an agreement for piggyback service. Ryan and TOFC Inc. spent $1.8 million on terminals in Jersey City (Croxton) and Chicago (51st Street). Croxton terminal was built with eight tracks, including one for Clejan cars. A young Tom Curry was one of the ramp managers. Eight regular tracks, two Clejan tracks and one reverse track (for "wrong way" trailers) were built at 51st Street. The costs of operation were recovered by Ryan on a per-lift basis.

TOFC Inc. consisted of a 50 percent ownership by Ryan's Rail-Trailer and six major trucking firms. Included were Cooper-Jarrett, Denver-Chicago Trucking, Eastern Express, Midwest Emery, Interstate System and Spector Motor Freight. It was a formidable gathering of power and talent. In the summer of 1961 Erie-Lackawanna President Milton McInnes announced the opening of service between Croxton and 51st Street with Plan I service for the truckers, Plan II, III and V for the Erie and Plan IV for contract forwarders.

Ryan next reestablished his contact with Roy Fruehauf. Fruehauf again agreed to finance the leases for a new trailer leasing susidiary of Rail-Trailer that, in time, grew to over 2,000 trailers. Ryan was now back in the piggyback business.

He continued to press for piggyback expansion, expanding the contract terminal loading/unloading business. The Erie terminal business extended to Buffalo and Cleveland. Freight Delivery Services was set up in Atlanta to handle terminal services on the Louisville & Nashville, Seaboard Air Line and Atlantic Coast Line. Additional service was started in Chicago for Baltimore & Ohio — Chesapeake & Ohio and in Jacksonville for Seaboard Coast Line. Operations under McDowall-Ferris Trucking were established in Orlando, Florida, for Atlantic Coast Line and Seaboard Air Line. These operations tied in with yet another Rail-Trailer subsidiary — Reefer Trailer Leasing. Ryan had teamed up with Linde to enter into a perishable trailer leasing pool. In the middle 1960's U.S. Van Lines, a mover of household goods, became a Rail-Trailer subsidiary and contributed a third of the company's revenue.

In a relentless drive to improve intermodal costs in the mid-1960's, Ryan again began to push for improvements in car technology. He formed the Con-

**Trailer Train initiated a National advertising campaign in business publications in order to promote piggyback. This two-color advertisement was to entice non-rail customers to the merits of Trailer Train piggyback. —
TRAILER TRAIN COLLECTION**

**This two-page spread which appeared in *Traffic World, Railway Age, Modern Railroads, Distribution Age* and the *Wall Street Journal*, was aimed at the anti-piggybackers on the railroads as much as it was to off-rail shippers. —
TRAILER TRAIN COLLECTION**

Bak susidiary of Rail-Trailer and pressed for the adoption of containers stacked on a depressed-well flatcar. The ideas grew out of a group of Chicago intermodalists. The group included Ryan, John Kneiling, the inveterate economics engineering consultant, D.H. Overmeyer, the largest U.S. public warehouseman of that time and Frank Macomber at A.T. Kearney. Macomber had done a consulting assignment for Matson Navigation Company (and made a report to the MH-5 Standards Committee). Macomber and Kneiling were able to interest West Coast canning companies, including Dole and Hunt-Wesson, in a container train service.

The concept of stacking up to six 20-foot containers or two 40-foot trailers on a depressed-well flatcar began about 1965-1966. It bore a striking resemblance to the X-15972. The whole idea percolated until the end of the decade when Overmeyer joined the fray.

Ryan visualized a new railcar equipment pool based on this new car type. Unit trains of cars would run between major cities that were served by Overmeyer warehouses. A major leasing company would provide the boxes and trucking company member would then provide the drayage moves. This world of intermodal in the 1970's, however, was changed from the tender world of the early 1950's when there were few railroads in piggybacking, to one of major competition. There were virtually no big dreamers by the 1970's, save for Ryan.

Now there were important stakeholders in the business of piggyback. By 1970 every railroad had an intermodal service. Battle lines had long since been formed within the various departments of each railroad. Shipper agents and freight forwarders were major players in the piggyback game, having a hefty market control. Steamship companies were still minor players, but growing steadily. Virtually every railroad was now a member of Trailer Train which was the industry's major railcar supplier. XTRA and Realco were established and between them they owned tens of thousands of pieces of equipment. Ryan was faced with a formidable array of companies who had big stakes and well-defined positions on intermodal.

The principal physical problem with the introduction of the new car, however, was the lack of mechanized terminals capable of handling the containers on and off the cars. In addition the maritime boxes and chassis were very heavy when compared to a standard highway trailer which would have cut into the payload over the road. The Ryan/Kearney/Overmeyer system would have required massive investments in cars, new lightweight containers and chassis and terminal mechanization — a massive capital challenge. While he might have overcome these obstacles, another challenge arose —

the U.S. economy.

Starting from about 250,000 units in 1955, intermodal grew at a heady pace for the first 20 years. It doubled to a half-million loads in the first four years, to a million the next four years and then in the next five years to two-million units. In two more years, up to 1969, it added another half-million. Just when it seemed that intermodal was invincible, and that Ryan, "The Prophet," was on his way back to reclaim The Empire, the bottom dropped out. Piggyback lost 300,000 loads over the next two years.

Piggyback, the golden boy of railroading, had taken a haymaker. It hit the deck. Stretched thin for capital and straining to keep the growth dream going, Ryan, in 1971, ran into a financial storm. The trucking members of TOFC Inc. were also hard hit by the recession. They returned leased trailers by the hundreds.

Ryan was hard-pressed to make his payment to Fruehauf, and with trailer sales off Fruehauf was forced to take the entire fleet back. The reclaimed trailers were managed by a freelancer named Ron Tackberry whose father had run the piggyback operation for the Pennsylvania Railroad.

Ryan had waited too long to pull in his exposed flanks. With volume down on the railroad, his trucking partners under financial pressure and the marginal U.S. lines bleeding cash, he hit a wall in 1972. Ryan was removed in favor of an accountant with a vision for diversification of Rail-Trailer. Mercifully, the experiment was short lived, and Rail-Trailer also went down for the count, but without Ryan.

Intermodal, however, gained its second wind and in 1972 began to rebuild its traffic base.

As Trailer Train's advertising campaign wore on, the boxcar mentality of some of the firm's board members caused Trailer Train to pull back on marketplace advertising. Once this ad had run in Business Week, Traffic World, Distribution Age, Traffic Management, U.S News & World Report, Modern Railroads **and** Railway Age, **the program was cancelled** — TRAILER TRAIN COLLECTION

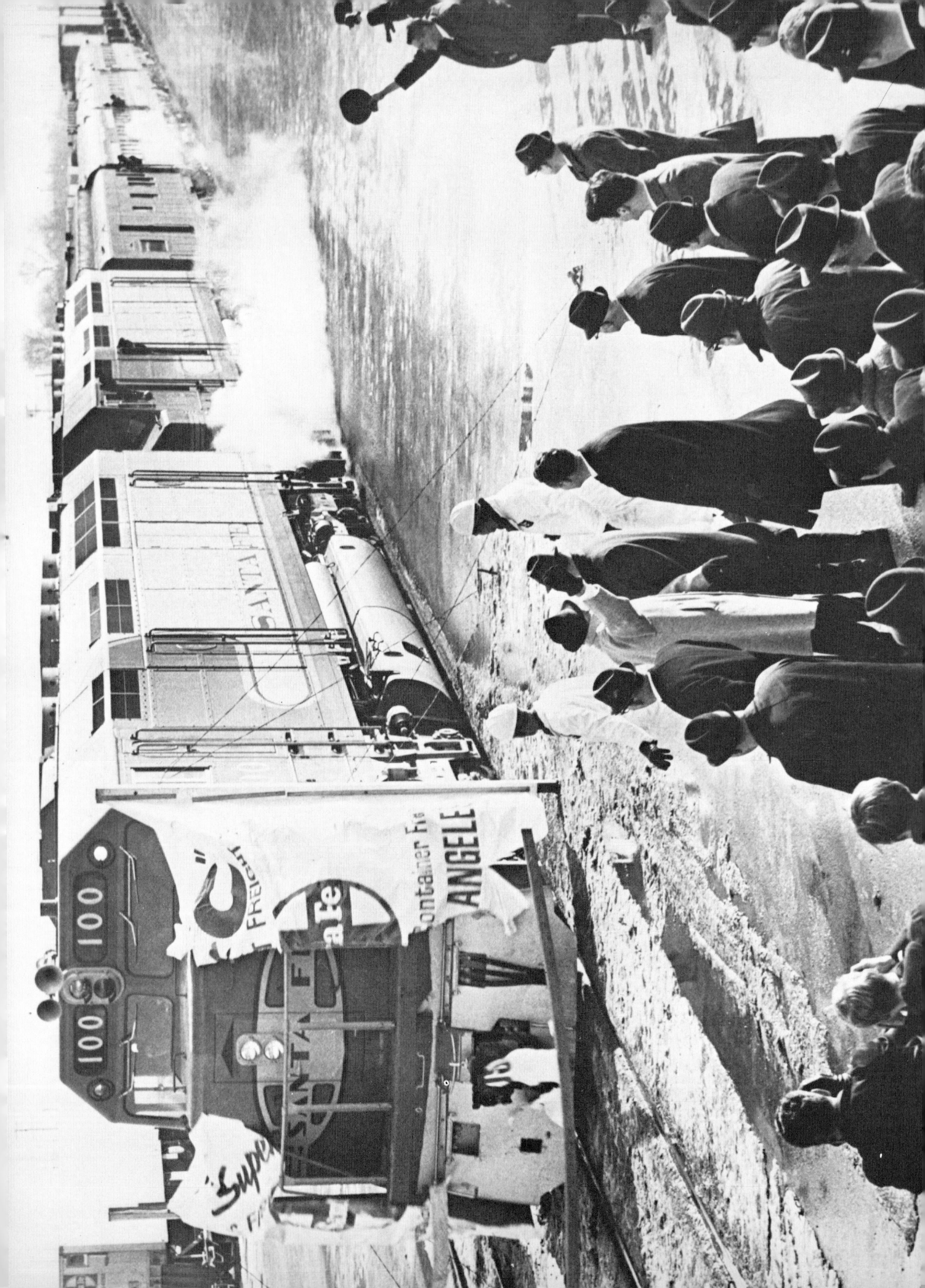

While the New York Central withdrew from the concept of high-speed intermodal service, the Santa Fe pressed forward with "Super C" service. On January 17, 1968, at 2:00 P.M., the first "Super C" train burst through the banner at Corwith Yard in Chicago headed for Los Angeles. It would arrive 34-1/2 hours later.
— SANTA FE-KANSAS STATE HISTORICAL SOCIETY

Chapter 13

Santa Fe
Super C and the Coax Train

Intermodal concepts, emerging in 1965-1966, planted the seeds for projects that would bloom for the following 5 to 10 years. One such idea came forth from an alliance with a major consulting firm and a major railroad. Another was expressed by a group of young interline rail brats, suitably protected and nurtured by mentors who supported change and improvement.

The first was a project done for the Santa Fe by Bob Nueschel of McKinsey & Company. Neuschel was a visionary who saw the vast potential in moving goods between modes in a "box without wheels." He proposed and was awarded a contract to look at the possibilities of moving containers from Asia to Europe by inserting a rail move (a "rail bridge") across the United States. The study was coordinated by Santa Fe's John Grygiel, director of Market Research.

Grygiel was bred to be the ultimate Santa Fe traffic man. I met John in his Market Research role in the early 1960's. He was a proper, conservative, by-the-book Santa Fe Vice President-Traffic-in-training. In poker terms he "held-em-close and played-em-tough." A standing industry joke of the era was the "Santa Fe split." That meant the Santa Fe ordered a T-bone steak while everybody else ordered a hamburger — and we split the check evenly. Santa Fe traffic officers wore hats and understood how to work the traffic bureau process. Grygiel worked that process extremely well.

Nueschel's concept was simplicity itself. Pacific containerships were operated three ways. (1) As Pacific-United States liners direct to a West Coast terminal; (2) as Pacific-United States liners direct to an East Coast terminal by way of the Panama Canal; (3) or Pacific-Europe liners also by way of the Panama Canal or in some cases the Suez Canal. Neuschel's theory was that the U.S. rail system could defeat the all-water route by operating a Land Bridge (his term) across the U.S. in place of the water route — particularly in terms of elapsed service time.

Grygiel liked the idea. In those days the containership was more of a competitive threat than a potential intermodal partner. Sea Train operated a service from New York to the U.S. Gulf Coast. Sea-Land operated New York-West Coast and New York-Alaska services in direct competition with rail service by way of the Panama Canal.

Neuschel would concentrate the forces where rail and containerships could be most easily welded together. This would ultimately take the form of land bridge movements, i.e., a rail move with both prior and subsequent steamship moves.

While visionary, the land bridge system took a long

time to start for a number of reasons. First, the traffic that moved between Asia and Europe was relatively sparse to begin with. Second, the Soviets were also developing their own land bridge from Asia to Europe westbound over the Trans Siberian Railroad. Finally, many of the new containership operators were truck-line veterans for whom the thought of working with the railroads was anathema.

Other ideas were being developed for joint rail-containership service. Sea-Land, for example, attempted to put trainload rates into effect on the Pennsylvania Railroad between St. Louis and New York. This move led to a predictable thrashing of the eastern rail piggyback rate structure. Competitive railroads as a defensive measure had put in two trailer rates at the trainload rate level in order to keep the piggyback traffic from being diverted to the Sea-Land container train.

The great potential for crossover moves from high-rated domestic trailers to low-rated international containers, through the use of Freight-All Kinds (FAK) "boxload" rates, dogged containerization in its early days. While land bridge was generally palatable because the traffic moved between ports, the rail movement of container traffic from a port to an inland point was still greatly feared by railroaders. Some containers, however, were handled on chassis as TOFC moves (at TOFC rates) to inland points.

The next proposal from the steamship companies caught up in looking at the potential for rail container moves was to eliminate a ship's port call through the substitution of rail. If a ship, for example, was on a Pacific run, it made a call at Oakland, Long Beach and then transited the Panama Canal for a call at Houston. What harm could there be in running the Houston traffic by ship into Long Beach and then operating it by rail to Houston? The operating logic struck a chord with operating railroaders. Thus mini-bridge, i.e., a port-to-port rail move with only one prior or subsequent containership move, was born.

The rationale of a mini-bridge made the extension of container moves by rail, from a port to or from anywhere inland in the U.S. (or micro-bridge), akin to being a little bit pregnant. Micro-bridge movement spread rapidly. The land bridge or mini-bridge moves were generally made as belly moves, i.e., without their chassis "on the belly" on a railcar. They were made between ports and, thus, had instant access to a chassis supply. Micro-bridge moves were most commonly on chassis due to the general lack of chassis at inland points.

Slowly through the years as international trade increased with the Pacific Rim countries this segment of intermodal grew. One critical element, container volume, began to move into place to set the stage for a monumental breakthrough.

Meanwhile, in the 1960's, the Santa Fe, New York Central, Burlington, Southern Pacific, Southern, Great Northern and to a limited extent the Missouri Pacific and the Northern Pacific had embarked on a hiring campaign of young MBA graduates. The new MBA group and the old rail traffic group who hired them were clearly of different tribes. And tribal culture of all kinds was critical in the railroad business.

The early recruiting efforts of the Santa Fe produced two young men, Bill Paul who would remain with the Santa Fe throughout his career and ended up as Vice President of the computer group, and Dave Gunn who would leave the Santa Fe for distinguished career in the transit business in Boston, Philadelphia, New York and Washington D.C. This pair of intrepid young Santa Fe analysts concentrated on the domestic side of the intermodal business.

In those days the young tribesmen formed interline support groups like the now defunct Rail Systems and Management Association and the Transportation Research Forum. Most of us knew our counterparts on those railroads who hired young people at other than clerical positions. Through the network Gunn and Paul met Jim McClellan who was a young Industry Planning Analyst for merchandise at the Central.

An exchange of thoughts and phone calls led to an interchange of visits, ideas and data. The latter resulted in a seven-page white paper from Gunn and Paul entitled *The Potential of a High-Class, Quality, Transcontinental Merchandise Service for the Santa Fe*. It identified markets for high-speed service, such as Kodak shipping film out of Rochester, hanging dry goods westbound from New York, imported goods eastbound out of Los Angeles, IBM products, and even transcon air freight over the weekend.

The Santa Fe was interested in the speed and cost trade offs between trailers and containers that the high-speed trains would require. The two groups lined up a test run over Santa Fe's Illinois Division on October 9, 1966, using 31 of Central's Flexi Van cars and five new passenger-geared U28 CG's for a 7.8 hp. per ton ratio. They needed to set out 10 cars in order to break 90 m.p.h.

Three days later the tests were repeated with 29 standard trailer cars with 8.1 hp. per ton ratios, setting out ten cars and hitting 86 m.p.h. This train also had 5.15 m.p.h. tail wind while the Flexi Van train had a 10-17 m.p.h. head wind. Santa Fe's test engineer John Angold calculated that the TOFC resistance was 31 percent greater than the Flexi Vans. These tests were intently scrutinized by Larry Cena, an up-and-coming operating officer.

On June 8, 1967, the Santa Fe and New York Central ran a train of 18 loaded Flexi-Van flatcars from New York to Los Angeles in the fastest time of any coast to coast train in history. The trip was made in 54 hours and 21 minutes. This led to the Santa Fe's ill-fated "Super C." — SANTA FE-KANSAS STATE HISTORICAL SOCIETY

The best Santa Fe service at the time was No. 59-53 which ran from Chicago's Corwith Yard to Hobart Yard in Los Angeles in 61 hours. The Central's SV-1 ran from New York to Chicago in 23 hours. The proposed schedule from New York to Los Angeles was 60 hours. The targeted market was to be service sensitive highway freight.

At that point in time the capability of the two roads to put the service together was unclear. Also, questions arose as to what the true size of the market was for such a service. To determine the former, Santa Fe and New York Central set up a joint test run on June 8, 1967. A train of 18 loaded Flexi Van flats behind four GP-40's left the Central's 30th Street Yard in New York at 10:24 P.M. McClellan and Paul rode the cab on the trip. The Central's run was made in 18 hours 51 minutes to McCook, Illinois. The Santa Fe run to Los Angeles was made in 34 hours 46 minutes for a total elapsed time from New York to Los Angeles of 54 hours 21 minutes.

Meanwhile, at the Central's Market Research Department, I had set about trying to help quantify the market. In New York I had scheduled an interview with O.D. Madison, the sales vice president of Navajo Freightlines — a service sensitive trucker whose route pattern looked like a New York Central-Santa Fe merger planning map. He showed up at the third floor Market Research office with his New York sales manager.

After introductions I proceeded to give them the details of the transcon test train run. Madison was already aware of it. Prior to this meeting I had talked to our pricing people, suggesting to them that we use $1.00 a car mile (or 50 cents per trailer mile) as a bogey price. "Hell, there's nobody in the world who would pay a dollar a car mile for rail service," was the response. The levels suggested by the pricing people were what we used to call MOS in Market Research — more-of-the-same.

Madison listened politely. I asked what would he charge to move a trailer a day for a year, transcontinental, if I gave him a checkbook with blank-signed checks, allowing him to fill in the amounts? What kind of schedule could he guarantee? He said, "Probably $1,500-2,000 per load. I would do it in 70 hours, except in the winter, and I'd probably kill three drivers a year doing it."

Was he interested in putting his freight on a fast guaranteed train? Not really. He had Teamster driver board and customer problems that would preclude that.

I was crestfallen. He was closing his briefcase and preparing to leave when he paused and asked (in the mode of a good negotiator), "What were you thinking of charging for this service?" Using my "they'll never pay" number I said, "Probably a dollar a car mile, or about $1,500 per box, transcon."

Madison sat down, opened his briefcase and said, "If you give me a six month head start on my competition, I will guarantee you the following base load business..." and proceeded to lay out traffic on a Navajo route map that would make the service instantly profitable to both the Central and the Santa Fe. "What about the Teamster problem," I said. "Give me 90 days lead time to solve it," he said. Yes, Jimmy Hoffa *was* in control of the Teamsters in those days.

I called McClellan and reported the good news. Unfortunately, he had been drawing fire from the forwarders and the Southern Pacific. The SP had a much longer route to Los Angeles via a St. Louis connection with the Central than did the Santa Fe who travelled

"Super C's" high horsepower units were geared to high-speed passenger running. Test engineer John Angold calculated that the trailers had 31 percent greater resistance than the containers - critical difference even with 10 cent per gallon diesel fuel at high operating speeds. (LEFT) The last "Super C" arrived at Checkpoint Chico-Corwith Yard in Chicago after eight years of service. No longer would truckers need the special directions provided by this sign. — BOTH SANTA FE-KANSAS STATE HISTORICAL SOCIETY

direct from Chicago. To make up for this disadvantage the SP wanted the Central to delay its delivery to the Santa Fe. McClellan and the New York Central Marketing Vice President Jim Sullivan flew to San Francisco to meet with SP President Ben Biaggini, and Traffic Vice President Bill Peoples. The trip was a waste of time. By the time the Central men returned from their trip, Biaggini had called Al Perlman, Central's president, and threatened that if Central did not bend, the SP would cut off its 50,000 annual carloads of perishables.

"But the perishables don't make any money for us," urged the Marketing Department, "and the future lies in breaking out of the commodity business and into the service sensitive merchandise business." It was the middle of 1967 and a recession was clearly on the way. "With business in a slump, I need the car count," said Perlman. And the high-speed container network on the Central died aborning. It also appeared to be dead on the Santa Fe. After all, Santa Fe's major partner had withdrawn and their largest customers were also against the idea.

They, however, did not count on John Shedd Reed. On September 22, 1967, Reed, the tall, patrician president of Santa Fe fired off an uncharacteristically sharp memo to the troops, noting his "surprise that our people had not moved more aggressively. . . Perhaps I am just not up to date on what has been accomplished.

In any event this is a reminder that our operating people should be looking into all aspects of the mechanics of handling this new service and I should consider such questions as a name for the service and/or the train, and plans for an advanced sales campaign, including eye-catching publicity such as signs at the terminals, and perhaps simple leaflets and even lapel buttons for use in connection with calls on potential customers."

It did not take a rock to fall on them (or at least *another* rock) before the departments that had been highlighted in the letter sprang into action. The Operating Department set a 40-hour schedule. The public relations and advertising people began to search for a train name and do advertising layouts. In the meantime Grygiel was taking a real beating from the freight forwarders. My recollection is that at the time there was $35-40 million considered at stake for the Santa Fe in forwarder revenues. Even though the Santa Fe service to forwarders between Chicago-Los Angeles and Chicago-Bay Area was impossible for any other railroad to match, the $35 million was viewed by Santa Fe's Traffic Department as an unacceptable risk.

On the other hand Reed's expectations had obviously been raised to a high level and then further bolstered by the other department's activity at the railroad. The answer was to schedule and price the service so that it was non-competitive in the majority of the marketplace, i.e., for forwarders straight truckload or

"Super C" rolling westbound out of Needles, California between Goffs and Fenner. On this day the "Super" had a pretty fair load, but most of the time it only had a handful of cars. — DONALD DUKE

partial truckload business.

The rate between Chicago and Los Angeles was pegged at a safe $1,400 (just $100 less than what we were planning from New York to LA). The schedule was set for an earlier than required arrival in Los Angeles (4:00 A.M.) and for most Chicago freight an impossible departure time from Chicago (2:00 P.M.).

That definitely got the forwarders off the Traffic Department's back. The forwarders needed to be on the street for morning deliveries by 8:00 A.M., but then spend the afternoons on pickups. Nothing earlier than 6:00 P.M. departure would harm them in the least.

Reed asked David Gunn what he thought of the rate. "This train will fail — no one will use it," he replied. "That opinion is not shared by your superiors in Traffic," said Reed. Little did he suspect the sidebar game actually going on.

With great fanfare, but with fatal flaws already built in, *Super C* was introduced on January 17, 1968. The initial run was made in a little over 34 and one-half hours. It arrived in Hobart Yard at 10:36 P.M. on January 18. While the Operating Department received high marks from Reed, the Traffic Department continued to take a pounding due to an obvious lack of volume.

Traffic basically consisted of mail (at lower rates), some auto parts and seasonal strawberries. Schedules were moved to a morning departure with arrival in Los Angeles at 11:00 P.M. for the convenience of the Post Office.

Early in 1976, however, the Post Office put the mail up for grabs again. The Union Pacific-Chicago & North Western captured the business which would have a slower schedule, but at a cheaper rate. The handwriting was on the wall for the remnants of *Super C*. On May 20, 1976 the last *Super C* arrived at Corwith Yard in Chicago at 3:30 A.M. And the train that more people didn't want than did, came to an end.

Intermodal innovation still lived on in the Operating Department, however. In his enthusiasm for progress in all things railroading, and especially for his favorite segment intermodal, Cena pursued ideas with vigor. One day in early 1972, in his office, Bill Paul showed me a model that looked like a log car with a hitch. "We're playing around with it to see if we can scare up some intermodal branch line traffic," he said. "You should also see what Mr. Cena is doing with GE."

What Cena was doing with General Electric was working on the opposite end of the Santa Fe intermodal scale — the *Super C* service. The old Angold Flexi Van tests had shown that high-speed freights took lots of power and required good acceleration and braking. Once you got those you could talk about trade offs. Trade offs like trailers versus containers, net to tare ratio, air drag coefficients and fuel economy.

As a Santa Fe background paper pointed out, Santa Fe felt that a breakthrough was needed to handle heavier intermodal loads at higher speeds. They established eight guidelines for the new technology:

1. A low center of gravity
2. Minimum wind resistance
3. An alternative to a rigid axle
4. Better weight distribution
5. Modular construction (for ease of repair)
6. Smooth ride — elimination of slack action
7. Power distribution throughout — even acceleration
8. Redesigned braking

An artist's drawing of the coaxial train appeared on a Santa Fe brochure. The concept envisioned a train of low center of gravity, modular individually-powered wheel units every four feet, a common center sill the length of the train with no couplers and other innovative features. The goal was to develop a train capable of high speeds on existing roadbeds. — DONALD DUKE COLLECTION

Santa Fe's coaxial train was also dubbed "the centipede" or the "snake full of boxes." The train was designed with all of its wheels being powered by electric motors from "distributed power" generated by the power module. Here a simulated bad order wheel is cut out to allow continued operation of the train. — SANTA FE-KANSAS STATE HISTORICAL SOCIETY

This 1/8th-inch scale model of the Coaxial Train was built as a result of studies by General Electric for Santa Fe. The power module, looking more like a duckbilled platypus, was on display at Santa Fe's Topeka Shops. — SANTA FE-KANSAS STATE HISTORICAL SOCIETY

This unique advertisement for Santa Fe's "Land Bridge," appeared in *Forbes* for May 15, 1969. — DONALD DUKE COLLECTION

GE issued a report to the Santa Fe in May of 1973. Its solution was revolutionary. As described by the Santa Fe: "A prototype coaxial train will be headed by a diesel-powered generator car, with electric current distributed the length of the train......The cab structure has been designed in the shape of a platypus, moving just above the railbed and sweeping up to create a desirable aerodynamic effect." The GE writeup continued, "The Coaxial Train conceptual design selected consists of a 2 x 12-inch steel spine to which individually powered and suspended 24-inch diameter wheels are attached every eight feet on either side." Thus every 40-foot cargo deck had five sets of wheels, all motorized.

The performance specs called for the new train to cut 20 percent off the running time of *Super C*, i.e., a reduction from 36.5 hours to 29.5. Other than cutoff times, this reduction would have provided little real benefit to shippers. Coax was projected to cost about two and one-half times the standard technology and to operate with a two-person crew.

Power and suspension of the train was radical. The entire train was revolutionary. A 1/8-inch scale model was constructed and tested in the Topeka Shops. Unfortunately, as the numbers came together on estimated maintenance costs and the cost of a prototype, it became apparent that the Coaxial Train was too great a reach from a risk standpoint. What was needed was more of an incremental approach. And that would come.

Illinois Central Gulf's "Slingshot" train roars between St Louis and Chicago with 15 cars, two-man crew, and no caboose. This was the first of the "short crew" intermodal trains. — ILLINOIS CENTRAL GULF

Chapter 14

Federal Railroad Administration

In an industry that spent very little money on research and development, Trailer Train stood out. The research and development budget at Trailer Train had always received good board of directors support. In allocating for the budget, a decision needed to be made as to whether it should be used on strategic or tactical research. Would money be spent to develop new, more efficient "breakthrough" cars and car adjuncts, or concentrating on items such as the knockdown hitch or on centerplate wear liners and more efficient car elements that would directly affect Trailer Train cost?

Trailer Train's answer from the board was clear. Money spent by the company should directly benefit Trailer Train. The primary interest of Trailer Train was in more efficient cars with components that would reduce maintenance cost, not contribute to the old "nonstandard" problems and threaten the existing fleet. Until intimidated by development of member railroads and others, Trailer Train would follow the safe path of tactical research. Thus, a potentially potent force for intermodal strategic R&D would remain untapped. Innovation would continue to fall to others in and around the struggling intermodal industry.

One of those to pick up the cudgel was a seemingly unlikely source — the Federal Railroad Administration.

A small fledgling agency when created in 1967 was about to grow dramatically. The FRA attracted many young railroaders to its ranks as Congress turned its attention to the "failing railroads problem."

Penn Central, which resulted from the 1968 merger of the venerable Pennsylvania Railroad and New York Central System, collapsed in June 1970, creating at that point the largest business failure in American history. The Penn Central bankruptcy ranks were rapidly joined by the Central Railroad of New Jersey, the Erie-Lackawanna, the Reading Company, the Ann Arbor, the Boston & Maine, the Lehigh Valley and the Lehigh & Hudson River.

In 1971 a meeting was called at the Federal Railroad Administration by Policy Deputy Bill Loftus to discuss the economic research budget. The FRA's mission was to assist and promote the railroad industry, and to decide where resources should be concentrated. A wish list was drawn up to include work in rail costing, labor management relations, industry economics, yard operation concepts, a rail network analysis model and intermodal research. The budget was to be divided among these worthy enterprises — but it was a meager $50,000. Fortunately, most of the young ex-railroaders were too inexperienced in the governmental process to realize the futility of the task and, consequently, they plunged ahead.

The task of labor management, yard economics and network modeling fell to John Williams who was then on loan from the Southern Pacific. The balance of the jobs, including intermodal, came to me. It was a presumption on my part that the seeds of many earlier FRA reasearch projects had fallen on barren ground. Previous research had been conducted with very little industry input or participation, and then was sprung on the industry as a surprise. Hardware projects seemed to often be as one wag put it, "An engineering solution in search of a problem." If we were to do any good we would need the full participation of the industry and supporters of the industry. From the beginning we would also need to make this a joint industry FRA R&D/Economic effort.

The first thing I did was to seek out a friend, a New York Central comrade-in-arms, Bill Edson. This tall, gaunt, good-natured New Englander had been the Central's highly competent Chief Mechanical Engineer, and had joined the FRA R&D section a couple of years earlier. We joined in an R&D/Economic Intermodal Task Team — an effort that was to go on for seven years. It lasted through an economic intermodal network analysis, an intermodal terminal management information project, several R&D projects and a six-million dollar intermodal labor/management demonstration program.

At that point the "official" contact point for the FRA was the Association of American Railroads. Next to the AAR board of directors (made up of railroad presidents or chairmen) the most powerful element was the Operating-Transportation General Committee, consisting of railroad vice-presidents of operations. Attached to this committee, and designed to deal with intermodal operating matters, was the Intermodal Steering Committee. The chairman of that committee was Tom Fante, intermodal general manager of the Southern Pacific. It was to Fante that I turned in an effort to establish the first FRA intermodal liaison group.

Tom, although not Irish, was the epitome of an Irish leprechaun. He was bright, quick-witted and had a ready smile. Would he be interested in a joint industry/FRA effort designed to look at how to improve intermodal efficiency and profitability through the Steering Committee? He certainly would. Would he help us, through the Steering Committee, keep the consultants (and us) "out of the weeds?" He certainly would.

In those days Tom was a rather rare offshoot of the typical intermodalist. Unlike most in the 1970's, he had responsibility for both intermodal operations and intermodal marketing and sales. The balance of the Steering Committee was largely made up of people with only intermodal operating responsibilities. To strengthen our intermodal commercial input, I reached out for the most creative intermodal commercial officer of that time. Both Fante and I agreed that the right man for that job was Paul Reistrup of the Illinois Central. If he could be convinced to join the effort, we would be immeasurably strengthened.

Fante contacted Reistrup and set up a meeting for me. Located in Chicago's old Illinois Central Office Building with the huge green diamond sign on the roof, Reistrup greeted me with enthusiasm and candor. He was a graduate of both West Point and the Baltimore & Ohio Technical Training Program. His physical appearance displayed an oblong face, modicum of hair and large glasses. I was later to find that Reistrup typically greeted all projects with enthusiasm, candor and intelligence. In other words you could expect him to be either "in or out." After my initial description of the project it was clear that he was "in."

Finally, it appeared that the one group that would be key to the success of the project was the Operating-Transportation General Committee — that hard-bitten bastion of top operating officials. The O-T General Committee was known as one of intermodal's major stumbling blocks. The chairman of the O-T General Committee at that point was Dick Dunlap of the Norfolk & Western. Dunlap was clearly not a supporter of intermodal, and it became readily apparent that we needed an approach to the O-T Committee other than through the top.

While the O-T General Committee generally contained operating vice presidents of an anti-intermodal stripe, it did have three notable exceptions — Larry Cena of the Santa Fe, Stan Crane of the Southern and Dick Spence of the Southern Pacific. I had previously had the privilege of meeting all three earlier in my career. I knew them well enough to call on each one for ideas concerning the "chairman problem."

As it turned out, in addition to being intermodal boosters to one degree or another, they were all great friends. Would they like to help? You bet. How would we duck the "chairman problem?" "Don't worry, I'll call Stan and Larry and you send the chairman a letter request and let us handle it." said Spence with a puckish grin. After the next O-T meeting I got a call from a puzzled O-T Committee Secretary, John Robinson, informing me that my letter requesting an operating vice president's Intermodal Liaison Committee had been granted, and that the members were Messrs. Cena, Crane, Spence and Dunlap. "I figured this was a pro forma no vote," said John. "But you got yourself a helluva interesting committee. Good luck," he said and hung up.

In 1973 with the liaison committee in place, we moved quickly to let contracts that would examine all aspects of intermodal operations, economics, technology and their application to the "improvement of the breed." Edson set to work with FRA's Arne Bang, looking at ways to improve the intermodal technology of the then current 89-foot 4-inch flatcar weighing 72,000 pounds (36,000 pounds per trailer). I let a contract entitled National Intermodal Network Study which was designed to look at baseline economics and practices and potential benefits.

We decided to bring the Labor-Management Project (then working on yard projects) together with the Intermodal Project. The United Transportation Union Secretary-Treasurer, Dan Collins, had kept a close eye on the Labor-Management Project from its inception. Collins, a short, stocky, good-humored Irishman with a bit of temper and at times a brogue so thick you could cut it with a trowel, was cautiously optimistic about the intermodal project, but nevertheless provided the leadership we needed to move forward. With the balance of the labor side on the Labor-Management Committee, it looked to me like the main interest was in tracking the activity of the committee and maintaining good notes for the file. Whether or not we could make progress remained to be seen. Collins, meanwhile, maintained a level of enthusiasm that increased as the project went along.

In 1974-1975 as work progressed, we held regular meetings with the Intermodal Steering Committee and O-T Intermodal Committee. Both proved to be extremely helpful.

From the Steering Committee, two members developed suggestions for new projects. George Stern of the Illinois Central Gulf (also a B&O Technical Training Program alum and successor to Reistrup) was looking at the negotiation of short, fast-service, dedicated intermodal trains or short-haul routes.

The second area of interest was expressed by Reggie Short of the Norfolk & Western. Short, an old-school rail (former Pennsy and Wabash), was (and remains) "Mr. Perpetual Motion." His interest was in the establishment of an intermodal Management Information System. On the FRA side, a newly hired young man with an interest in Management Informations Systems, Bill Bourque, worked with the N&W's Larry Keoughan.

Reggie Short had an Operating Department more attuned to long, slow coal trains rather than light, fast intermodal service. With no direct service east of Buffalo, the Norfolk & Western had forged a piggyback service over the old "Alphabet Route." It had previously been used by carload shippers looking for an alternative to the Pennsy and New York Central between the Midwest and the Northeast. This had been a combination of Nickel Plate, Wheeling & Lake Erie, Pittsburgh & West Virginia, Reading, Central of New Jersey and Western Maryland, which produced most of the letters of the alphabet when translated to a shipper routing instruction on a waybill. The N&W controlled most of the route through merger. The exception was the Baltimore & Ohio who controlled the Western Maryland which ran from Connellsville, Pennsylvania (near Pittsburgh), to the East.

As mergers occurred carriers increased their own competitiveness by offering direct, single line hauls. This often cut out cooperative deals made by predecessor roads. No more "everybody plays" atmosphere. Now it was "run fast — but run with your team."

The Chessie System (C&O, B&O and WM) consolidated the merger partners and cut Norfolk & Western off from the east end of the Alphabet Route. Chessie intermodal was headed up by a big, tall operating rail named Gordon Volkers, also a B&O Technical Training grad. "Gordie is a real gentleman," said Short. "But he effectively slammed the gateway shut and cost N&W 26,000 loads a year." Things were tough as everyone in intermodal increased the competition a notch. One response by Short was development of the intermodal Management Information System to improve profitability of N&W's business.

Meanwhile, Edson and Bang were examining equipment options. They looked at the earlier work done by General Electric for the Santa Fe at the American Car & Foundry Lo Deck Car and at a car built by Pullman-Standard for container service. That, plus the experience gained by Edson with the low-profile, lightweight Flexi Van equipment, indicated that significant potential existed in car tare weight reduction, improved aerodynamics, better ride quality and lower center of gravity.

Between the Network Study, the Labor Management work and the R&D work, the Intermodal Team spent a lot of time on the road in 1974-1977, working with industry groups and individual railroads. In those days most Intermodal Departments received such low priority from the Management Information System groups that little if any progress was made with computer applications.

At the Santa Fe Larry Cena had hired Bill Paul who had worked on the NYC/Santa Fe container project as a special assistant. Paul took an interest in the terminal aspects of trailer handling on the Santa Fe. As he talked to the intermodal operating people, it became obvious that intermodal could benefit greatly in an application of computers. Unable to budge Santa Fe's Computer Department (which he was later to head) Bill Paul looked at employing a small computer to be placed directly in the terminal rather than using a mainframe. In an era of the ubiquitous Personal Computer this is no big deal. However, in the 1960's and 1970's it was revolutionary. Cena supported both the concept and the purchase of a small computer, and the Santa Fe improved its intermodal terminal paperwork by an order of magnitude over everyone else in the industry.

Of the O-T group Cena was the most interested in the improved, lightweight technology. He ran a long-distance, high-speed railroad where fuel costs, acceleration and braking were important. Crane's intermodal service, while extremely consistent, was slower due to numerous curves and grades on the Southern Railway.

In attempting to keep everyone informed on the progress of the work, we met with all of the car builders. Of the "majors" of the era only Pullman-Standard's Dr. Bill Manos expressed both an interest and a willingness to work on the project. He had lots of ideas on reducing car weight and construction costs. In fact he had developed a box girder construction container car he called the "Land Bridger" with just such an idea in mind. But Pullman had been unable to sell it to the railroads. Their concept was to eliminate weight from full-length car decking and cushioned draft gear with a bare bones car operating between mechanized terminals.

Edson and I went out to the Pullman Works at Hammond, Indiana, for the purpose of a tour, idea swapping and a look at the "Land Bridger" (actually two prototype cars, TLDX 61 and 62). We were impressed by what we saw and decided to try the ideas with Trailer Train.

I called Curt Buford, president of Trailer Train, whom I had known briefly at the Central and asked for an appointment. We were received by Buford, Rene Brodeur, head of engineering, Sheldon Landy, head of planning and a couple of other people. After briefing them on the progress of the various projects to date, we launched into what we had seen at Pullman-Standard with the lightweight developments. We got a very interesting response from Buford. "You know," he said, "we have a really large investment in our Trailer Train intermodal fleet and obsoleting it overnight would not be wise. In addition we have looked at lighter weight cars and the 25 cent per pound saving in steel costs would be more than offset by increased production costs."

I offered that some car builders thought reduced weight would reduce, not increase production cost. "We're sure that is not the case," was the response.

Pullman-Standard had been the largest of the nation's car builders, but had fallen on hard times by the 1970's. Dr Bill Manos had designed a lightweight container car called "Landbridger" which was modified for trailers and used in Santa Fe's "Super C" service. It led to the development of the third generation of intermodal equipment. — PULLMAN-STANDARD

"Besides, maintenance costs would probably increase."

It was clear that hardware progress lay in a different direction. Our next attempt was back with the Operating-Transportation group. In our meeting with them we brought up the "Land Bridger" car. Spence had tried it and wasn't impressed. Crane still had a hilly railroad. Dunlap was courtly. Cena said he was interested in putting it in *Super C* service, but only if it hauled trailers.

I went back to Manos. Could he modify TLDX 62 with hitches and running gear pads? "Could you pay for it," he asked? What would it cost? "About $25,000," he said. I could, but it would take a couple of years to work through the bureaucracy and we didn't have the time. Although it cost him a large percentage of his discretionary budget, Manos modified the car and it went into service between Chicago and Los Angeles on Santa Fe's *Super C*.

Edson in the meantime had also been trying to interest locomotive builders in developing power for high-speed, light-tonnage intermodal service. Santa Fe had flirted with aerodynamic locomotive fairing on its F-45 cab units of the 1960's. In addition to improved aerodynamics, why not design a locomotive for intermodal that was lighter in weight since much of the locomotive weight for general service units comes from concrete ballasting?

Calls to the Electro-Motive Division of General Motors went unanswered. Calls to General Electric produced an invitation to come to Erie to talk. We took a tour of the Erie plant and were given a session with top engineering people that was a basic repeat of the Trailer Train session. "We don't see the market, and we don't see the economics."

Based on our studies we found that 80-90 percent of the economics was in the car side and 10-20 percent was in the locomotive. With a car costing $40,000 (but with 75-100 of them in a train) and a locomotive costing $400,000 (with 2-5 per train), it was obvious that the leverage lay with the cars.

Progress had been made with the Steering Committee, the Operating-Transportation group, individual railroads and the Labor Management group. As headway was shown we were able to gain support to go to Congress for an appropriation for an intermodal corridor demonstration. The idea was to shift traffic from the all-highway to intermodal by showing the economic lessons from the Network Study, combining it with a labor-management short crew arrangement and following up with new technology equipment. The potential even existed to try high-speed, lightweight locomotives since Paul Reistrup had moved to the Amtrak presidency and was about to try a Canadian-built LRC train set.

In exploring potential routes in 1974 an interesting possibility emerged. George Stern of the Illinois Central-Gulf had conducted market research into the St. Louis-Chicago lane. As a Steering Committee member he saw the potential of the combined projects to reduce costs, improve service quality, create a breakthrough with labor by increasing jobs and business and make real progress.

Bill Thompson was then Vice President and General Manager of Operations at the Illinois Central-Gulf, and left to become Director of Operations Planning at the Norfolk & Western. Familiar with both routes, Thompson suggested that Stern and I take a ride and discuss "possibilities." An inspection run was set up in early 1974 from the N&W Landers carload yard in Chicago to Decatur and then to St. Louis.

Could train miles be traded evenly enough that employees from both roads would have a fair share of the work? It appeared that they could. Would the terminals work? Current N&W intermodal operations in Chicago ran out of Calumet Yard. Reggie Short took a lot of kidding in the Steering Committee about issuing a free set of water wings with every trailer for his often-under-water terminal. Short had capital plans in for an intermodal terminal at Landers that would correct the problem.

Stern ran the planning "through the chairs" at ICG and then decided to test the idea at the Interstate Commerce Commission. He called Virginia Mae Brown, affectionately known as "Peaches," the first woman Chairman of the Commission, for an appointment. His Law Department had told him that a joint Illinois Central-Gulf and Norfolk & Western move would require a pooling agreement which would take several years at the Commission. Stern wanted to test the theory himself.

Outlining the program, Stern asked if this made sense. Without committing one way or the other, Brown indicated that the Commission was always interested in promoting efficieny in transportation.

Satisfied that it was worth the effort, Stern had ICG submit a potential pooling agreement with the N&W. The Commission approved the pool within two weeks. Planning moved forward at ICG, both as a joint line effort and as a single line ICG effort. The latter resulted in "Slingshot" service between Chicago and St. Louis over the old Gulf, Mobile & Ohio route.

Stern, in an unpublished letter to a rail trade magazine a few years later, describes the details:

> As so often happens, the people behind the story are as fascinating as the story itself. I thought you and your readers might enjoy knowing some of them.

Slingshot started on December 19, 1974, in the office of Dave DeBoer, then Chief Economics Program Division, Federal Railway Administration. DOT had just completed the feasibility study of the National Intermodal Network. The meeting was to brainstorm how to move from the study phase to implementation. Dave exclaimed "We need a demonstration route — short, frequent, low cost trains in a high volume corridor." The ICG initiated the "Jobs Commission,' intensive labor management meetings to search for new business opportunities. If the government offered some seed money, would the ICG initiate such train service?

Scott Harvey, ICG's Assistant to the President and Chairman of the Jobs Commission' program took the plan to John Lange, ICG's Director Labor Relations. John immediately said it would be a mistake to develop any train service without labor input. Labor involvement was needed from the inception even before Market Research.

One of the most fateful sessions in railroad history was held on January 14, 1975. Eugene Abbott, General Chairman, and Jim Clarke, Local Chairman, represented the UTU at the meeting in the Holiday Inn Coffee Shop in Bloomington, Illinois. The idea was put on the table. Two-man crews, no caboose, three trains per day, no overnight lodging — almost four days pay for 8 hours work, six days per week. Gene Abbott was 62 years old with a bad heart. Over several cups of coffee and a nitroglycerin pill, he told of being a union leader for 25 years. During that time he said 2/3 of the work had disappeared. The 1975 recession was at its worst. The rank and file were asking him what he was doing for them.

Better motels and electric cabooses were nice, but what was he doing about jobs?

Gene said he would like to believe he could put his men to work, but how could he trust management? Would management run the new train service for one week right then? If management would run one train for five days right then, even though there was no traffic, he would negotiate and assist in development of the new service.

John Lange extended his hand across the table. Two men, one not knowing if his management would run the trains, the other not knowing if his men would accept his decision or if his union leadership would accept his revolutionary work rules in the face of a sold national position, joined hands for mutual help.

Would railroad management recognize and capitalize on this unique concept? In early 1975, the ICG was losing more money then ever in its history. Cash was at a critical level. New financial officers and control systems were the watch word of the company. The market for new service had to be poor; competition would never allow new service to gain a foothold. Economic analysts showed the corridor from Chicago to St. Louis was too short to break even at revenue which sales said were required. Corporate officers said the company could not afford investment in risky ventures. The market was to tenuous. The cash loss at the nadir too severe.

Allen Boyd, the first Secretary of Transportation, now President of Amtrak, president at that time of the ICG, summarized the conversation, then declared the project was a go.' Furthermore, he said, "If the program was not successful in the first six months, or in the second six months, he would be in favor of giving it a third six months."

He had seen the same situation once when Pangara had requested the CAB for new service and knew success would come if management was patient.

One final hero needs to be mentioned. In mid August, the tariffs which called for a 43 percent reduction in price were approved by the Interstate Commerce Commission on an experimental basis. At that point labor said it was time to start the train service. ICG management had authorized a cash ceiling but no base customer in sight and the summer lull due to last at least another 30 days, disaster was imminent. The cash limit was bound to be exceeded. On August 7, one week before start up Bob Maisch, United Parcel Service, agreed to buy 1/2 of one train. Even though he would lose several hours safety margin in his transit from New York to St. Louis, he felt UPS had a stake in the piggyback business and should support innovation whenever and wherever it reasonably could.

Government, labor, rail management, shippers, all cooperated to make the "Slingshot" possible.

Stern was hoping that this display of private initiative would convince Congress that an intermodal demonstration was a good idea, deserving support, and that ICG should be awarded the contract. I had tried to convince him to hold off a bit. Washington had a way of declaring the problem fixed if a demonstration was already in progress using private funding. But at that point the Slingshot was stretched to far to stop. Stern gave us strong support on the Hill with prepared testimony, and Collins worked the Committee behind the scenes. We got a $6 million appropriation to try our ideas. Collins dubbed me the "Six Million Dollar Man" similar to a popular TV series of that name, and we were off and running, looking for a demonstration railroad. But the FRA contract people made it very clear that the existing ICG Slingshot service would not be a potential candidate.

What was needed was a willing railroad with determined operating unions and a good track, operating on a lane of less than 800 miles, but over 400 miles. As it turned out, giving away the $6 million was tougher to do than it had been to get it from Congress in the first place.

With both the Vice President-Operating's Committee and the Intermodal Steering Committee following the project, the interest level was high. Initially, 16 roads requested preliminary information, but by the time we were ready to ask for serious expressions of official interest, the candidates list had decreased to five.

The best candidate looked like the SP's route between the Bay Area and Los Angeles. Tom Fante had been involved with the project from the beginning and understood the nuances of dealing with the FRA. Several meetings were held with various elements of the SP, but in the end they could not work it out within the company.

I also learned a valuable lesson about union politics. Although Collins was more than willing to exercise his Irish charm on the General Chairman and Local Chairmen, if the local people had their heels dug in, union headquarters in Cleveland couldn't directly order them to do anything. The power of Cleveland came in stopping a potential project, not in starting it.

So we moved on. The Illinois Central-Gulf's St. Louis-Chicago lane looked great (although a bit short), but we couldn't do it because it was already in business. Detroit-Chicago was a candidate, but Conrail presented a dual problem. First, Conrail was incapable of doing the project based on physical condition. The alternative was Grand Trunk Western, but funding a competitor to Conrail was a problem when the Federal Government was trying desperately to keep Conrail afloat. And besides, the Grand Trunk had a great deal of difficulty tracking through the program.

Conrail had filed an interest in the New York-Buffalo corridor. We had offered to cover up to only 60 percent of the starting losses of the program due to strictures placed on us from departmental budget officers. We had, however, defined the costs so that all out-of-pocket losses were covered. This was done through costing equipment on replacement rather than on a depreciated basis. Conrail attempted to have the New York Department of Transportation (DOT) fund the remaining 40 percent. The end-run attempt failed. A strong case could be made that Conrail had a full plate without this additional project.

The Richmond, Fredericksburg & Potomac suggested a Richmond-New York service, using trackage rights over Chessie and Conrail. The difficulties of this plan were readily apparent and led to a withdrawal.

The Detroit, Toledo & Ironton had proposed a Detroit-Cincinnati route. They had also looked at an extension to Atlanta. The DT&I route traffic looked very thin for a multiple train operation. And working on through traffic when the connecting carrier was not a part of the demonstration, produced a real problem. The combination of problems caused the route to sink.

Finally, there was the Chicago-Twin Cities corridor. We visited the Burlington Northern, but between a new terminal with the normal shakedown bugs in Chicago and an under-construction terminal in a muddy cornfield in the Twin Cities area, the Burlington Northern had its hands full. The SOO Line clearly had neither the track nor the willingness to run a showcase operation. A visit to the Chicago & North Western revealed a hard-core bastion of rock-ribbed conservatives who wanted absolutely nothing to do with government bureaucrats — even if they had a $6 million bag of money. Not only that, they didn't want anyone else in the lane doing business with us either.

Just to polish off the route we also called on the Milwaukee Road. We found an interest in the intermodal and trucking company side through Laurin Cowling and Clarence Goldsmith, but elsewhere in the company the project seemed to bog down. It did,

Pacific Fruit Express was a company jointly owned by the Union Pacific and Southern Pacific to provide and service refrigerator cars for hauling of perishables. It was formed by E.H Harriman in 1906 to cut dependence on independent refrigerator car carriers. As technology improved, PFE began to offer piggyback refrigerator trailers called "Tempco-Van Service." — DONALD DUKE COLLECTION

The Milwaukee Road participated in the FRA Intermodal Demonstration Program by establishing highly successful "Sprint" trains between Chicago and the Twin Cities. — WILLIAM D. MIDDLETON

A Conrail piggyback train "under the wire" of former Pennsylvania Railroad territory at Wilmington, Delaware. It won't be long before the cabin car (PRR's terminology for a caboose) will be replaced by the ubiquitous automatic "fred." — HARRE DEMORO

The Milwaukee Road seemed to try to make use of anything to improve its traffic base. This ad, explaining about their piggyback service, appeared when not much about piggyback was shown in the print media.

however, spark curiosity on the part of the C&NW when they heard of the attention from the Milwaukee.

We were fast running out of potential routes for the demonstration. During the time the intermodal program had been put together an old friend from the Great Northern, Paul Cruikshank, had come to Washington to work at the United States Railroad Administration, helping put together what eventually became Conrail. At the end of the USRA process Pete had become senior vice president-operation for the Milwaukee Road.

I phoned Pete in Chicago in 1976 to talk about the intermodal demonstration project. We discussed how it might fit on the Twin Cities route, and how we seemed to be bogged down in "the process" at the Milwaukee. "I'm taking the car to look at that route next week," he said. "Why don't you come out and ride it with me and we'll talk about it."

The next week we boarded the car *Wisconsin* at Union Station for a ride to the Twin Cities. The route itself was in what could be described as adequate shape at that point, and the Milwaukee Road still had the horses to turn it on — especially with Pete Cruikshank.

About two-thirds of the way to the Twin Cities, after I explained what we expected and what we could do in return, Pete simply said "Sure we're interested," and the Milwaukee Road Sprint Demonstration was born.

As word leaked out about the demonstration, the Chicago & North Western made one more political run to try to get the route changed or to have it go between Chicago and the Twin Cities over the C&NW on their terms. This in actuality meant no multiple frequencies (beyond the second frequency they wanted us to fund), no tight schedules, no special marketing or sales effort and no minimization of equipment costs. But the path and the message was clear — "If you want to play, we welcome you to the game. If you don't want to play, don't rain on someone else's game." With that the program was launched with the Milwaukee Road to demonstrate new concepts and new technology.

At this point the Department of Transportation formally recognized intermodal as a legitimate transportation form, worthy of promotion. The thousands of hours that had been put in by the railroads, the Operating-Transportation liaison committee, the Intermodal Steering Committee, the suppliers, the FRA staff and the contractors finally bore fruit. John Barnum, deputy DOT secretary, gave a policy kickoff speech outlining the national benefits to shippers, carriers and employees if the demonstration succeeded and was emulated.

Lots of details were left to be worked out before the startup. The union had agreed to a three-man crew with extended districts. Next, the railroad looked at setting up the Chicago terminal at Harvey to facilitate connections. But the bulk of the new traffic was projected to originate in northwest Chicago. Thus, the Franklin Park facility was chosen as the Chicago terminus. Franklin Park had three Packers and a Le Tourneau overhead crane in place. Very minor improvements were made for the new trains.

Facilities in the Twin Cities, however, were a far different matter. The old St. Paul facility was truly something to behold. As the terminal superintendent gave us a tour new wonders emerged around every bend. The facility had originally served as a passenger coach yard and had five usable short track circus ramps in view. It also boasted an ancient "Piggypacker" for mechanized loading and unloading. Tucked away on slightly higher ground was a sixth stub track "for high water" according to the superintendent.

From its meager treasury the Milwaukee Road purchased a second "Piggypacker" and rebuilt two tracks as run-through tracks capable of handling 22 or 23 cars. There was no question of the spirit of cooperation and can-do attitude on the part of the Milwaukee Road people to make the demonstration a success. Our choice looked like a good one.

The Milwaukee had run one mixed, but primarily it ran a piggyback train a day on the route (Nos. 210 and 211) that averaged 538 trailers a week. The demonstration would allow them to really go after the highway business. Spurred by the ICG's Slingshot, the Milwaukee dubbed the coming demonstration trains *Sprint*.

A test train was run May 18, 1978 on a ten-hour schedule. This was designed to allow a round trip per day for most of the train equipment. The service was initiated with 32 trains a week — three trains each way Monday-Friday and one pair on Saturday.

The first departure left Franklin Park at 8:00 A.M. on June 5, 1978. In the first six months *Sprint* trains averaged 757 loaded trailers a week. Initially, the Milwaukee ran the trains with two locomotives to assure over-the-road reliability. However, as the Milwaukee gained experience and confidence in the service (and rebuilt some SD 40-2's) the consist was cut back to the designed one unit.

In August of 1978 an early afternoon departure was added from either end which increased the weekly trains to 42. Early in 1979 severe weather let the Milwaukee Road show its stuff as highways snarled to a crawl. Traffic grew to 1,100 trailers a week. Commitments by both UPS and the U.S. Postal Service in the early days made the *Sprint* train a success.

The on-time performance (measured in actual trailer availability) was a solid 95 percent. It was clear that everyone on the Milwaukee cared about their *Sprint* trains. In an owner-operator "sickout" in June of 1979, *Sprint* averaged 1,600 trailers a week. Using an "all in" cost at replacement cost of capital, the Milwaukee made a ten percent return on its capital. To a cash hungry Milwaukee it was a Godsend. The FRA found that two-thirds of the *Sprint* traffic had been attracted from the highways.

The demonstration was renewed for another year at the request of the Milwaukee Road. The train frequency was increased to six pairs of trains per day. This resulted in a train every four hours. Unfortunately, the U.S. economy went into a steep recession that year. The Milwaukee *Sprint* demonstration suffered traffic losses despite the additional frequencies.

As the demonstration ended Milwaukee dropped the schedules back to 34 trains per week, made minor adjustments and continued the project on its own on the ten-hour schedule. Similar programs over the years, involving intermodal trains with special labor agreements, were initiated by Burlington Northern, Norfolk Southern, Santa Fe and Southern Pacific among others.

From the standpoint of the Milwaukee Road the *Sprint* demonstration was termed a success, and from the standpoint of both the FRA and the U.S. Department of Transportation the *Sprint* demonstration was also considered a success. It proved a test bed for trying new concepts, validated costing techniques, brought rail labor in as partners to intermodal progress and stimulated the creative juices of the rail and supplier industries. All in all, not a bad use of Federal funds.

Norfolk Southern No. 7150 leads the Triple Crown RoadRailer train No 248, down cemetary hill at Danville, Virginia. Danville is on the main line and a junction with the NS route to Norfolk, Virginia. On this day, March 28, 1992, the RoadRailer train has a consist of 45 cars. — CURT TILLOTSON, JR.

Chapter 15

RoadRailer

In 1976 in conjunction with a United States Railroad Administration project to study intermodal service for a startup Conrail, Bob Reebie began to look for an alternative to the then current 89-foot, two-hitch trailer car system. He had previously worked as a consultant on the original Flexi Van project for the New York Central before joining the company's Marketing Department in 1960. In 1974 he commenced the two-year Intermodal Network Study for the Federal Railroad Administration. In his technology search he reviewed all of the previous systems used in rail intermodal. Included was the Chessie's Railvan system.

In the interim since leaving the New York Central in 1965, Reebie had established a successful transportation consulting business. Central's former Executive Vice President Wayne Hoffman, with whom Reebie had worked closely, had left the Central in the mid-1960's to become chairman of the Flying Tiger Line, a cargo airline. One element of the Flying Tiger Line was North American Car Company. Reebie became convinced that an updated design of Railvan was the railroad's answer to competing against the all-highway mode. He would ask his old friend Hoffman to fund the prototype through North American Car and then participate in its success.

Reebie established Bi-Modal Corporation in 1976 to develop, market and operate the new product. He contacted Ken Browne about the product and brought in Alan Cripe to help re-engineer the basic concept.

Hoffman agreed to have North American put up seed money, and as a result a new version of the Chessie Railvan was developed. The two prototype units were built in 1978 and called the Mark IV RoadRailer. the unit, a 45x96-foot trailer, also carried a set of single-axle rail wheels behind the tandem highway axles. Following extensive testing at the Association of American Railroads facilities in Chicago and Pueblo, Colorado, and road tests on the Canadian National in revenue service, North American then advanced more money, and Bi-Modal ordered 250 Mark IV units in 1980 from Budd Trailer.

Next, Reebie approached several railroads in order to operate RoadRailer. Initial revenue tests were run between Alexandria, Virginia, and Jacksonville over the Richmond, Fredericksburg & Potomac and Seaboard Coast Line. First to respond for full revenue service was Intermodal Manager Peter Novas of the Illinois Central-Gulf Railroad. It had planned a service between Louisville and Memphis, a 370-mile haul.

Reebie had urged the carriers to use the new technology to negotiate with rail labor. This was to reduce the extreme spread between the manning of trains and the manning of trucks in all-highway moves. Not only were single owner-operator truckers hauling 8-10 hours per day which equated to 400-600 miles per day, but they also made less than half of what a railroader did for operating only 100 miles a day. The railroaders generally also shared the job with three to five other line-haul employees per 100 miles.

The ICG attempted to negotiate a short (2 or 3 person) crew on extended districts with no caboose in exchange for a limited length RoadRailer train. Unfortunately, United Transportation Union Chairman Spencer Stuckey dug in his heels. The scheduled August 5, 1981 startup of RoadRailer was postponed in an attempt to reach an agreement.

When the Illinois Central-Gulf's RoadRailer *Supermode* train started up on September 28, 1981, it did so with a four-man crew and a caboose. It did not take many months to prove that an expensive piece of equipment with standard labor agreements could not make money in a less than 400-mile corridor. The abortive project was quietly terminated after a year of operation.

Next on Reebie's list was Conrail. He approached them for a corridor operation. Conrail was not interested in acquiring and operating the equipment, but said that it would not object to Reebie running RoadRailer equipment on Conrail through Bi-Modal.

The corridor that Reebie agreed to was between Buffalo-New York City. The route was slightly over 400 miles long and had substantial truck traffic. In addition a good highway, i.e., the New York State Thruway, ran on an almost parallel route and charged a stiff toll. Unfortunately, it also allowed turnpike doubles, i.e., two large twin trailers per tractor.

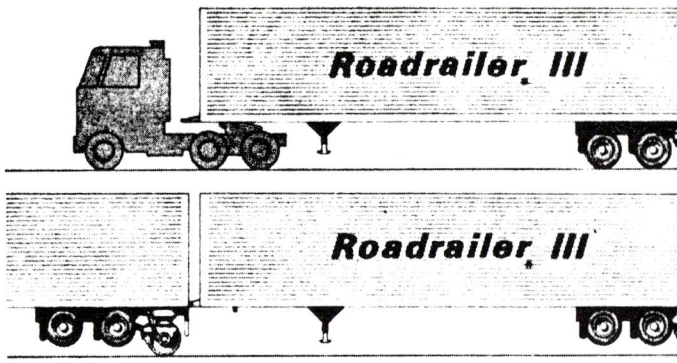

Drawing of a 45-foot by 96-inch RoadRailer from Bob Reebe's Bi-Modal Corporation booklet showing the concept of RoadRailer in highway and rail mode operation. — BI-MODAL CORPORATION

Fifteen Mark IV RoadRailers leave Alexandria, Virginia, on a revenue test run in 1980. The test was conducted on the Richmond, Fredericksburg & Potomac Railroad and the Seaboard-Coast Line. — PROGRESSIVE RAILROADING

The Bi-Modal 45 x 96 Mark IV RoadRailer train prepares to depart in Illinois Central Gulf "Supermode" service in 1981. The service was short-lived due in part to the lack of cooperation by the United Transportation Union. — ROADRAILER

Nonetheless, Bi-Modal initiated its *Empire State Xpress* on November 2, 1982. Conrail had negotiated three-man crews for the service. Initial traffic was substantially overbalanced eastbound, and the train operated in the red.

In 1983 Bi-Modal began to work with Inter-Rail Xpress, a new startup company established to haul perishables between Orlando, Florida, and the Hunt's Point market in the Bronx. The service was to operate over Seaboard Coast Line, Richmond, Fredericksburg & Potomac, Amtrak and Conrail. Coordinating the interline move was proving difficult. Objections were raised by the Long Island Rail Road which feared a tie up of its commuter traffic. A lack of ability by Inter-Rail to raise capital to purchase RoadRailers ultimately ended the project.

Meanwhile, Bi-Modal's deep pockets, North American Railcar, was running into financial problems completely unrelated to Bi-Modal. Early in 1984 North

The Bi-Modal Corporation press kit for 1977 contained this photograph of Mark III RoadRailer. The company was a part of North American Car and updated Chesapeake & Ohio Railvan technology. — BI-MODAL CORPORATION

American informed Reebie that he would have to make it on his own with both RoadRailer and the *Empire State Xpress* operations. With an operating deficit running more than a million dollars a year, Bi-Modal closed down the *Empire State Xpress* in July of that year. North American Car went bankrupt in December of 1984. A year later Thrall Car bought the RoadRailer plans and continued to market the carless technology.

At that point another candidate entered the carless technology arena in the form of Railmaster Corporation. Headed by Monte Riefler, the new concept substituted a two-axle rail truck with adaptive castings. This truck was in lieu of the Mark IV RoadRailer single-axle rail truck that was integrated into the van. RoadRailer also worked on a similar unit, the Mark V which was put into prototype in May 1984. The new technology reduced tare weight of the van from 17,900 to 16,200 pounds. Railmaster was later bought by Thrall and integrated into its RoadRailer unit.

Despite the financial trials, Reebie continued to press other railroads and shippers. General Motors had responded — particularly on plant-to-plant moves where RoadRailers could be loaded beyond highway weight limits.

The Burlington Northern and Grand Trunk Western had been running short-crew *Expeditor* standard piggyback trains between Detroit and St. Louis, largely for GM Freight. GM asked the BN to substitute RoadRailers. BN was willing, but the GTW balked. So in January of 1986 the BN started up with two-man crews between Chicago and the General Motors' plant in Wentzville, Missouri. The dray from Detroit to Chicago, however, made for very marginal operations.

The Norfolk Southern had also been looking at the

The original test of RoadRailer was held at the Department of Transportation (later Association of American Railroads) Test Track at Pueblo, Colorado. Much later in time, an advanced version Mark V unit riding on modified rail bogies is being tested. — ROAD RAILER

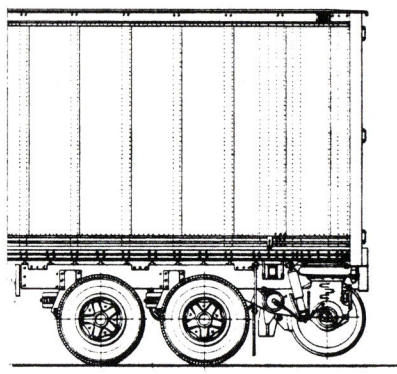

At the left, a photograph showing the RoadRailer trailer in the rail mode. Note that by lowering the rail wheels it raises the highway rubber tires a foot off the ground. (RIGHT) A drawing from a RoadRailer brochure showing the trailer on the rubber tires with rail wheels withdrawn. — ROADRAILER

The Norfolk Southern leased all its RoadRailer units for use over its network. They did turn back the original Bi-Modal units. In this photograph of RoadRailer train No 248 at Swann, North Carolina, in 1991, a Union Pacific RoadRailer unit is in the train's consist, after being released to the Norfolk Southern. — CURT TILLOTSON, JR.

service. Unlike the Burlington Northern the NS had a direct Detroit-St. Louis line (the old Wabash route). Ed Kreyling, Norfolk Southern's Vice President of Marketing, took up the case for RoadRailer and sold the corporation on establishing the operation. NS took over the BN operation in July of 1986 and subleased the 220 RailRoaders units under a short-term lease. With a plant-to-plant operation things went better, and NS was in a unique position. As Tom Finkbiner explains, "We had a problem with intermodal in 1986. We faced declining revenues on our short hauls. Our intermodal facilities were in bad shape; many were old circus ramps. RoadRailer was the obvious choice." The circus ramps were largely inherited from the Norfolk & Western by merger. Although the Southern ramps were largely mechanized, they were only able to handle trailers since the ex-Southern "home-built" cranes did not have twist locks on the spreaders and were too short to clear a double-stack car.

Tom Finkbiner, a bright, acerbic, young trucker inherited by Norfolk Southern with the North American Van Lines acquisition, was exactly what Reebie and RoadRailer needed. Finkbiner had served a stint with Roadway and understood the complexities of both Less-Than-Truckload and Truckload trucking. He began to build a RoadRailer network under the Triple Crown Services Organization, i.e., a Norfolk Southern subsidiary. The service was retailed directly to the shipper, using a separate sales staff hired mostly from North American and headed by Kevin Donohue.

The network grew with the addition of Detroit-Atlanta, Chicago-Atlanta and St. Louis-Kansas City legs. At this point CSX also initiated a Detroit-Atlanta RoadRailer service (Xpress Railer) using Mark IV units.

Norfolk Southern added Fort Wayne, Indiana, to Cleveland and Buffalo service and additional routes from Alexandria, Virginia, to Atlanta and Jacksonville, Florida, to Atlanta. The Union Pacific established a service using the Mark V unit between Chicago and Dallas in December of 1987. Both CSX and the Union Pacific discontinued their respective services in 1988.

Clearly, a major drawback of the carless technology is its high initial capital cost and its need to operate in dedicated trains from day one. One attempt to overcome these problems is through the use of standard domestic and international containers via a ChassisRailer.

This device separates the box from the highway and rail unit. The rail/highway unit is essentially a highway chassis with fittings that allow a Mark V truck set to be used on the railroad. With special FRA permission, a custom hitch on a stack car also allows the ChassisRailers to be moved on the rear of a stack train as domestic container feeder service from low density points.

Carless technology in a modified version was offered in a joint venture between Strick (who built the vans) and Sambre at Meuse of France (who built the rail bogies). The units were introduced in 1988 and remain in the test mode.

At Union Pacific's East Los Angeles yard, a Drott crane unloads a 20-foot I.S.O. box and lowers it on a chassis.
—UNION PACIFIC

Chapter 16

New Technology

Just as we saw ideas for intermodal technology spring forth in great profusion in the 1950's, the Third-Generation technology of the 1980's responded to the needs and opportunities presented in the mid-1970's. As was true of the 1950's, not all ideas would be successful, but some would drive technological progress at an unprecedented rate.

The dawn of intermodal's Third-Generation technology began in many places and all at once. But as we have seen many times in intermodal, it took committed intermodalists to get in started, and others to really make it a force to be reckoned with.

THE TRAILER SPINE CAR

The initial thrust into the Third Generation begins with the Santa Fe at 80 East Jackson Blvd. in Chicago. Larry Cena, while an active member of the Federal Railroad Administration's Operating Advisory Committee, had borrowed the modified trailer version of Dr. Bill Manos' Pullman-Standard "Landbridger" (TLDX 62) in 1974. The Santa Fe had the physical plant and the traffic base to make substantial gains with the new intermodal technology.

Tucked away in the Mechanical Department, Cena also had a very competent mechanical man named John Angold (the same test engineer of the New York Central/Santa Fe Flexi Van test days). Larry Cena was a practical railroader, but with a difference. He was possibly the most restless, curious railroader I ever knew — with Stan Crane and Al Perlman running a close tie for second. When Cena came upon a good idea, he would become very impatient until it was converted into successful hardware.

Cena told Angold to design and build a lightweight, lower center of gravity intermodal car. In order to do this, Angold teamed up with Ted Wade at the road's Topeka Shops. The result was a lightweight, centersill articulated car that came in six sections — each holding one trailer and immediately dubbed by shop forces as the "six pack." During 1976 the "six pack" was tested in high-speed service on the Santa Fe. It was cheap, lightweight, easy to load and unload, tracked well in high-speed service, saved fuel and dramatically reduced slack action in trains. It was just as Angold and Wade had planned.

Cena had a series of them built as ten-unit cars, again on a trial basis. This time they were referred to as "ten packs." They too performed so well that, as Cena put it, "Six months into the *experiment* we had stopped tracking them altogether." In his mind it had stopped being an experiment when the "ten pack" had worked out. Santa Fe named the cars "Fuel Foilers," reflecting

Four tracks full of Santa Fe's Ten-Pack Fuel Foilers. This is a result of Santa Fe's move to lighter weight intermodal equipment. — SANTA FE RAILWAY

the nation's energy consciousness in the 1970's.

Pullman-Standard now had received the "Landbridger" back and watched the new Santa Fe car with interest. One P-S'er suggested that the "Landbridger" had been pulled out of the train for a weekend and had been "gone over" in Topeka with a fine toothed comb. Other than being lighter in weight, of course, the two cars had very little in common. When Cena heard the story he replied in characteristic good humor that, in fact, the Topeka Shops had gone over the "Landbridger" with the "world's largest Xerox."

Unfortunately, Pullman-Standard had become so debilitated by this time that they were financially unable to respond to the Santa Fe opportunity. They were instead pursuing the Trailer Train Research and Development plan — the development of a single-axle trailer car.

Cena reserved Santa Fe's right to use their new design free and then allowed Angold, Wade and Chief Mechanical Officer Ted Mason to negotiate a personal licensing agreement with Itel on the construction and sale of the car to others. This was not an ordinary arrangement in the railroad industry, but then, Larry Cena was not an ordinary railroader.

Santa Fe was not alone in pursuing new intermodal designs. Several parties had followed the Federal Railroad Administration studies with great interest. Neil Paton, an inveterate inventor from Seattle, had an idea for improving intermodal through the use of specialized trucks. In 1977 he approached the Budd Company at Red Lion, Pennsylvania, to see if they were interested in financing the concept.

Budd officials bucked the ideas to their Tech Center for an evaluation. In 1978 the Center came back with several problem areas they thought needed work before proceeding. Inventors and chefs often share a common temperament when it comes to their trade — and as such are very sensitive to what they perceive as a criticism of their creations. Paton was not pleased with the Tech Center's suggestions for improvement and decided to take the ideas to Youngstown Steel Door.

THE BUDD LO-PAC 2000

A German company, Thyssen Industries, had taken control of the Budd Company. Early guidance provided by the new management was that Budd was too dependent on auto and truck products and needed to increase projects within the rail industry.

With that mandate, the Tech Center nominated two candidate projects — an inexpensive, fabricated three-piece freight car truck and a low-profile, lightweight intermodal trailer car. The first was in response to the great fear that Budd's casting plants would not keep

The Budd-built car was named the Budd Lo Pack 2000 and the prototype model was given BUDX-2000 as its reporting marks. Seen here in Conrail's Kearny, New Jersey, intermodal facility, it is loaded with six Budd-built trailers. — TRANSIT AMERICA INCORPORATED

Encouraged by FRA studies in the 1970's, the Budd Company designed a low-profile, lightweight trailer well-car to replace the standard 89-foot double-hitch car. — TRANSIT AMERICA INCORPORATED

up with the need for wheels, axles, truck frames and bolsters. The latter was in response to the Federal Railroad Administration's intermodal work of the time.

Dick Behrend from the Rail Division and Mike Pavlick of the Tech Center had concluded in 1979 that a cheap, fabricated truck was not possible from a competitive cost standpoint, and recommended that Budd focus on the low-profile lightweight trailer car. They had watched Angold's articulated car on the Santa Fe and liked the idea, but still felt that the low-profile car made more sense.

Thus encouraged, Budd officials allocated $1 million for construction and testing of a six-unit prototype. The unit was to be built at the Tech Center since the railcar plant at Red Lion was set up for shotweld, a stainless steel welding process for passenger cars, and not for carbon steel freight cars. The goal was a car that would haul trailers and fit within a Plate B, i.e., a very tight clearance profile.

By 1980 the prototype had been fabricated at the Fort Washington, Pennsylvania, Tech Center. Since the facility had no tracks, the units were trucked to a nearby Tank Car Corporation of America facility where BUDX-2000 was assembled and painted.

A revenue run with Budd's flatcars was made in December of 1980 from Kearny, New Jersey, to Chicago in Conrail's TV-II train. Shown here is BUDX-2000 being loaded next to an 89-foot car at Kearny. — TRANSIT AMERICA INCORPORATED

Youngstown Steel Door Company built this prototype "Backpacker" well car for both trailers and containers, but never built the car in production lots. The car carried containers single loaded on pedestals located on top of the side sills. Only trailers fit into the wells. — YOUNGSTOWN STEEL DOOR COMPANY

Behrend had been dealing with Conrail's marketing people, Mac Sanders and Jim Hagen, in order to get a series of tests run on Conrail. He and Pavlick had run into resistance from the Conrail Mechanical Department. After four months, and with help from Hagen and Sanders, the test was run on Conrail just prior to Thanksgiving 1980.

A full set of impact, high-speed stability, rock and roll, braking and curving tests produced the expected results. Budd officials were encouraged and set up a multi-division group with manufacturing to be from the Trailer Division, engineering from the Tech Center and marketing and sales from the Rail Division.

In December of 1980 BUDX-2000 ran its first revenue run on Conrail's train No. TV-11 from Kearny, New Jersey, to Chicago. The runs continued successfully during the next few weeks. However, it had become apparent to Budd that the two markets they initially had targeted would be a real problem.

Conrail, as primarily a receiving carrier, felt that it had all the intermodal equipment it could use and was not in the market for new cars. Amtrak was less than enthusiastic over additional freight trains traveling the Northeast Corridor, and the BUDX-2000 idea never got off the ground.

Youngstown Steel Door Company came out with a trailer well car in 1981. This car carried containers single stacked. It never found a sponsor.

Budd next turned to Trailer Train to market their BUDX-2000 car. The Budd engineers worked with Tom Harley who had just arrived at Trailer Train as vice president of equipment and with Rene Brodeur and Boris Terlecky of the engineering staff. After several months of work in which Budd thought it was making progress, a meeting was held with the engineering group and Trailer Train's President Curt Buford. The reception was almost a carbon copy of that held with the Federal Railroad Administration five years before. Brodeur summarized by stating that Budd "had not demonstrated to Trailer Train that the low profile, lightweight car was a good thing."

Budd was thunderstruck. The stainless steel passenger car business had turned sour, the freight car business was rapidly falling apart and now their new million dollar bet looked like an orphan. Thyssen officials ordered the Tech Center to market the car design to another car builder.

Interest in the design was expressed by American Car & Foundry, Berwick, Fruit Growers Express, Thrall and Portec. The group narrowed itself quickly, as Fruit Growers Express, Berwick and Portec were all economically on their last legs. This left American Car & Foundry and Thrall. Budd knew that ACF was working with Trailer Train on a single hitch car. And Carl Icahn was talking takeover of the American Car & Foundry.

Thrall was without an intermodal design and, consequently, looked like the best bet to market the Budd design. An agreement was signed with Thrall in 1982. Dan Domigez of Brae Corporation also had an interest in the design. Earlier, Brae had bought the "Fuel Foiler" design from the Santa Fe design group. Budd also signed a sales agreement with Brae.

THE ACF DOUBLE STACK

At this point we leave Budd and Thrall with the BUDX-2000 Lo-Pac, struggling for a foothold in the intermodal marketplace. It is here where we pick up the next thread in the Third-Generation story. The second "Western connection" to contribute to a Third-Generation breakthrough was the Southern Pacific. The SP had contributed two outstanding intermodal supporters to the FRA effort — Vice President of Operations Dick Spence and Intermodal General Manager Tom Fante. Both caused a lot of conceptual work to be done by SP's Research & Development Chief Paul Garin for an improved intermodal design. Unfortunately, Spence left the Southern Pacific in 1975, leaving Fante without support at the SP.

Studies had been going on for some time at the SP. In 1970 I saw a group of nine of Garin's comparative designs at 65 Market Street, showing estimated tare weights, carrying capacity and costs. The last design on the sheet was for an articulated double-stack container car. Now, five years later, what the SP needed, absent Spence's support, was a customer to push for building the design.

An early and growing intermodal customer for the Southern Pacific was Sea-Land. They had developed a large flow of Minibridge containers between the West Coast and the Gulf (i.e., the movement of containers between ports by rail rather than by ship). In the process of developing Minibridge, Sea-Land had reached into the rail industry and hired a tall, brash young man named Bob Ingram. Ingram had spent short stints with the New York Central, Norfolk & Western and Central Railroad of New Jersey.

Ingram was interested in everything intermodal, and viewed all things that were inefficient with sharp disdain. Fante found Ingram to be the ideal customer to help him press for progress. Ingram had earlier been intrigued with the old General Motors/A.T. Kearney depressed center flatcar for stacking containers.

Fante introduced Ingram to Bill Thomford, Southern Pacific's tall, patrician engineer from the Mechanical Department. Thomford, considered by many to be the industry's leading expert on car design, had worked with Garin to develop the alternative intermodal car concepts. With Ingram, they worked the choices down to two or three basic stacked container designs, and Thomford set to work. He tapped Wally Greb as SP Project Engineer.

Thomford got together with George Reed, Director of Engineering and Bob Billingsley, Chief Engineer of American Car & Foundry to develop a prototype. The car was very different from the solid floor, heavy, depressed center flatcar others had previously envisioned. The car had no center sill. It had side sills to support the load attached to the end bolsters. This was a box design as opposed to a center sill bridge girder design common to "normal" piggyback cars. In addition it was a single platform stand alone car with 70-ton standard trucks. The car carried reporting marks of SP 513300.

Eugene Cordani was appointed American Car & Foundry's Project Engineer. With a high center of gravity it was not certain that the stacked container car design would work out on the road. Then, too, it needed to work efficiently in the terminal. In 1977 ACF turned out the first single unit 40-foot double-stack bulkhead container car and placed it in service on the SP with Sea-Land for testing. Fante assigned his Assistant General Manager Lloyd Nations to follow the tests.

The car worked well on all accounts, leading Thomford to try Paul Garin's next thought, a three-unit articulated car. Garin had been fascinated with the potential of articulation he had seen on an earlier visit to Europe. With the concurrent success of Santa Fe's "Ten Packs" this appeared a natural progression.

By 1979 American Car & Foundry had the three-unit articulated double stack in iron and on the road. Each unit was 40 feet long with bulkheads, and it had flipper container guide accommodations for Sea-Land's 35-foot units. Interestingly, the intermediate units on this experimental car had 125-ton, not 100-ton trucks, increasing the car's load carrying capacity by about 20 percent. It was an innovation that would not reappear in a production car for another eight years.

The Southern Pacific ordered the first 42, five-unit production stack cars from ACF in 1981. They had 40-foot wells with the capability of handling 40-foot or 35-foot containers using 100-ton intermediate trucks. And the first part of the double-stack revolution — the international container stack car was born.

The first articulated double-stack prototype was built in 1979 by American Car & Foundry Company for Southern Pacific and Sea-Land. It was a three-platform car. Seen here with test containers from XTRA, it was the logical step up from the single platform produced in 1977. — SOUTHERN PACIFIC

A Trailer Train "Front Runner" is being loaded by Conrail. The "Front Runner" is a single-axle, lightweight car (this one is 25,000 pounds) that follows in the footsteps of Adapto and Portager. Trailer Train ordered over 3,000 of these cars. (BELOW) In 1979 Trailer Train produced the 4-Runner, a four-platform car with single-axle trucks. The car developed tracking problems, which led to the development of the "Front Runner."
— BOTH TRAILER TRAIN COLLECTION

THE FRONT RUNNER

Trailer Train, meanwhile, had been busy developing a single-axle trailer car. While not anxious to make obsolete their large first- and second-generation fleet, Trailer Train began pressing forward on a new trailer car design. Santa Fe's order for additional "Ten Packs" or, as they had been renamed, "Fuel Foilers," only quickened Trailer Train's effort.

Boris Terlecky had watched the European experience with single-axle trucks for years. The high-speed tracking qualities were extremely good. European railroads would not risk derailment of freight traffic which might interfere with the more dominant passenger moves. Cost was a less relevant factor for the Europeans than in the U.S. Another important difference was that the U.S. railroads permitted far heavier axle loadings.

Trailer Train, in 1979, introduced a 48-foot, two-platform prototype car with European style single-axle trucks. It was called the 4-Runner. This was followed in 1981 by 102 production cars that were placed on the Union Pacific for testing.

The single-axle cars displayed serious tracking problems while in service on the Union Pacific, requiring an expensive retrofit. Trailer Train was convinced, however, of the value of the single-axle design and pressed forward. In 1981 Trailer Train ordered a modified four-unit 4-Runner, a three-unit "Fuel Foiler" and a three-unit Thrall/Whitehead and Kales center sill, articulated, skeletonized trailer car. It was clear that, although late to the game, Trailer Train was getting serious about understanding the overall technological tide that had begun to wash over the intermodal industry in the mid-1970's.

In December of 1982 Curt Buford, president of Trailer Train since 1969, relinquished the presidency, becoming chairman until his retirement the following July. During his tenure, Buford largely weaned Trailer Train from the shadow of the Pennsylvania Railroad, moved the company to Chicago and set up independent repair facilities. When Buford assumed command from Newell, the decision as to car type was largely set for the company. Trailer Train concentrated on refinements, enlargement and protection of their fleet of cars until events forced them from that course.

It now fell to Raymond C. Burton, Jr. to guide the company through the turbulent 1980's and beyond. Burton, formerly of the Santa Fe and Burlington Northern, would be the first non-eastern, non-operating executive to assume and control the helm of Trailer Train. Early on he would successfully tackle and solve the financial problems of Railbox and Railgon, both Trailer Train subsidiaries. This critical situation had threatened the very existence of Trailer Train. Solution of those problems allowed Trailer Train to return to intermodal basics. By the end of the 1980's equipment decisions would be made that would change the face and the character of the Trailer Train pool more than in the entire history of the company.

At this point, however, the industry stabilized briefly. In addition to the large number of "Fuel Foilers" ordered by the Santa Fe, a small number of the multiple-

unit, articulated trailer cars were ordered by the Southern Pacific and Burlington Northern. Trailer Train also acquired the five-unit articulated trailer cars from Thrall and FMC. Trailer Train continued to refine and develop the single-axle trailer car, now called the Front Runner, and by 1983 the car was in full production.

The acquisition of Third-Generation cars proceeded very unevenly. The large acquisitions of the articulated trailer car by Santa Fe, Southern Pacific and Burlington Northern pushed that car type into an early lead. Santa Fe also moved into the development of something they called the A-Stack.

Behold, the entire fleet of Santa Fe A-Stack containers ever built. They pose in the sun on five units of 10 Pac Fuel Foiler cars. — SANTA FE RAILWAY

THE A-STACK

One evening Larry Cena was with an old friend from a major Japanese trading company, who remarked that he felt what was really needed was some type of container that could be loaded with merchandise freight in one direction and high-quality grain or soybeans in the other direction. Thus, the A-Stack was born.

The A-Stack was a big fiberglass or metal container that looked like a large pair of saddlebags draped over the center sill of a de-hitched "Fuel Foiler." It had an end door, and from the end it looked like a squat letter A. When loaded on the car, the top container nested on the bottom which, in turn, rested on the car.

Unfortunately, when loaded with grain the container far exceeded the highway weight limit and thus could not legally move over the highway. Like many great baseball hitters, Cena had his share of strikeouts, one of which was the A-Stack. In intermodal and other areas, however, he hit more than his share of home runs for both the Santa Fe and intermodal.

A-Stack containers being loaded aboard an unhitched Fuel Foiler car. These container's had a low center of gravity and boasted a trough hatch for grain loading and an end door and grating for package goods. — SANTA FE RAILWAY

Four trailers ride on four ICI bogies in a 1984 demonstration of a Ford tractor with Hi-Rail equipment. The bogies were meant to provide cheap gathering service with non-mechanized loading from light density areas to intermodal hubs. Light rails, lack of ballast, and weeds, indicate the market originally visualized for this equipment. — ICI PHOTO

THE BOGIE CONCEPT

Two other developments of the early Cena years was an idea for intermodal branch line service units. The concept was to develop a cheap rail bogie to carry and support the running gear of a trailer on the railroad. This would allow the trailer to move from a low density area to a major intermodal hub for transfer to a main line intermodal train. The idea was to supplant expensive, over-the-road drayage with cheaper rail moves.

The initial idea was developed by Wayde Furlow who had originally been with the Baltimore & Ohio's Mechanical Department. In 1970 while at Chessie, he presented his idea to George Kirwan — another ex-B&O'er who agreed to work on the advancement of the concept.

Furlow and Kirwan submitted their completed idea to Chessie's review committee for consideration. They declined to accept the project due to Chessie's short-haul market, and returned it to Furlow and Kirwan for further development. They, in turn, enlisted the help of Walter Pogue and Jim Hennessy, owner of a railway supply company.

The rail bogies were designed to be pulled by a highway tractor modified with retractable rail wheels (called high rail equipment). They would then be uncoupled and deployed. The unit was called ICI for Intermodal Concepts Inc. It required the trailer to be backed up a ramp, over the rails and onto the rail bogie

Here a trailer is being placed on bogies at Greenville Yard in New Jersey to be loaded on car floats for a trip to the Long Island Rail Road in Brooklyn, then by rail to Farmington - far different from the original market thrust for the equipment. Note that the inexpensive loader has returned to an "all-weather" cab for operations — ICI PHOTO

unit. From there, it would be coupled to units ahead of it and made into a mini-train hauled by the tractor. Berwich Forge produced five test bogies. For obvious reasons it was informally nicknamed the "Pogie Bogie" by the intermodal fraternity.

Initial service was scheduled on the 183-mile route of the Rock Island between Chicago and Silvas, Illinois, using United Parcel Service trailers and a UPS tractor. Unfortunately for ICI, the Rock Island ceased operation before the test got off the ground.

Bill Greenwood, then head of the Burlington Northern's intermodal unit, hosted a National Railroad Intermodal Association meeting for the opening of BN's new intermodal facility in Minneapolis. As a side treat, he lined up demonstrations of the new intermodal technologies of the day. One of those was the "Pogie Bogie."

The idea of the unit was to go from a cheap, low-volume terminal to a hub, minimizing cost wherever possible. Thus, plywood sheets were used as ramps to get the trailer from the ground up over the rails.

Iowa Interstate Railroad commissioned a bogie prototype called Trailer Railer. It is shown here with a CSX/Sea-Land Intermodal trailer. — BRUCE HARMON

The Trailer Railer prototype is shown here being readied for Atlanta's Intermodal Expo. In this view, the wheel chocks are being set. — BRUCE HARMON

Watching the trailer sway as it was loaded on the system was interesting. The concept was demonstrated on the Burlington Northern, the Pittsburgh & Shawmutt and the Iowa Interstate.

To improve on this concept, Paul Banner, president of Iowa Interstate, supported Charlie Bakka, also from Iowa Interstate, in critiquing improvements. A design engineer, Roger Sims, was hired to design a modified bogie with steel ramp loading. The prototype Trailer Railer unit was shown at the Atlanta Expo in 1988, but stirred little interest. The problem seemed to be that trailers needed to be drayed by highway to even a mini terminal. In most cases, the trucker preferred to go direct to the hub. Here, he could get a return load rather than take the shorter route to the mini terminal where a return load was much less likely due to lower volume.

Interestingly, the "Pogie Bogie" later reemerged in a totally different market. Rather than being used to solve rural access problems, it was used to solve an urban access problem.

There had always been a problem getting around within the boroughs and suburbs of New York City. In a word, the problem was congestion.

Being short-haul traffic in nature, the railroads of New York City did not have an incentive to solve the problem. An exception was the Long Island Rail Road. Owned by the state of New York, the LIRR is, by definition, a short-haul and mostly passenger railroad. Short-haul freight solutions were thus looked at somewhat differently.

So in 1989 truckers began using the LIRR as a dedicated truck bypass route around congested highways. Loadings on the bogie were made with inexpensive cranes at Farmington, Long Island and

Looking like a coiled snake, a technician attaches the air line connecting the brake shoes between Trailer Railer bogies. — BRUCE HARMON

Bayonne, New Jersey. The train was moved from Farmington to Brooklyn for transloading to cross-harbor barges and movement to Bayonne by the New York Cross Harbor Railroad.

Usage was discontinued in early 1990 in a dispute over who should be responsible for capital costs of the rail technology. Later in the year, New York State funding was provided to purchase the existing twelve bogies and two lifters and to buy an additional 33 bogies for the service.

THE IRON HIGHWAY

The Association of American Railroads, in 1983, launched an economic and mechanical team to evaluate technologies that could be developed for the rail industries two top commodities — coal and intermodal. The effort was dubbed H-PIT for High Productivity Integral Train. Goals were set and suppliers were asked to design hardware to meet the objectives. The AAR would provide analytical assistance along the way. They then would validate any test results at the AAR's Pueblo, Colorado, test facility.

Scott Harvey led the staff effort for the AAR. He retained John Williams of Woodside Consultants for cost analysis. Jim McClellan from Norfolk Southern and I, then at the Southern Pacific, served on the economics group chaired by Peter Detmold of the Canadian Pacific. In the intermodal area line-haul savings of 40 percent appeared well within reach for double-stack technology. Distributed power (the concept of powering the wheels of the cars, using the payload for traction similar to the Santa Fe coaxial train) appeared worthy of exploration. We estimated a ten percent additional line-haul saving for a total goal of a 50 percent intermodal savings versus the current 89-foot technology.

The mechanical task group led by Santa Fe's Ted Mason seriously questioned whether we should set a goal of 50 percent in cost savings. They suggested something on the order of 15 percent. At that time Southern Pacific's double-stack, cost-savings experience was not generally well known in the industry.

In general, by the time H-PIT had finished its work in 1987, the double-stack revolution was well under way. While no immediate technology sprang forth, technological spurring events such as H-PIT had a way of scattering seeds that matured in their own good time.

One of the intermodal concepts developed for H-PIT was a New York Air Brake (NYAB) entry called the "Iron Highway." The idea was conceived by Tom Engle, general manager of new development, as a radical departure from any existing technology. The concept was to get away from fixed length railcars, allow the loading of standard highway trailers (without intermodal lift pads or other beefing up) and reduce the break-even length of haul by allowing an "unload anywhere" capability.

The result was different in almost very respect. Standard railcars have always used a wheel set that was fixed on an axle and rotated on a bearing. NYAB designed a wheel that rotated independently with no solid axle. Steering linkages guided the wheels.

New York Air Brake adopted the idea of distributed power. However, rather than DC motors it opted for AC with twin 800 hp. engine-alternators, using an automatic transmission with a fluid torque converter.

The units are designed to use movable knock-down hitches on a series of continuous, slack-free platforms. A series of powered and non-powered platforms are joined to a "ramp platform." The "ramp platform" is intended to allow trailers to be loaded and unloaded from the ground level with a hostler tractor. It is meant to operate at a break-even distance of 350 miles with 20 trailers. Initial testing was under way at Pueblo in 1990-1991. Further testing is planned.

Whether this ambitious concept is able to be brought into production remains to be seen.

REBUILDS, RETROFITS, AND REMAKES

After Trailer Train worked the main bugs out of the single-axle car, this car type became a major order item. As seen in the chart on page 60, acquisition of the Third-Generation technology was very uneven, but pressure from the railroads on Trailer Train was becoming

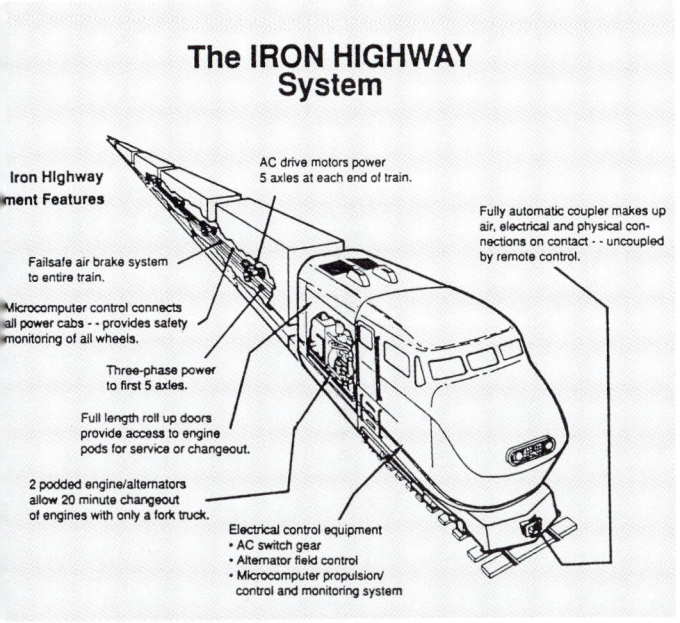

intense. As the 45-foot trailer was introduced, hitch utilization on the Second-Generation 89-foot fleet began to suffer. It was physically impossible to fit two 45-foot trailers on an 89-foot flatcar. While a 40- and 45-foot trailer could be loaded on an 89-foot car, the wave of 45-foot units and attendant lack of 40-footers led to loading one trailer per flatcar — a financially ruinous situation.

This led several railroads and Trailer Train to initiate a retrofit program on existing 89-foot cars to move the hitches which allowed the nose of the trailer to "hang out" over the car end. Some carriers such as the Southern Pacific, deracked obsolete multi-level cars and added hitches to produce "Twin-45" conversions.

The "Iron Highway System" was the New York Air Brake Company's intermodal concept. The units were designed to use moveable knock-down hitches on a series of continuous, slack-free platforms.

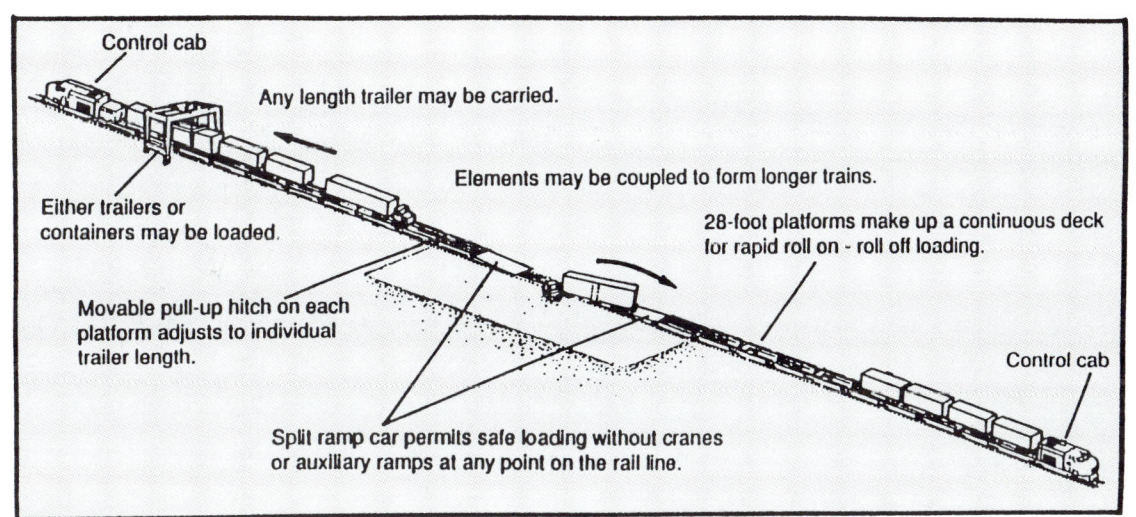

Trailer Train cut the deck out of an 85-foot TOFC car to lighten the car's tare weight and then added bolsters to handle containers as Pacific Rim container intermodal traffic picked up. — TRAILER TRAIN COLLECTION

Trailer Train also did major "Twin-45" rebuilds. Other railroads, such as the Southern, Missouri-Kansas-Texas and the Chicago & North Western cut down boxcars to produce single-hitch intermodal cars. The Santa Fe removed the bulkheads from plasterboard and lumber flatcars and added a single hitch. Some carriers and Trailer Train rebuilt short flatcars into container cars. These stop gaps met with varying degrees of success. Some of the boxcar conversions tracked poorly and some of the former bulkhead flats were twice as heavy per hitch as a standard 89-foot Trailer Train car. They were immediately dubbed "lead sleds." With the larger 45-foot trailer (and 48- and 53-footers on the horizon) and major growth in containers, no clear direction presented itself. Inexorably, the Third-Generation cars began to make their presence felt in the intermodal fleet. The only question was — would the ultimated car be one that could handle containers, trailers, or a mix?

Seaboard Coast Line "pig train" roars through Selma, North Carolina, while crossing the diamonds of the Southern Railway's Greensboro-Goldboro Line, back in 1978. — CURT TILLOTSON, JR.

Chapter 17

Deregulation — Free At Last

While the nation's railroads and their suppliers had been investigating hardware, things were happening in Washington D. C. that would have an even greater effect on the future of intermodal.

Congress, in its debate of the myriad of railroad legislation of the 1970's, had indicated a strong interest in rail deregulation. During the short time I spent at the Interstate Commerce Commission, all staff groups were requested to look at areas in which deregulation might be tried. Chairman George Stafford had been chairman for a greater length of time than any other person in the long history of the Commission. Stafford was short, with a shock of white hair and a pronounced limp. He was not known for innovation, but clearly attempted to be responsive to the Congress.

Our policy group looked into the areas where competition was keen between rail and trucks, and we submitted a long list of commodities, including fresh fruits, vegetables and intermodal. I can still recall another staff group's list. It included all "safe" commodities, i.e., those no longer hauled by rail. One example that stuck out and typified the list was "human remains." Since human remains, i.e., corpses, traveled only in passenger trains, and passenger service had been turned over to Amtrak in 1971, except for the Southern Railway, the Georgia Railroad, the Denver & Rio Grande Western and the Rock Island, it certainly was a non-controversial commodity. The policy staff concluded that serious deregulation at the Commission was not going anywhere soon.

I left in 1978 to form a market planning group at Southern Pacific. As sometimes happens in Washington, Stafford, as chairman, was followed by a very pro-active staffer from the Senate Commerce Committee, A. Dan O'Neal. The dark and striking O'Neal was a total contrast to the quiet, white-haired Stafford. And it was not long before he put his personal stamp on the Commission.

I was on a panel at a meeting in 1979 held by the Western Growers Association to discuss theories of how railroads and shippers might react to perishable deregulation. I leaned over to ask Chairman O'Neal, "You wouldn't be about to drop a dereg bomb by any chance would you?" Not only would he, but he did, announcing that the Commission had voted the day before to deregulate perishable shipments by rail. Bob Thull, who was Southern Pacific's Market Manager for Foods, then gave our carefully prepared talk on how the Southern Pacific planned to deal with deregulation. With that meeting the railroads were off and running in the new world of meeting our customers face-to-face

Lettuce grown in the Salt River area, near Phoenix, is loaded aboard flatcars which will carry the refrigerated vans to dockside in New York City for overseas movement in Santa Fe trailers all the way to Sweden. Perishables became the first ICC deregulated commodity, followed by all intermodal shipments. — SANTA FE RAILWAY

The venerable Interstate Commerce Commission building located at 12th and Constitution Avenue in Washington, D.C. Created April 5, 1887, it is the nation's oldest regulatory agency. — LIBRARY OF CONGRESS COLLECTION

in the marketplace, as opposed to the time-honored, formalized and long-drawn-out rate bureau process.

The rate bureaus often took over a year to revise railroad rate structures for even non-controversial items. Where a fight was involved (either with a shipper, another railroad, any other transportation mode or the ICC) the process could take five or ten times as long. In the interim, the full truckload trucker had long since set his rate and service package and had taken the freight.

At the Southern Pacific we labored long and hard to make deregulation work. We made frequent trips to Washington to assure both Congress and the ICC that we definitely liked dereg and that we considered it to be a success.

It was clear that many Commission stalwarts from the staff ranks viewed O'Neal as a "Commission wrecker" and a heretic. His youth and freewheeling style just did not sit well with some of them.

Little did they know what lay in store for them. Looming on the ICC horizon was Darius Gaskins, the next chairman. He was a broad and sharp-witted person with a tongue to match. Gaskins had spent a short time at the crisis-established Department of Energy as a young economist and policy guru. Things moved rapidly at DOE and Gaskins was in his element. If O'Neal was considered a freewheeling chairman, Gaskins was downright swashbuckling.

Unlike the quasi-judicial approach taken by most of the past Chairmen and Commissioners, Gaskins had a program and a mission. He was determined to bring the Commission into the 20th century before the century ended which meant a *lot* of cobweb removal.

Those who tried to delay or defer the new chairman's program felt the sting of his sarcasm or worse. Many was the staffer who longed for the relative calm of the "good old days under Chairman O'Neal." Clearly, everything in those days was relative.

As Gaskins stepped into the Chairmanship, Congress was passing the Staggers Rail Act of 1980. While important on many fronts in opening up rate flexibility for railroads, it was particularly critical to intermodal. Much of the legislative history for deregulation exemptions of the Staggers Act dealt with the perception of Congress that deregulation of intermodal might make a dandy experiment.

Gaskins did not need the Capitol dome to fall on him. This one was right up his alley. A notice of proposed rule making had been issued on August 21, 1979, before Gaskins' arrival. Identified as Ex Parte (sub5) *Improvement of TOFC/COFC Regulation*, it had languished on the Commission's back burner. However, with Gaskins elevation to chairman, that quickly

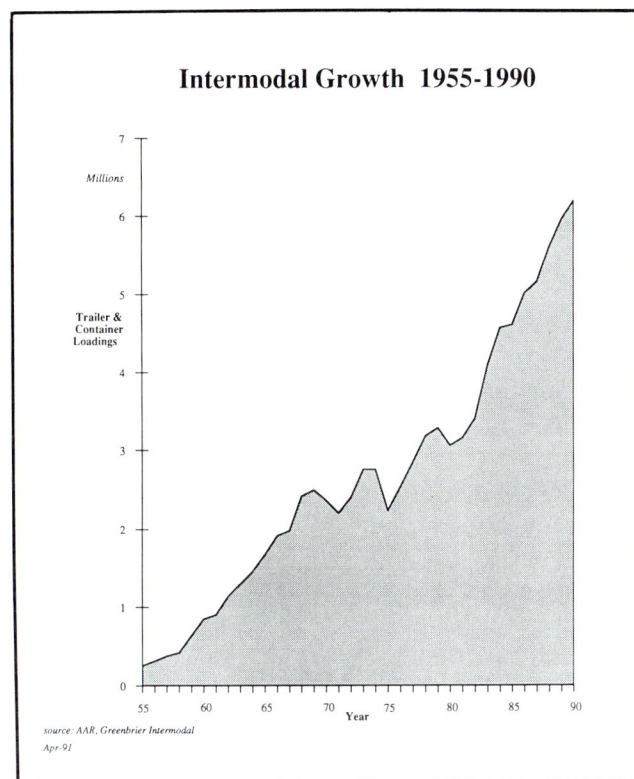

The successful deregulation of perishables finally led to total deregulation and major growth for intermodal. In this scene, trailer loads of potatoes from the San Joaquin Valley arrive at the piggyback ramp at Bakersfield in leased Transamerica trailers. — SANTA FE RAILWAY

changed. He wanted it done. Now!

The decision was issued on November 19, 1980, and some of the language of the determination was vintage Gaskins. "The Congress expects us to undertake a careful examination of railroad regulation and eliminate or reduce restrictions on railroad price and service changes. In particular, the legislative history focuses on the need to pursue vigorously opportunities for exemption. Congress has stated it is anxious for us to remove existing regulation barriers and reserve judgement on potential problems until after exemptions have been granted." Rarely has a single paragraph telegraphed more accurately a preview of a decision or a Chairman's overall policy for his term.

The balance of the argument stated the historically obvious. First, the potential for rail abuse of market power in TOFC/COFC service is virtually nonexistent. Second, intramodal competition is "a significant factor in the market for TOFC/COFC service. . . .[since] the operational flexibility of the motor carrier portion. . . .permits numerous railroads to serve areas beyond their fixed system of tracks." So much for the feared and long-debated argument of invasion of territory.

The last major problem cited in the decision was the desire of many traffic people, both rail and customers, to hold on to the antitrust immunity granted rate bureaus. The rate bureau process was comfortable and it was a known quantity. Deregulation was an unknown — and thus was to be feared by many.

The Commission had faced and rejected the proposed allowance of antitrust immunity in the perishable case under O'Neal. The same solution was applied to intermodal under Gaskins. Railroaders and their partners were forced out of the comfortable surroundings of the rate bureau and into the marketplace. The results were spectacular. The adjoining chart tells the story. The stagnant growth of the 1960's and 1970's was replaced by a real growth spurt. Being out in the marketplace clearly agreed with intermodal.

The effective date of the final order was March 23, 1981. The initial order had dealt only with domestic intermodal. In the final order the Commission included both domestic and international intermodal traffic, and with that the era of railroad intermodal regulation came to an end.

Sea-Land containers are being loaded aboard prototype double-stack cars produced by FMC Rail and Marine for Greenbrier Intermodal and Southern Pacific in 1984. A bulkhead car with massive (note sloping top chord) side sills, was the only car of this exact design built, but it led to follow-on Twin-Stack, Maxi-Stack and Husky-Stack designs. — BRUCE HARMON

Chapter 18

Putting Technology To Work

The seeds of change sown in 1977 by the Southern Pacific and Sea-Land were about to receive a liberal watering and nurturing from another major U.S. flag container company. American President Lines brought stack service on stream in 1983. Like Sea-Land, APL had reached into the ranks of the railroads, in this case the Denver & Rio Grande Western, to draft talent to run its landside service. Don Orris came aboard at APL in 1977.

At that point, steamship companies had been shipping containers by rail since the late 1950's. In the 1950's, 1960's and 1970's the roles of major particpants in intermodal was clear cut. If you were a third party, you maintained a sales force to retail intermodal, but were generally careful to avoid any capital investment. If you were a railroad, you owned or leased cars, engines, terminals and track and operated all of them. If you were a steamship company, you owned or leased containers, chassis and ships and operated them between ports. Each element of the intermodal chain "did its own thing." Slowly, but surely, Orris would change all that.

American President Lines moved an important segment of its traffic to Chicago and then east of Chicago via Conrail. During the winter of 1978 Conrail was in its early years, struggling to rebuild and unite the segments of railroads that went to make it up.

During Penn Central's bankruptcy, the winters had been generally mild. Snow removal expenses had been far lighter than usual. With the huge task before them, Conrail could use all the good weather and expense savings that Providence might provide. That, however, was not be be. Instead, nature whipped up some of the worst winter storms of the century.

Drifting and blowing snow came in record amounts. It inundated most points on the railroad from Chicago to the Atlantic Coast. The worst area to be hit was Buffalo.

Stories of heavy winter storms of the past abounded among railroaders along Lake Erie and Lake Ontario. At Frontier and Bison yards in Buffalo, the wind was strong enough to blow freight cars back up the hump. I recall talking to a yardmaster at DeWitt in 1965 about moving grain fleet cars, for which I was responsible.

"Son," he said, "we've had a little snow up here."

"How bad is it?" I asked.

"Up to the car roofs," he said. "But we'll have 'em out in a couple of days."

If you have the proper snow removal equipment and personnel, cars can be moved when it snows and then stops. This time the snow just kept coming. The wind raged, causing heavy drifts. The weary people of the various bankrupt railroads that Conrail was comprised of were yet to be pulled together into a cohesive team. As a consequence, the railroad was locked up tight.

An opportunity presented itself during the snowdrifts of the storm of 1978-1979. At American President Lines, Don Orris was convinced that APL needed an organization to shadow manage the rail operations. It also needed its own railcars in order to give the quality service needed to differentiate itself from others in the steamship business.

That idea gave the webfeet managment of APL heartburn. "Not our primary business"..."too expensive"..."not proven"..."nobody else does it" were among the reasons given. Besides, APL was part of a conglomerate — Natomis. The one thing that the webfeet team didn't count on was the ingenuity of Orris — and the giant snowstorm.

When the storm hit, nothing in Chicago or east of there moved. Orris had most of his traffic in Chicago on the Union Pacific and Chicago & North Western. Conrail was paralyzed. In desparation Orris went to the B&O/C&O's (Chessie) Gordon Volkers. "Is there anything you can do for us?" asked Orris. "We'll do everthing we can, but it's really tough," said Volkers. "Is there anything I can do to help?" asked Orris.

Volkers had been working on C&NW's Vice President Ed Burkhart to build a Chessie intermodal block for setout at Chessie's Forrest Hill, Chicago intermodal facility. "I'd really like to work with you Gordon," said Burkhart, "but I won't make that move 'til Hell freezes over or I'll have to do it for everybody."

"If Burkhart would shove your block to us at Forrest Hill, we could save a day or two," said Volkers. "Done," replied Orris. Hell was a little chilly that year.

Meanwhile, back in Oakland, Orris used the disasterous storm and service interruptions to sell his dedicated train ideas to management. "If we had had our own equipment and train service, we would have come out of it a lot faster. We wouldn't be just another customer."

The argument carried the day, and Liner Train was born, using 89-foot cars in dedicated train service. In addition Orris was given responsibility for inland backhaul sales at American President Lines.

This move established the first breach in the intermodal partners' traditional Chinese Wall. The railroads conceded, and the APL gained an intermodal function. APL established a new standard for the ability to control end-to-end intermodal service.

Orris, round-faced and affable, had a single-minded purpose and, like Ingram, had long been fascinated by the potential for double-stack technology. Moreover, he had pursued it at the Rio Grande, but it was too small a carrier and, thus, the car builder's were not interested in putting up the capital needed for prototype development. Once Orris arrived at American President Lines he gained instant credibility with the car builders, due to the huge traffic base he now controlled.

Orris went to the Southern Pacific, the only operator of stacks at that time, and attempted to negotiate a rate package for APL that reflected stack economics. The SP had negotiated a rate concession with Sea-Land as an original partner to the technology, but planned to offer common-user stack service to steamship lines at current rates and harvest the economic fruits of its creativity. Both the Southern Pacific and Sea-Land, thus, had a real incentive to minimize publicity on their "New Mousetrap." Unfortunately, two elements conspired to defeat this goal.

The first was the explosive growth of Pacific Rim imports in the 1980's. The volume increases produced the ability of steamship lines to tender full trainload volumes of container traffic. This produced a corresponding rate negotiating lever in the hands of the steamship companies.

The second was Orris himself. He had already generated trainload volumes, traveling in his own equipment, on his own dedicated Liner Trains. In addition he was fully aware that the economic power of double stacks would immensely benefit the first intermodal company to seize those economics.

Orris next approached the Santa Fe's new Traffic Vice President Jim Wright. Orris would bring his substantial traffic base and new stack equipment to the Santa Fe's high-speed Chicago-Los Angeles route in exchange for a rate that reflected a sharing of the stack economics. "APL will take the risk on the equipment," said Orris, "but Santa Fe needs to reflect a part of the cost savings in our rate."

"No, Don, I just couldn't do that," said Wright. "Our other third parties just wouldn't hold still for that."

"Your other third parties don't supply Santa Fe with equipment," said Orris. "We'll bring both the boxes and the cars, *and* we'll bring you totally new traffic."

"Sorry," said Wright.

"What about stack economics?"

"Sorry," said Wright.

"Jim, you are forcing me to go to the UP," said Orris.

"They won't give you the rate either," said Wright. Shades of the Santa Fe split.

Rebuffed by the Southern Pacific and the Santa Fe, he turned to Union Pacific's Don Shum. Would the UP be willing to work with APL in order to develop a new stack car that it would place into their Liner Train service? The answer was "yes."

Interestingly, a small predecessor of the current Union

Pacific, the Western Pacific, had been working with the Budd Company on the Lo Pac design. John Gray, head of WP's Intermodal Department, approached Budd for a car to carry trailers westbound and containers eastbound, but he wanted the containers to be double stacked like the SP. Pavlick suggested a bulkhead design similar to the American Car & Foundry/Southern Pacific design, but Gray wanted "something different."

Unfortunately, the Western Pacific was devoured and digested by the Union Pacific before much progress could be made on the design. Gray, considered a major annoyance in Omaha, was relegated to head up the Real Estate Department. He would later escape and reenter the intermodal business as a major contract terminal operator.

Orris assigned Dennis Richards, Charlie Green and Dick Wade to work with the Union Pacific, Budd and Thrall. The UP named Chief Mechanical Officer Jack McDonough to work on the double-stack car. Budd assigned Mike Pavlick and Dick Behrend and Thrall chose Vice President of Engineering Ted Dancu, Project Engineer Jim Schuller and Sales Vice President Jack Lynch.

Orris, seeing a major opportunity for APL, relentlessly drove everyone on the design team. Whatever was suggested either wasn't good enough or lightweight enough. Most of the early work fell to the Budd Company. Thrall was not convinced that a car order would result from this less-than-orthodox process.

Richards, Green and Wade continued working the process to develop the Lo Pac into a double-stack car. Pavlick developed an early version of the interbox connector car (IBC) and he made enough for a full car set for testing at the Association of American Railroad's Pueblo, Colorado, test facility.

Tested for stability, curving and rock and roll, all went well. But in the impact tests, the interbox connector (a means of locking the upper containers in position) froze up under impact and were difficult to disengage.

American President Lines' group suggested the use of existing seagoing interbox connectors. In the meantime, Orris approached railroads, then operating APL Liner Trains, to test the Lo Pac in double-stack configuration. The SP agreed to the test, but countered with a suggestion that an entire double-stack train be run with the Lo Pac, and that the rest of the train be filled out with Southern Pacific bulkhead double stacks. Orris agreed, and in August of 1983 the test train left SP's temporary Los Angeles Valla Container Yard.

Orris, however, was sold on the interbox connector stack concept. He pressed everyone in sight to get the lightest weight design possible. At the UP McDonough, whose temper was legendary, finally blew his stack. "If the SOB wants lightweight, I'll give him lightweight." He ordered the shops to build an articulated car "with trucks, coupler, draft gear, center sill, container pedestals and nothing — repeat nothing else." And out of the Omaha Shops rolled the first container spine car.

While light in weight, the car missed the point. It did not have the operating or capital cost savings of a double-stack car. Orris continued to drive his people on the Lo Pac double-stack specifications.

In October of 1983, Thrall's Sales Vice President Jack Lynch, big, completely bald and a seasoned veteran of the freight car wars (for which he credits his hair loss), pressed Orris to stop refining his engineering and instead order some cars. Orris responded with a request for bids on three train sets of 20 five-platform cars and five five-unit spares, all to be delivered within six months.

Budd's Rail Division had decided that they did not want to be involved in production of the Lo Pac car. Thrall had sent them a bid on the project, and at the last possible moment Budd licensed the car to be built by them. Thrall then went to work on building the first production interbox connector (IBC) stack cars for American President Lines.

Orris proceeded to negotiate a completely "bare bones" rate contract for movement of APL stack trains with Union Pacific's Don Shum. The contract called for APL to furnish the cars, containers and chassis. The Union Pacific was to supply terminal services and "hook and haul" road service. With control of the pricing, equipment and service, combined with the bulk of the savings from double-stack equipment, Don Orris

American President Lines double-stack train hurtles through the midwest on its way to Chicago & North Western's "Global One" yard in Chicago. — TRAILER TRAIN COLLECTION

American President Lines operated a test train containing the Budd Lo Pac 2000 between Los Angeles and Chicago. Left to right, David DeBoer of SP, John Hyder of Stor Door, Gary Towell of Transway, John Joyce of Western Carloading, Norman Kirsch of SP and Don Orris of American President Lines. — GARY TOWELL

was in business. Shortly after, in exchange for more volume from American President Lines and a major main line siding extension investment by UP, Orris extended the initial UP contract to a ten year period.

Meanwhile, at the Southern Pacific, Tom Fante had retired. In his stead, I was attempting to have the American Car & Foundry design a 40-foot well car that would also load 20-foot boxes in the well and larger boxes on top. Unfortunately, ACF was facing a corporate takeover bid from Carl Icahn and, thus involved, they could not respond to the opportunity.

Southern Pacific's Mechanical Department next went to FMC Corporation's Portland-based Rail and Marine Division for help. Sitting for two extended sessions to work on the problem were myself, Bill Bourque and Bob Yates from the SP's Intermodal Department and Bob Austill, Dick Lenz and Norm Ferren of the Mechanical Department, also the FMC Rail Division Engineering Department led by Chief Engineer Bob Landregan, Roger Hawkins, Gary Kaleta, Greg Saxton and Bill Galbraith. Within two weeks the group came up with a conceptual design.

I was impressed by the FMC Corporation Marine and Rail Division's response to our critical need for container cars to meet the exploding import container business. Since FMC had never built a stack car, I wanted to see and test a prototype before placing an order. Unfortunately, FMC had fallen on hard times and did not want to commit the required half-million dollars to build and test a prototype for what they felt was an uncertain market.

Bill Furman had once worked for FMC and was now head of Greenbrier Leasing, with whom we had done business. He approached me to ask whether I would have a problem if he funded a prototype and did a joint venture with FMC. I did not.

Furman made the deal, and in May of 1984, he hired Bob Yates from the Southern Pacific to do a Greenbrier startup subsidiary, Greenbrier Intermodal. The company would market FMC's double-stack car. In July FMC produced the GBRX-1984, a five-unit, bulkhead, double-stack car. At that point I left the SP to join Greenbrier Intermodal so I could remain in the intermodal business.

Thrall had cemented its relationship with American President Lines. At Greenbrier Intermodal we began by tackling all other potential stack customers. This included the Port of Seattle, Sea-Land, Burlington Northern and, of course, the Southern Pacific. Before any of these orders materialized, FMC Corporation's corporate offices decided to spin off six of their divisions, including FMC's Rail and Marine Division in Portland, Oregon.

After a bit of scrambling, a group consisting of Bill Furman, Bruce Ward, who had run the division a number of years before, and Standard Insurance Company bought the plant from FMC in May of 1985. It was renamed Gunderson, Inc., a throwback to the Gunderson Brothers who had originally built the plant.

The irony of the stack car pioneers was thus complete. American Car & Foundry, the builder of the initial order of Southern Pacific's double stacks, was taken over by Carl Icahn. The plant in which the stacks were built was sold, along with all jigs and fixtures. Budd, the designer of the second prototype stack car, never built a commercial stack car or filled an order. Now FMC Corporation, who built the third stack prototype, sold the plant before building another car. Thrall and Gunderson, however, would be the major beneficiaries of the new technology beginning in 1984.

It was in 1984 that some of us discovered a southern cousin we never knew we had. In that year a diminutive, bell-ringing, hard-charging chap named Nat Welch invited the intermodal world to Atlanta to display their wares and to "parley." Nat was Director of the Southern Freight Tariff Bureau in an era when powerful deregulation forces roamed the land. Only 300 people took him up on his offer to attend his first Atlanta Intermodal Exposition. Needless to say, it was hot in Atlanta and it also rained a lot. Besides, who was this guy? If ignored, he'd probably go away.

Wrong! The following year railroad and intermodal company presidents came to Atlanta. It goes without saying that if something in the intermodal area was good enough for Chief Executive officers, then it certainly was good enough for intermodalists. Besides, there was a lot of interesting hardware to look at, plus old friends to talk to so you could catch up on all the latest news.

The Atlanta Intermodal Exposition soon ranked as the premier intermodal event of the year. Top executives from domestic and international intermodal companies from around the world began to attend and participate. Manufacturers often purposely pointed their new equipment designs or improvements to be exhibited at the Atlanta Expo. Nat had clearly moved a backwater organization and the intermodal industry into the forefront of what had truly become a world community business.

In 1984 the American President Lines brought double-stack technology into the public spotlight with the onset of full page color advertising. The same year a service with three trains each week was initiated between Union Pacific's Los Angeles Intermodal facility and Chicago & North Western's venerable Wood Street facility in Chicago. APL instantly began to funnel its eastbound import containers to the new double-stack service. Refilling the majority of the boxes that did not return with export freight became an immediate priority. While stack car economics has kept the costs of empty container return under control, real profit leverage existed in operating loads in both directions — and that meant domestic freight.

For an old line steamship company like American President Lines this was a major departure from its core business. But Don Orris had already initiated Liner Train service, using standard 89-foot cars, and APL itself was being run by someone who definitely was not a "webfoot." APL, through its acquisition by, and later spinoff from Natomas, acquired a tall, quiet, extremely

These two American President Lines' advertisements appeared in *Distribution* magazine. APL got very aggressive with double-stack technology, owning containers, cars and terminals, and contracting for hook-and-haul service only. — DONALD DUKE COLLECTION

The first prototype double-stack car was a joint effort between American Car & Foundry, Sea-Land and Southern Pacific. SP No. 513300 is shown here being loaded with demonstrator 40-foot containers. — SOUTHERN PACIFIC

In August of 1990, Maersk Line and the Santa Fe joined forces to create a unique train for the filming of advertising photographs. Santa Fe's No. 146, a new GP60M, was painted in blue, silver, and white, together with a string of Maersk double-stack cars all freshly painted. The action took place on Southern California's Cajon Pass. — MIKE MARTIN - SANTA FE RAILWAY

At Tacoma, Washington, a Valmet straddle machine loads a Maersk 45-foot container on the end platform of a Gunderson built Maxi car. — GREENBRIER INTERMODAL

competent Chief Executive Officer in the person of Bruce Seaton. He saw the leverage and the potential of turning his "steamship company" into a true intermodal company.

Reloading was accomplished by offering cut rates to third parties for westbound domestic freight on the days the Liner Trains operated. Limited day of the week operations led to customer coordination problems with pickup of boxes, loading and scheduling for train departures. Railroads who operated daily service had a distinct advantage.

The only single-line rail carrier in the lane was the Santa Fe, but they decided to stay with trailers rather than compete head to head with American President Lines containers. The Traffic Department maintained the high westbound trailer rates — and provided APL with a rate umbrella. In addition the Santa Fe's Operating Department determined that trailers were more efficient than containers. Larry Cena felt that without center sills stack cars would probably not hold up in service.

These decisions allowed Don Orris almost a free rein in the marketplace. Nevertheless, he still required a massive jump in traffic in order to build up to daily train frequency. To accomplish this he pursued two goals. First, he began to move "beyond Chicago" traffic in blocks on his existing trains. While this helped to build his eastbound volume, it merely added to the empty westbound woes. However, in 1984 he played his key trump card. In order to build both bidirectional volume and fill his Chicago westbound empties, APL bought the largest existing third party, National Piggyback. This was a company built by R.C. Matney, a self-effacing, extremely bright man.

At the time when the purchase price of $65 million was announced, many observers thought that someone at American President Lines' Oakland headquarters had "slipped a cog." All that money for assets consisting of "telephones, desks and folks who went home at night." Strategically, however, it balanced up the existing APL trains, allowing them to move to daily departures, and it gave them a critical mass that would allow APL to survive if things became highly competitive.

Sea-Land, meanwhile, was also becoming aggressive in the double-stack business. Bob Ingram had returned from an overseas assignment and took over the helm of the intermodal function. He, too, envisioned a network of dedicated double-stack trains to control service quality.

Unlike APL, who offered trans-Pacific service only, Sea-Land operated in the Pacific, Atlantic and the Mediteranean. Its anchor terminal was at Elizabethport, New Jersey.

This presented Ingram with a problem. To compete, he needed competitive rail service into New York Harbor. The only thing available to him on the New Jersey side of the harbor was served by Conrail and the New York, Susquehanna & Western, a small carrier, locally known as the "Susie Q" that was barely scratching out an existence.

Conrail had effectively used its lack of competition in the New York area to keep intermodal rate levels high. It, however, failed to solidify the advantage by

A peek into the empty well of a TTX articulated car shot above the truck frame shows the criss-crossed "floor" of the car. — GREENBRIER INTERMODAL

What does an articulated connector look like? Well, here's one viewed from above resting between two platforms of an articulated stack car. It connects over the center bowl of the truck (forming the "H" in the photograph). — GREENBRIER INTERMODAL

Sea-Land's Tacoma intermodal facility qualifies as the first "on dock" ramp to be built before there were on dock facilities. — GREENBRIER INTERMODAL

not offering new intermodal technology. This left a perceived void in the marketplace. As we have seen throughout the history of intermodal, voids of this kind tend to become filled in one way or another.

Ingram's way was to route trains into New York Harbor over the Susie Q. He not only brought the boxes and railcars, but he went Don Orris one better by striking a deal with NYS&W's Walter Rich to build an exclusive Sea-Land rail terminal at Little Ferry, New Jersey. Initial routing consisted of the New York, Susquehanna & Western, the Delaware & Hudson and CSX between New York and Chicago. Sea-Land, as a result, could control the quality of service from end to end. At the Norfolk Southern, Ed Baughan, using a small private facility at Resources Terminal just south of Little Ferry, would similarly "back-door" the Conrail "New York Monopoly."

After an initial shakedown period in the east at Little Ferry, Ingram moved in on the west with a dedicated Sea-Land intermodal terminal directly across from their new berth in Tacoma. Debates would rage for years about the relative merits of "on dock" intermodal terminals. Ingram built this one, separated from the Sea-Land quay only by a local street, long before the idea became fashionable. He had planned to locate a third terminal in Chicago.

Sea-Land was then threatened by a takeover bid from a Texas investor and, consequently, most of the capital plans were shelved. The company moved to fight the acquisition. Ultimately, CSX entered the fray, serving as a "white knight" and eventually acquiring Sea-Land. This gave Sea-Land access to the new modern CSX Bedford Park facility at Chicago and ended the need for a separate Sea-Land terminal in that city. The CSX intermodal and Sea-Land intermodal units were integrated to become CSX Sea-Land Intermodal Company. Ingram left shortly thereafter to become Vice President of Sales and Marketing for the Soo Line.

CSX Sea-Land Intermodal Company continued to develop and integrate into a full service carrier. McNeil Porter from Sea-Land took over at CSLI. In addition to its CSX terminals east of the Mississippi, and the Little Ferry operation in New York Harbor and

Tacoma, CSX Sea-Land Intermodal Company also operated over other rail carriers. As a result it was able, like American President Lines, to price its services directly to customers and third parties on a nationwide basis. With the National Piggyback group now a part of APL, the firm rapidly increased its business to a daily service between Los Angeles and Chicago.

At the Chicago & North Western, Jim Ronayne had long been an advocate of containerization. He had pressed for a major Chicago facility to take the place of the cramped, old Wood Street terminal. Working with American President Lines and the Union Pacific, Ronayne sold his management on a large state-of-the-art intermodal facility to be named Global One. Ironically, CSX, before buying Sea-Land, sold a large portion of its subsidiary Baltimore & Ohio Chicago Terminal's Robey Street rail yard acreage, adjoining Chicago & North Western's Wood Street. This made C&NW's expansion to Global One possible. Don Orris immediately made full use of the facility to increase APL's business.

As APL and Sea-Land rapidly expanded use of double-stack technology, other steamship carriers took particular note. The Pacific Rim steamship companies were the first to feel the impact of stack technology.

The Japanese had set up auto assembly plants in America's heartland. Nissan and Honda already had plant locations and were early users of rail containers. The movement of containers on standard 89-foot cars produced a certain amount of unavoidable product damage due to slack action, the crack-the-whip impacts inherent in trains made up of individual cars.

The problem was also made worse by draft-gear cushioning built into the 89-foot flatcars which had originally been designed to prevent damage to the cars from impacts as they were switched in a classification yard. The end-of-car cushion device was essentially a large shock absorber built into the draft gear on each end of the car. While this device absorbed switching shocks, in actual train service it reacted just the opposite.

A 150 feu (40-foot equivalent unit) container move required 75 standard 89-foot flatcars which contained about 200 feet of potential train slack action. The length of a 75-car train spreads out over the railroad for a mile and one-half. Over that distance, the railroad may not only go up or down hill a couple of times but also around a curve or two. This means that a part of the train is moving uphill (and stretching out) while another part is moving downhill (and compressing). This run-in and run-out with 200 feet of slack in the trains acts like a big 5,000-ton Slinky toy. The whip action produces predictable results on the freight. To offset this harsh environment, the steamship operators tended to ship

CSX Intermodal grew out of the CSX and Sea-Land intermodal departments and established a nationwide intermodal service network. This advertisement appeared in *Distribution* during May 1991. — DONALD DUKE COLLECTION

K Line Railbridge car is a Maxi I 40-foot articulated well car made primarily for international traffic. Two 20-foot containers rest on the right hand platform in the well with a 40-footer resting above. On the next platform a 40-footer rests in the well as a Cat top pick machine loads a 45-footer on the top position. — GREENBRIER INTERMODAL

many of their containers on a chassis (as a trailer) on the railcar in an attempt to absorb some of the shock with the chassis, tires and running gear.

Articulated cars, i.e., both spine and stack cars, do not have end-of-car cushioning. They remove the car slack by using a device called an articulated connector which is placed between the center units of the cars. These connectors swivel to allow the car to negotiate curves (and to connect the car body to the car's truck sets), but they have little fore and aft "give."

Dick Frick, an early Southern Pacific intermodalist, left the company to join Honda, but he still kept his intermodal hand in from the customer side. Through the use of an add-on to a consultant's study at Honda, Frick promoted a test of stack cars destined for its plant in Marysville, Ohio, using motorcycles and auto parts. The ride quality of tests were outstanding, and as a result containerized parts movements began to shift to stack cars. In Asia word quickly spread. Many Asian shippers began to insist that their freight also be moved by stack car rather than TOFC or COFC on 89-footers.

Overseas Orient Container Line, Mitzui OSK Line, Hanjin, Evergreen, NYK and K-Line all responded with dedicated stack operations and many hired intermodal veterans to run them. K-Line hired Ray Ascencio who had been the Pennsy's terminal manager in Chicago. In addition to setting up train operations, Ascencio designed and built the first modern, Third-Generation terminal in the high-volume New York — New Jersey area at Port Elizabeth. The New Jersey K-Line terminal was quickly followed by another modern terminal built by APL at the old Pennsylvania Railroad Kearny facility. With these steamship facilities, the Sea-Land at Little Ferry and private Resources Terminal container facilities at North Bergen, the New Jersey side of New York Harbor would never again be the same.

From the Atlantic side, Maersk Line was an early entrant into the "do it yourself" stack-train market. Maersk's entry also utilitzed a dedicated train terminal in Tacoma. Unlike its Pacific Rim counterparts, the move to stack technology by Maersk and Sea-Land did not produce a stampede on the part of other Atlantic seaboard container lines.

The equipment rush generated by the Pacific carriers, however, was unprecedented. Historically, the rail industry adopted major technological changes very slowly. As an example, the move to dieselization required three and one-half decades. The steamship lines would see to it that the integration of stack technology would come to pass much sooner. This, in spite of the rail "experts."

In the period from 1984-1986, for example, it was very fashionable for some to dub stack technology as

A perfect intermodal mix is shown in this photograph at Southern Pacific's Market Street yard in Oakland. Note the TTX single-axle piggyback car. — HARRY DEMORO

1994 Intermodal Capacity*

Year	Total Spaces	1st/2nd Generation Slots**		Third Generation				RoadRailer	
				TOFC Slots		Doublestack Slots			
1983	110,000	109,000	99%	200		400		300	
1984	112,000	109,000	97%	700		2,000	2%	300	
1985	119,000	109,000	92%	2,900	3%	7,000	6%	300	
1986	118,000	102,000	86%	3,100	3%	13,000	11%	300	
1987	116,000	93,000	80%	4,800	4%	18,000	16%	1,400	1%
1988	118,000	88,000	75%	5,800	5%	24,000	20%	2,300	2%
1989	116,000	75,000	65%	9,000	8%	30,000	26%	2,300	2%
1990	127,000	70,000	55%	15,000	12%	40,000	31%	2,050	2%
1991	135,000	64,000	47%	20,000	15%	48,000	36%	2,450	2%
1992	143,000	57,000	40%	22,000	15%	61,000	43%	2,775	2%
1993	154,000	50,000	32%	29,000	19%	72,000	47%	3,065	2%
1994 est	167,000	47,000	28%	35,000	21%	82,000	49%	3,065	2%

* Measured in "spaces" or "slots", defined as capable of carrying one box (container or trailer, depending on car type).
Example: 89' flatcar = 2 spaces; double stack = 2 spaces per well, 10 spaces per five-pack.

** 85 Foot, 89 Foot, 89 Foot 4" Cars

Source: Greenbrier Intermodal

a "niche" or "boutique" market. Major policy speeches were delivered pointing out that stack "had to" move in trainload lots between one origin and one destination. And surely, a container based challenge to the highway trailer for domestic freight was unthinkable.

Fortunately, railroad intermodal operating people and knowledgeable intermodal marketing people were too busy to listen to the "policy." They went about their business operating blocks of cars to smaller en route points to build the service. This led to an exceptional rate of introduction for the stack-car technology. The adjoining table shows how quickly this equipment was integrated. The table greatly understates the overall importance, since the early stack equipment averaged 50 percent higher mileage per car than its first- and second-generation counterparts.

As we have seen, after the initial American Car & Foundry stacks were built, the fleets from Gunderson, Thrall and Trinity quickly standardized on a five-unit car with articulated connectors replacing couplers over the intermediate units. Each intermediate well (and one adjacent end of each end unit) shared a 100-ton truck. The coupler end of each end unit had its own 70-ton truck.

This produced a nominal carrying capacity for each well of about 100,000 pounds. To some that was counter intuitive, since cars with 100-ton trucks generally carried 200,000 pounds of lading. The secret lies in the fact that since each well *shares* a 100-ton truck, the capacity is effectively halved to 50 tons. In fact each end of the end unit with a 70-ton truck, theoretically, has greater capacity since the truck is not shared with another unit. A look at the outline drawing will quickly confirm this.

Initially, the major difference between the manufacturers was that Gunderson built a bulkhead car and Thrall and Trinity built an Interbox Connector car (IBC). Top containers on the bulkhead car were held in by container guides or the bulkhead, while the IBC car secured the top box to the bottom box with interbox connectors. The basic tradeoff was between the terminal savings of the bulkhead car and the greater payload of the IBC car.

The cars were built with either all 40-foot wells or with 40-foot end units and either 45- or 48-foot intermediate wells. Some carriers initially resisted having the intermediate units of the cars built to carry 20-foot containers. Thus, many cars were built with 20-foot carrying capacity in the end units only. On the top chord of the side sill of each car is a device called a birdhouse. This is to guard against damage from side-lift machines to the top chord. On units that cannot handle a 20-foot container the birdhouse is painted the same color as the car body. On units that can handle 20-footers, it is painted white to help the terminal loadout crews identify whether or not a given well can handle 20-foot containers.

As stack movement continued to grow, the need for

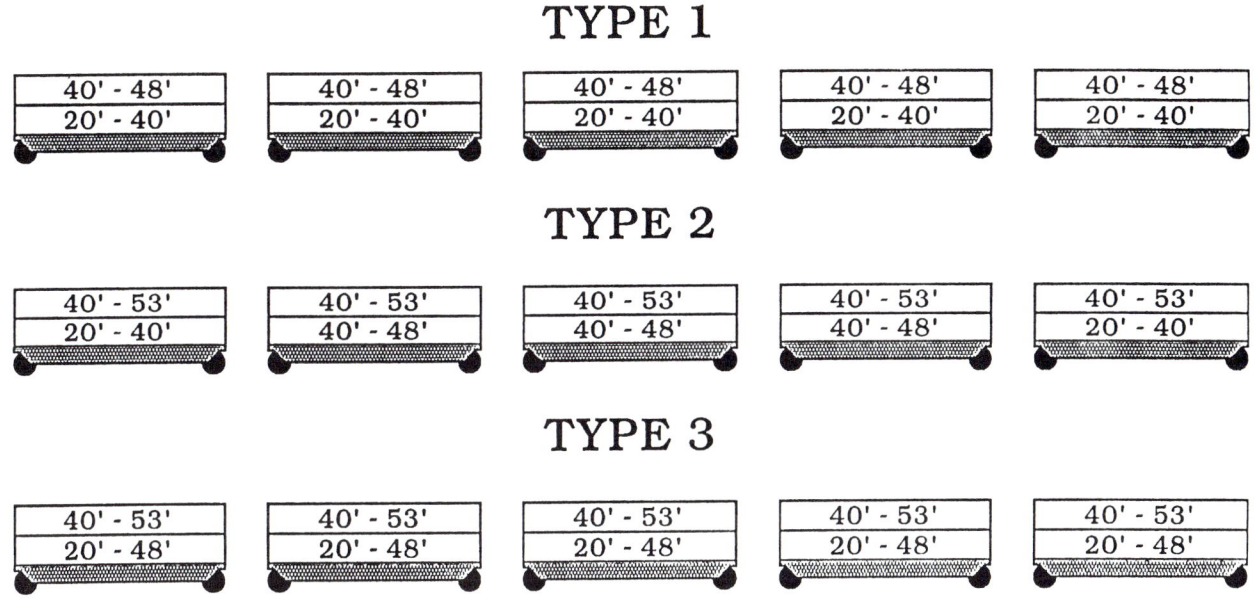

The 125-ton double-stack cars were produced in three basic types - a 40-foot well car (Type I), a 40-foot end unit/a 48-foot intermediate unit (Type II) and (Type III) an all 48-foot well car. This chart shows the loading capabilities of each car.

more car-carrying capacity became apparent. This led to the manufacturers offering a 125-ton intermediate truck version stack car. In addition to the need for greater carrying capacity, the growth of container choices from the 20- and 40-foot International Standards Organization (ISO) versions to 45-, 48- and 53-foot domestic containers forced Gunderson to abandon the bulkhead and design an 125-ton IBC car.

The cars quickly settled into three and then two versions. The Type I car was a 40-foot well size with a 20-foot carrying capacity throughout. It was designed for heavy international movements and offered a well capacity up to 124,000 pounds. The car was popular with steamship companies in that it was the shortest stack car available which allowed them to place two or three more cars in an average train with no train length penalty.

The second version or Type II car was one that was initially preferred by American President Lines. This car had 40-foot end units which also accommodated 20-foot containers. The intermediate units were 48 feet long and could carry a 40-, 45- or 48-foot container, but could not handle 20's. A drawback of the 40-foot end units was that the terminal loading the car needed to have outbound ISO boxes available in order to load those end units. Often just the larger domestic boxes were available and they could only be loaded on the top position.

The Type III car was an all 48-foot well car with 20-foot capacity in the wells. It permitted complete flexibility for loading everything from a 20- to a 48-foot container in the well and a 40-, 45- or 53-footer on top. The flexibility made this car type by far the largest double-stack seller. Its only drawbacks were a slightly lower payload capacity per well and its somewhat greater length. When the Type III car was produced, the greater flexibility made the Type II car obsolete.

While the articulated five-unit double-stack cars were a great success for handling the majority of the international containers, two separate needs were not being well-served by the articulated cars. Both had to do with the problem of the inefficient use of articulated cars. The first involved the difficulty with weight.

In international business some traffic lanes have very heavy commodities which are generally loaded in 20-foot containers. This often results in stack cars being single-level loaded since the addition of a top load would exceed the weight-carrying capacity of a five-platform car.

An additional weight problem was presented by the Burlington Northern's development of 28-foot "pup" containers. The idea for this unit was developed by Bob

Gunderson/Greenbrier advertisement for their Maxi III car. The Maxi-Stack III car is a double-stack car built for versatility and extra capacity in domestic containerization. This advertisement appeared in *Modern Railroads*. — DONALD DUKE COLLECTION

Ingram as a result of his visit to the 1989 Atlanta Intermodal Expo. He had stopped by the Maxi III car display at the Gunderson outdoor exhibit where they were showing 40-, 45-, 48- and 53-foot containers on the top tier of the car.

"Would two 28's fit on top all the way across?" he asked. "I don't know, but let's get our engineers and a steel tape and find out," I said. After some quick measurments and some curve calculations by Gary Kaleta, Gunderson's chief engineer, we said O.K.

Twenty-eight-foot highway units are important to both the United Parcel Service and Less-Than-Truckload highway carriers. To develop a workable 28-foot container that could be efficiently loaded on a stack car (this means two containers on top) would result in a huge potential market for intermodal.

Bob Ingram and I had previously kicked around the idea of 28's with a back to back, horizontal locking system to allow a single pick for two unit top loading on a stack car. Ingram, working with Jim Jimenez of Stoughton Trailer, had come to the conclusion that the horizontal locking system would not be stiff enough to keep from bending the center of the top rails of the bottom box loaded on a stack car. Ingram's solution involved the theory of using a saddle that would sit atop the lower box which in turn supported the two upper 28-footers. In fact, to help people visualize the concept, he constructed a cardboard saddle in HO scale to fit a presentation model stack car he had been given. The device was immediately called the "Ingram Saddle" and the prototype was shown on the Gunderson car at the 1990 Atlanta Intermodal Expo. By 1991 the device and the 28-foot containers had moved into production.

The weight of a lower box, the saddle and the two 28-foot boxes potentially exceeded the capacity of the existing 125-ton articulated cars. In addition, as the domestic container business grew, the need to load fewer than ten boxes at a time to another location also grew.

International traffic tends to move in large blocks. Container ships that discharge a thousand boxes at a port are not uncommon. This traffic moves very efficiently on rail in five-unit cars. While domestic traffic in major traffic lanes, such as Los Angeles-Chicago, move in similarly large blocks, most domestic traffic moves in much smaller lots between either large terminals and small terminals or between two medium or small terminals. For example, Portland, Oregon, may originate 100,000 intermodal units per year. However, those units are split between three carriers and numerous destinations. This may result in only two or three containers or trailers per day moving from Portland to most destinations. This produces the need for a car that carries the fewest containers or trailers possible, consistant with basic economics.

Through the years, Trailer Train had worked on single-unit cars. In fact three double-stack cars had been commissioned in 1987. The initial cars followed the single-axle European truck development (i.e., two single axles per car) begun with the 4-Runner car in 1979. As payload requirements increased, Trailer Train developed a four, single-axle car design.

Beginning in 1986, the intermodal/engineering/manufacturing team at Gunderson wrestled with a "heavy-lift" design. The intermodalists were sold on articulation. This led to a look at both 125-ton and six-wheel intermediate trucks.

The engineering side countered with a standard two 70-ton truck stand-alone design car. All of us on the intermodal side were extremely reluctant to surrender the advantages we had been given by the articulated car. However, we were also drawn to the simplicity and cost advantages of the engineering proposal and the wonderful leverage of the two-box car.

As we crossed the line to embrace this "stand-alone heavy lift" concept, engineering began to back away. There were fears of instability in a two-truck stack car.

Trailer Train engineering was convinced that the European single-axle design was the answer, but due to the exotic trucks, its price tag quickly convinced the Gunderson intermodal team members that there had to be a better way.

When faced with uncertainty in an area in which I have no training, I have always sought help from people in that particular field who have evidenced the best track record. In this case, I called the "Father of the Stack Car" Bill Thomford.

Though long-retired from the Southern Pacific, Thomford is a vigorous and active engineer. At one of our semi-regular luncheons at the San Francisco University Club, Bob Yates and I told Bill about our studies and the trade-offs involved. "It comes down to everything favoring the two 70-ton truck car if we can get the ride quality. You built the only single unit 70-ton truck car out there (the initial American Car & Foundry 1976 prototype car), will it work?"

"Sure." (You can see why Bill is my kind of engineer).

"What if we have rock and roll problems (a violent swaying of the car)? I asked.

"I don't think you will, but if you do you can control it with snubbers. After all, the ACF car has over a million miles with no reported problems. Besides, I ran it through a battery of tests initially." That was good enough for me.

The initial car was rolled out at Gunderson in 1990. Bob Ingram cracked the obligatory champagne over the side sill and the "Husky Stack" was off and running. As an aside, the engineering test at Pueblo in 1990 validated Bill Thomford's 1986 luncheon prediction.

While the double-stack car came on the scene faster than almost any other major rail technology, it was clearly driven by international freight customer requirements. It may have looked like double stack had sprung forth spontaneously. However, several intermodal trends had been converging to make the rapid progress possible. The first was the great increase in international container volume. In the decade of the 1980's traffic from the Pacific Rim grew at two to three times the rate of our domestic Gross National Product (GNP). This rapid growth provided a huge base of traffic for direct service between terminals. The second trend was an ever-expanding mechanization of intermodal terminals across the U.S. which began in the 1950's. Mechanization was critical since without top-pick capability containers could not be handled in the intermodal terminal. Third, the container capacity was already in place. There were about five million international containers in existence in 1984.

Major investments in terminals, terminal mechanization and containers were, thus, not necessary to allow for a double-stack startup. The double-stack cars could be run either in regular freight trains or as unit trains. For a relatively small investment in cars, the entire system was now available to the container wave.

There were major intermodal traffic lanes (trackage) that could not accept the stack technology due to rail clearance restrictions. To compensate for this, Trailer Train and some of the carriers reexamined the Berwick spine car concept. Basically, the spine car was a Santa Fe "Fuel Foiler" with container pedestals in place of trailer hitches. The car was articulated for a smooth ride and, loading single level, had no clearance problems.

Problems with container floor failures in a very few severely overloaded containers had led railroad mechanical forces to insist on "floors" in the stack cars.

Here is a view of the future from the 1987 Atlanta Intermodal Expo. Domestic 48-foot boxes sit above a 20-foot liquid container and stacked empty flat racks and a 40-footer in an adjoining well of a TTX bulkhead Twin-stack car. — GREENBRIER INTERMODAL

A K-Line stack train rolls downgrade through Lugo, on the desolate eastside of Cajon Pass. The Santa Fe uses their new "Super Fleet" motive power on container and piggyback trains. The date is December 18, 1989. — MIKE MARTIN - SANTA FE RAILWAY

The man with the schoolmaster's bell clutched firmly in hand was a familiar figure at the International Intermodal Expo. Our favorite southern cousin, Nat Welsh, brought us to Atlanta each spring to see the latest intermodal technology. — INTERNATIONAL INTERMODAL EXPO

A compromise produced a framed latticework in stack cars. The container spine car was substantially beefed up to guard against container floor failures and, consequently, lost much of its early weight advantage over 89-foot First-Generation cars.

Trailer Train was faced with a multi-faceted demand from railroads to cover several needs. First was a major policy thrust led by the Santa Fe to convert Second-Generation technology to slackless Third-Generation technology. A second group suggested a need for "clearance cars" for non-stack routes. A third group addressed the requirement of a transition car that could load trailers in one direction and containers in the other.

The Trailer Train engineering function was assumed by Bob Hulick on the retirement of Tom Harley in 1988. Hulick set the department to melding the trailer spine version with the container spine version, developing what old timers would call an A or "all purpose" car. Considered by Trailer Train management as a way to

A Genstar-leased 40-foot container is loaded aboard TTX 100-ton double-stack car. The car is a Gunderson-built Twin-stack car with bulkheads used to hold the upper container in place. — GREENBRIER INTERMODAL

cover trailer equipment demands with slackless technology and hedge against a downturn in stack car business, the all-purpose spine car began to be purchased in quantity in 1990.

As the 1980's drew to a close and customers clamored for articulated cars, the railroads and Trailer Train responded by scrapping out the 50-, 70- and 85-foot fleets and by converting many of the 89-foot cars from trailer cars to multi-level cars. The number of old First- and Second-Generation cars that remained, consisting of 50,000 cars (with 100,000 "slots" or spaced for a 40-foot trailer or container), were reduced by over a third in five short years. In that same time frame the Third-Generation fleet share increased from a negligible amount to over half of the fleet. For an industry that took more than three decades to dieselize, the intermodal shift in technology came in the relative blink of an eye.

Two Santa Fe Dash 8-40BW locomotives handle the road's intermodal operation at San Bernardino, California, in 1990. — MIKE MARTIN - SANTA FE RAILWAY

One look at intermodal's domestic future. Burlington Northern's "BN America" 48-foot containers are unloaded from TTX five-platform articulated cars by a Taylor "Big Red" unloader. —GREENBRIER INTERMODAL

Chapter 19

The Movement To Domestic Containers

When the growth of international containers began in 1984, the movement of domestic container traffic was largely confined to the filling of the backhaul of empty international ISO containers. When American President Lines absorbed the National Piggyback group into its organization, they began to take domestic containerization seriously. By offering daily container train service between Los Angeles and the Pacific Northwest with Chicago, Atlanta and New York, American President Lines was in a position to add to its domestic box fleet. While the general railroad industry gnashed its teeth over piggyback trailers vs. containers for the movement of domestic freight, Don Orris was busy updating intermodal technology and improving the ride quality of domestic container stack cars.

Domestic container service began to slowly move ahead in 1986 with the use of heavy containers equipped with small 103-inch high doors. In contrast piggyback trailers had doors 110 inches high. After containerization had slumbered for some 30 years, Don Orris and his American President Lines' international and domestic container business would change things. Too, Bob Ingram reemerged in intermodal at the Burlington Northern. Having gained a well-earned reputation for intermodal innovations under Bill Greenwood, the Burlington Northern had been very active in the adoption of international stack technology. Ralph Muellner had made the BN a major force in handling international containers. But as Greenwood was promoted to the top marketing job, the BN had languished on the application of Third-Generation technology to domestic traffic. It had flirted briefly with RoadRailer and other technologies, but had remained with trailers for its domestic moves — that is, until Ingram arrived. At that point a study was immediately launched to look at not only the adoption of stack technology, but a complete new program that would solve piggyback problems.

Major problems had developed in the domestic piggyback trailer business over the years. Slack action from normal train handling often resulted in cargo damage. The Third-Generation intermodal technologies could bring an end to that situation, but what the BN really wanted was to produce a package that would also address the difficulties encountered in the marketplace.

Obstacles for the railroads, as regulated common carriers, had developed from the early Interstate Commerce Commission requirements to treat all shippers equally. This created a "common carrier attitude" in many railroad commercial departments. They held that no differentiated programs should be offered. In intermodal this led to the do-nothing operator-broker being accorded the same service, equipment and rates as the best, high-service, third-party operator. When first time intermodal customers received poor service, they rarely came back. If third-party customers were going to be the railroad's commercial representative, then railroads needed to remove the bad apples from the barrel.

Intermodal was hampered by its limited arena. Truckers and other competitors had gone nationwide in scope, allowing them to give a shipper single responsibility coverage for all of his needs. Intermodal remained, like the railroads that handled the containers, regional in nature.

Another sore point was the casual way in which the intermodal industry treated drayage, i.e., the highway movement of containers and trailers to or from an intermodal terminal. Most often a small local trucker, under contract to either the railroad, a steamship company or a third party, was chosen based entirely on costs. This resulted in the draymen responding by using an inadequate number of worn out tractors and undertrained drivers. Service to customers then suffered.

APC 48-foot domestic box is loaded aboard a five-unit articulated car over two 20-foot boxes in the well by a La Tourneau side-lift machine. Interbox connectors (IBC's) can be seen set in the end of the 20-footer. — GREENBRIER INTERMODAL

As the 1980's progressed, the national trailer fleet fell on hard times. Leasing companies introduced shipper incentive programs — "Use an ABCZ trailer and receive $5 per load." This led to less than high-quality trailers being kept in service as carriers lost control of equipment quality. In turn, it reflected badly on intermodal.

The one function honed to perfection by truckers, and virtually unknown in intermodal, was processing and control. This included spot pricing, dispatching of equipment (both loads and empties) from terminals and prompt, accurate billing.

Burlington Northern's Bill Berry assembled, integrated and implemented the new approach. The "BN America" program would use a new, lighter weight 48 x 102-foot domestic container traveling in stack cars — all controlled by BN. Every box would be "BN America" (no pool boxes) in order to maintain consistent quality and regular maintenance and cleaning.

Third-party participation was to be by contract. It would be limited to those who met basic standards. The term "partner-shipping" began to take on a new and more reasonable meaning.

Draymen were selected on the basis of quality, service needs and price. Then, they were measured to assure compliance. When canned goods shippers complained that they could ship 3,000-4,000 pounds more by truck than by "BN America," the use of lighter weight drayage tractors solved the competitive issue.

Moving to off-line service areas was accomplished through Voluntary Coordination Agreements (VCA's) with other carriers. As two early examples, VCA's were extended to the Southern Pacific by Conrail, for service to Indianapolis and Columbus, and the SP extended the courtesy to Conrail for service to Texas. The Burlington Northern allowed the Santa Fe to go to Birmingham, Alabama, while the Santa Fe reciprocated by allowing the BN into Los Angeles from the southeast. Some host railroads provided a basic towing service and permitted the guest railroad to price the through service.

Through VCA's or through direct pricing of traffic blocks or trains, several intermodal companies began to build national domestic service networks. This enabled them to provide customized service to their customers either directly or through selected third-party agents.

Control and management also began to be exercised in an unprecedented fashion. "BN America" established a control center in Seattle that quoted rates, booked space and put tight control on assets.

Elsewhere, other railroads began to explore "control based" systems. Conrail established Mercury Motors in the east, and offered full retail service. Initiated as an intermodal trailer-based system, it aimed at very tight equipment and drayage control, lane balance and guaranteed service at truck-level rates. Mercury utilized its own separate sales force. Late in 1990 Mercury ordered their first domestic containers.

CXL Sea-Land Intermodal maintained its nationwide offerings of international and domestic containers and trailers in the east. The Norfolk Southern continued to offer "Triple Crown Service" within its region, utilizing RoadRailer, and retailing its own service. It

GBRX 1990 is the successful Gunderson prototype "stand alone" double-stack car shown with Transamerica 40-foot container loaded in the well. Above, is the "Ingram Saddle" (BNO 1996) with two 28-foot domestic containers used by UPS and LTL truckers in BNA livery. — GREENBRIER INTERMODAL

also offered a regional, but declining trailer service through third parties.

In the west in addition to the Burlington Northern, the Santa Fe established a joint high-quality service with full truckload carrier J.B. Hunt, named Quantum. Utilizing a separate 48-foot trailer fleet on spine cars, the service got off to a slow start, but later grew. By 1992, Hunt announced a conversion to containers and double-stack operations. Santa Fe also maintained regional international and domestic container offerings and a declining trailer service.

During this period the decrease in the national piggyback fleet was precipitous. From a high of 141,000 piggyback trailers in 1982, the fleet fell to about 100,000 by the end of 1990. It was projected to fall to 75,000 by 1993.

The growth of domestic containers was almost as abrupt. The first domestic 48 x 102-foot container was shown at the Atlanta Intermodal Expo in 1986. Built by Miller, it was heavy (i.e., 12,000 pounds) with small doors and large interior "knee braces" for the top pick castings.

The American President Lines immediately began to order 45-, 48- and 53-foot "big boxes" for domestic loadings. Others, including the leasing companies — Transamerica, XTRA and Itel, quickly joined in. The 102-inch wide containers were utilitzed almost exclusively in domestic service while the 45 x 96-foot boxes were swapped between U.S. domestic and international service.

The beginnings of domestic container service were akin to watching a baby take its first steps, with many fits and starts. There were mistakes and spills, but day-by-day the baby got stronger. Day-by-day domestic containerization became the way to go.

Two things drove the domestic container revolution. The first was the quality of the line-haul service. No longer did intermodal give a cheap ride that beat up the freight, or were shippers required to "build a house" inside an intermodal box to restrain the movement of their lading. The phrase, "build a house," comes from a major intermodal customer who claimed he discovered that he was the best customer of his local lumber yard, based on the two by fours purchased to build the blocking and bracing in a piggyback trailer in order to get his freight safely across the railroad.

In contrast American President Lines did an early test shipment of a container on a stack car by setting a dining room table with fine china and crystal. At the destination, the "dining room" emerged in the same pristine condition in which it was loaded.

Trailer advocates cried foul. "We have the same ride quality in spine cars as the stacks." True enough. But the stack containers had something else. Economics.

Granted economics conjures up two images to most people — boring and monotonous. For those who can't take boring — skip to Chapter 20. For the other brave souls — bear with it.

Train operating costs are fairly straightforward. Mainline trains are generally built based on the length of the shortest main line passing siding. If that is 6,000 feet, then the train you build as a yardmaster or an intermodal area manger had better not exceed 6,000 feet. Otherwise, you have what dispatchers refer to as a non-clearing train, i.e., *all* oncoming trains need to take a siding for the train you have just overbuilt. For this misdeed you have just guaranteed several late schedules across the railroad, plus more grey hair on the Chief Dispatcher. So let's stay within our template for clearing trains.

With a given limit let's now compare line-haul operating economics for candidate intermodal technologies. For our 6,000-foot railroad train we can choose the following:

1. Double-hitch cars — 91 feet long
2. Spine cars — 261 feet long
3. Double-stack cars — 305 feet long
4. RoadRailer — 48 feet long

Comparative intermodal operating costs are determined by the capital costs of the technology employed, the distance traveled, the weight of the train hauled and the number of containers or trailers hauled. Beginning with the weight of each system, it becomes readily apparent that a basic goal for any transportation entity is to obtain a reasonable line-haul vehicle. This includes the best balances of a low net to tare weight

Double-Stack Freight Cars

A Santa Fe Railway stack train rolls down the south side of Cajon Pass en route to San Bernardino, and Hobart Yard of Los Angeles. Warbonnets and lots of California sunshine produced this perfectly lighted photograph. —MIKE MARTIN - SANTA FE RAILWAY

A "Super Fleet" locomotive is attached to a group of 10 stack cars at Santa Fe's San Bernardino intermodal facility. —MIKE MARTIN - SANTA FE RAILWAY

A train of domestic containers (ie., those 102 inches wide) ride atop ISO international containers aboard a five-unit TTX type III articulated stack car. The units reporting mark "DTTX" stands for a five-platform articulated well-type COFC car which is capable of carrying double-stack containers. The length of the unit, over the end sills, is 304-feet. Note the Southern Pacific container, at the left, with the new style name design. — GREENBRIER INTERMODAL

The Greenbrier prototype "stand alone" Husky Stack car with an international box in the well. Above (with reporting marks BNO 1996) is an "Ingram saddle" which holds two 28-foot BN America boxes. The latter are designed for the LTL market and for United Parcel Service. — GREENBRIER INTERMODAL

Table 1
EQUIPMENT TARE WEIGHT — 6,000 FOOT TRAIN

Equipment Type	Car Weight	Trailer/Container Wt.	Number of Boxes	No. Cars Per 6,000 Ft. Train	Total Tare Trailing Weight	Total Tare Wt. Per Box	Total Trailing Weight
89' Trailer Car	2,275 T	910 T	130	65	3,185 T	24.5 T	5,785 T
89' Container Car	2,275 T	520 T	130	65	2,795 T	21.5 T	5,395 T
Spine Car-Trailer	1,804 T	770 T	110	22	2,574 T	23.4 T	4,774 T
Spine Car-Container	1,804 T	440 T	110	22	2,244 T	20.4 T	4,444 T
Stack Car-Container	2,043 T	760 T	190	19	2,803 T	14.8 T	6,603 T
RoadRailer	300 T	608 T	75*	75	908 T	12.1 T	2,408 T

*RoadRailer restricted train length

Car builders have a tradition known as "sample car day." It allows mechanical types to inspect last-minute details on the first car off the line and to generally celebrate the order between car builder and customer. In this photograph, Bob Ingram of Burlington Northern is speaking in front of a Gunderson sample car after four years of joint work. — GREENBRIER INTERMODAL

ration (i.e., the weight of the freight moved in the system versus the weight of the vehicle or vehicle system required to move it) with a reasonable purchase price and cost to maintain the system. This is the essential trade-off made by people who buy or operate lightweight cars. It also shows why a container system that "leaves the wheels behind" has held a fascination for operating people through the years.

As we see in Table 1, the Equipment Tare Weight Table, there is a 43 percent weight difference between a 48-foot container and a 48-foot piggyback trailer. That only amounts to about a 2 percent savings in operating line-haul costs with an 89-foot or an all-purpose spine car. When we examine the weight savings in cars, however, the weight savings begin to mount up. (It should be noted that the efficiency of Second-Generation 89-foot cars, that can only load 45-foot trailers or containers, is highly overstated compared to Third-Generation technology.) Third-Generation spines and RoadRailers load 48-foot units, the current highway standard. RoadRailers are limited by regulation to 75 RoadRailer units per train. Within those constraints, however, the lightest per box technology is the RoadRailer Mark V at 12.1 tons of tare weight per box, or half the weight of trailers on an 89-foot car. Stack cars come in at 40 percent under, and the all-purpose spine car at 17 percent.

When capital costs are considered things change somewhat. The capital cost of trailers on 89-foot cars appear at $17.64 per day. Again, however, the cars can not load 48-foot trailers and the car cost does not reflect a new purchase price. RoadRailer capital costs are very high which balances its light weight. Stack costs use both the cheaper container capital costs and the lower capital cost (per box) of the cars.

The ultimate measure is the overall effect of light weight and capital costs on over-the-road operating costs.

Table 2
CAPITAL COSTS PER DAY

	Capital Cost	No. of Boxes	Cost Per Box	Maint. Cost Per Box	Car Total Cost	Total Cost
89-Foot Car	$10.80	2	$ 5.40	$ 4.99	$10.39	$17.64
All Purpose Spine Car	42.00	5	8.40	4.99	13.39	18.29
Stack Car	72.00	10	7.20	2.23	9.43	14.33
RoadRailer Mk V						
Bogie	10.80	1	10.80	0	10.80	29.15
Box	18.35					
Domestic Container	4.90					
Domestic Trailer	7.25					

With the trailing weight and capital costs calculated let's now put our train on the road. For a hypothetical

1,000 mile haul the costs generally looked like this:

Table 3
COSTS FOR 1000 MILE HAUL — 6,000 FOOT TRAIN

	89 Foot Car/ Trailer	89 Foot Car/ Container	Spine/ Trailer	Spine/ Container	Stack/ Container	RoadRailer
Linehaul Cost	$46,800	$46,200	$38,600	$38,000	$51,000	$25,700
Car Capital/Maint.	4,050	4,050	4,420	4,420	5,400	2,400
Total	50,850	50,250	43,020	42,420	56,400	28,100
Box Capital	2,830	1,910	2,390	1,620	2,790	4,130
Total Ramp to Ramp	$53,680	$52,160	$45,410	$44,040	$59,190	$32,230
Cost Per Box	$413	$401	$413	$400	$312	$430

These are generalized costs. All rail costs are route specific and may vary greatly. This example does, however, show the cost differences between the technologies. When the "leave the wheels behind" idea is combined with stacking the boxes and fully utilizing the relatively tall rail right-of-way, costs decline dramatically. For example, the line-haul cost of the stacks runs about 31 cents per mile, compared with 40 cents for containers on all-purpose spine cars and 41 cents for trailers on spines. RoadRailers run 43 cents per mile, compared with efficient truckload highway carriers whose costs are about 75 cents per mile.

Intermodal line-haul costs suffer a competitive disadvantage in needing to add drayage (i.e., local trucking) costs at each end of the line haul. Depending on the area and the direction of the haul, this can be a substantial cost amounting to as high as $4.00 per mile in some areas. Balancing the charge of those pickup and delivery cost against the direct applicability of the more expensive all-highway truck service is a major task of intermodal.

The best chance for intermodal is to have a combination of low cost, intensively managed, well-marketed system. That would now appear to be a domestic stack system.

Just as the conditions of cost advantage, terminal mechanization, ride quality improvement, general highway vehicle size and terminal rationalization all converged to make things right for domestic containers after a 30 year hiatus, it will be interesting to see whether other threads of thought from the 1950's about containers reemerge. One school of technological and economic thought in those days looked at the container not only as a portion of a transportation system, but as an extension of a total logistics and production system. Recall the early Railway Express container system which used the container as a storage system with built-in legs on the box.

At Ford Motor Company a think-tank group, run by Foster Weldon in the 1960's, viewed the container as an integral part of future production lines. A container of fenders would move off its chassis into the plant, going directly to a point on the production line where fenders were needed, by-passing intermediate handling and damage.

An early containerization study for Marad declared that a containerizable commodity was "anything that would fit in a container." That was radical thinking in those days. Certainly, said critics, liquids would not travel in containers. The next year Sea-Land began transporting tank containers of olive oil from Italy and Scotch from Scotland.

The decade of the 1980's saw a firm base laid for intermodal to move to a container-based system both for international and domestic freight. By 1992, container loadings passed trailer loadings for the first time. But only the surface has been scratched with regard to the full potentiality of containers. Greater use of containers by Less-Than-Truckload highway carriers; the use of containers in the logistics function as cheap storage and warehousing; movement of bulk goods such as lumber and liquids, now in its infancy; and the integration of the container into the heart of the production line. These are goals worthy of the next generation of intermodal dreamers and doers.

A long Sea-Land double-stack train rolls eastbound out of Needles, California, on Santa Fe's Los Angeles to Chicago main line. In a few minutes time, this 64-car intermodal train will cross the mighty Colorado River, at Topock, Arizona. — MIKE MARTIN - SANTA FE RAILWAY

Chapter 20

End Of The Beginning

As intermodal entered its 55th year, one could look back on a maturing, but generally vital and changing transportation service. Intermodal was born in the crucible of the great depression of the 1930's. It was created to meet the challenge of the all-highway truck mode which, in turn, arose largely from desperate men trying to make a living during hard times. Low capital entry requirements and tough times have often spurred men to innovation. The result was over-the-road truckers waiting to capture railroad-hauled merchandise freight.

The building of trucks for highway transport was the offshoot of the auto industry, which had engineering funds and capital to burn. Plus the advantage just listed, throw in a paved right-of-way whose up front money was provided by all levels of government. It was no wonder that trucking was able to offer bargain basement prices, leaving the railroad struggling to develop a competitive system.

In reality, depending on your view of history, it was the price regulation policy initially designed to protect the public from the railroads — or the railroads from each other, that was the root cause of the problem. In any case it was an ideology that was slow and cumbersome. It was also a system which, when confronted by the trucking industry, spread a broad rate umbrella to protect the emerging transportation medium.

Finally, added to all the regulations was the entrenched bureaucracies of the railroads themselves. Operating officials strove to pitch an efficient game at any cost in the face of competition from high-priced, high-service truckers. In spite of the railroad's proficiency, truckers continued to knock them out of the box every year. Traffic officials who insisted on sticking with the boxcar syndrome were stuck with complex tariffs, in a marketplace that had long since declared itself bored with that game and switched to another.

It is a wonder that the intermodal system ever took hold, let alone survived. Yet, it did. It lived and it thrived. It grew because the people involved truly enjoyed their work. Those pioneer intermodalist would never entertain the thought of doing anything else.

Intermodalists looked after intermodal and each other. It made no difference on what railroad it happened to be. This kind of concern is how and why intermodal survived through the hard times and thrived in the good times. You have met many of the survivors of intermodal in this book. But for everyone you have met in these pages, there are still unmentioned thousands out there, working at the ramps, on the trains, in the general office and in the marketplace, who must be credited with making the system work.

Intermodal, during the embryonic 1920's, encompassed the fledgling fits and starts of containers handled by the interurban lines. In the 1930's the Chicago Great Western in the midwest and the New Haven in the east began the quiet birth of hauling trailers on flatcars and in gondolas. These early beginnings saw screw jacks, chains and binders which proved expensive, but provided almost bombproof-safe flatcar loadings. During the 1940's, these premature beginnings were almost forgotten when America joined the rest of the world in an international military conflict.

In the explosive 1950's, came the entry of many Class I railroads into the exciting "new" world of piggyback, accompanied by an uneasy attempt of railroaders to accommodate both current and new customers. In this same period specialized flatcars evolved. First was a 75-footer, then an 85-footer, and then a 50-footer. Also developed were the EMDX 15972, the Clejan car, Railvan, Portager, Adapto and the Flexi Van. The retractable hitch and the hostler tractor made life easier at the ramps. It was not long before new factors came along that needed to be understood and dealt with, such as car pools — Trailer Train and GATX, trailer pools — REALCO and XTRA, and the redoubtable Gene Ryan who seemed to do everything and be everywhere. The industry came to terms with the regulators at 12th and Constitution Avenue (the Interstate Commerce Commission) and added Plan I-V to its vocabulary. Next to come upon the scene was a trucker, Malcolm McLean, who brought with him the invention and implementation of the standard intermodal container. For the railroads, the container would grow slowly at first and, over the next 20 years, produce a love-hate relationship.

The 1950's were tempestuous. They were filled with innovation, experimentation and a try-it mentality. One thing was clear — the perfect way had yet to be invented.

The 1960's changed all that. Virtually, all railroads adopted some form of piggyback service. The 89-foot flatcar came to dominate car technology for the next 20 years, bringing stability to intermodal. The handling of trailers closed out competing technology. Trailer Train absorbed the members of the GATX pool. Unfettered innovations were replaced by consolidation, fine tuning and security.

Terminals grew in number, and major terminals were mechanized. Cars were improved, hitches were refined and trailers were fine tuned. But further breakthroughs in equipment or functional organizations were put on hold as the industry digested its gains.

The 1970's went through a period of consolidation which had an effect on intermodal. Corporate level mergers of the Chicago, Burlington & Quincy, the Great Northern and the Northern Pacific formed the Burlington Northern. Family Lines was an outgrowth of the mergers of the Seaboard Airline, the Atlantic Coast Line and the Louisville & Nashville Railroad. The Chessie System was put together by the consolidation of the Chesapeake & Ohio, the Baltimore & Ohio and the Western Maryland railroad, Chessie and Family Lines, became CSX. The Southern Railway and the Norfolk & Western Railway merged to form the Norfolk Southern Railway. The Union Pacific expanded its system by absorbing the Missouri Pacific, the Western Pacific and later the Katy. The 3R and 4R Acts of the federal government pulled together the northeast bankrupt railroads of the Penn Central, the Central Railroad of New Jersey, the Erie-Lackawanna, the Lehigh Valley, the Lehigh & Hudson River and the Reading Lines to form Conrail (Consolidated Rail Corporation).

For intermodal, the 1980's were indeed explosive. New technology seemed to burst on the scene every year or two — and much of it was radical. The Six and Ten-Pack, the 4 Runner and Front Runner, the spine car, the double stack and the born-again RoadRailer. The 45x96-, 45x102- and 48x102-trailers were built. Containers of 45x96-, 45x102-, 48x102- 53x102- and 28 x 102 were built.

In the pre-1980 period, it was easy to tell the difference between railroads, containership companies and third parties. The railroads operated ramps, engines, cars and trailers within their own, i.e., rail tributary territory. The steamship people operated ships, docks, containers and chassis in and around port areas and on the high seas. Train and truck personnel took care of the container boxes inland. Third-party accounts worked "out of their hat," had few if any assets and did the intermodal sales work for the railroads. It was not always a comfortable relationship, but everyone was used to their service and knew what to expect.

In the 1980's two Class I railroads bought two major truck lines. One leading railroad bought a major steamship line. Two ranking steamship lines purchased third-party firms. Two steamship lines (or part of them — or the companies that were formed out of their acquisition) established domestic nationwide networks. Four steamship lines, their heirs or successors, (to borrow a legal phrase) established their own captive intermodal terminals. Several steamship lines leased double-stack container cars.

Two railroads in the 1980's established full retail operations that excluded third-party participation.

Another established a highly selective third-party operation. At the request of the railroads, the Interstate Commerce Commission, threw intermodal railroaders out of the comfortable confines of the rate bureaus and into the marketplace.

The results, once again, placed intermodal on a major growth cycle. For the first time in intermodal history it could be shown that intermodal was significantly cutting into over-the-highway freight traffic. Intermodal was now moving toward nationwide intermodal companies and partnerships.

Within the decade of the 1980's a tremendous spurt of progress for intermodal was seen, setting the stage for a meaningful leap into the 21st century.

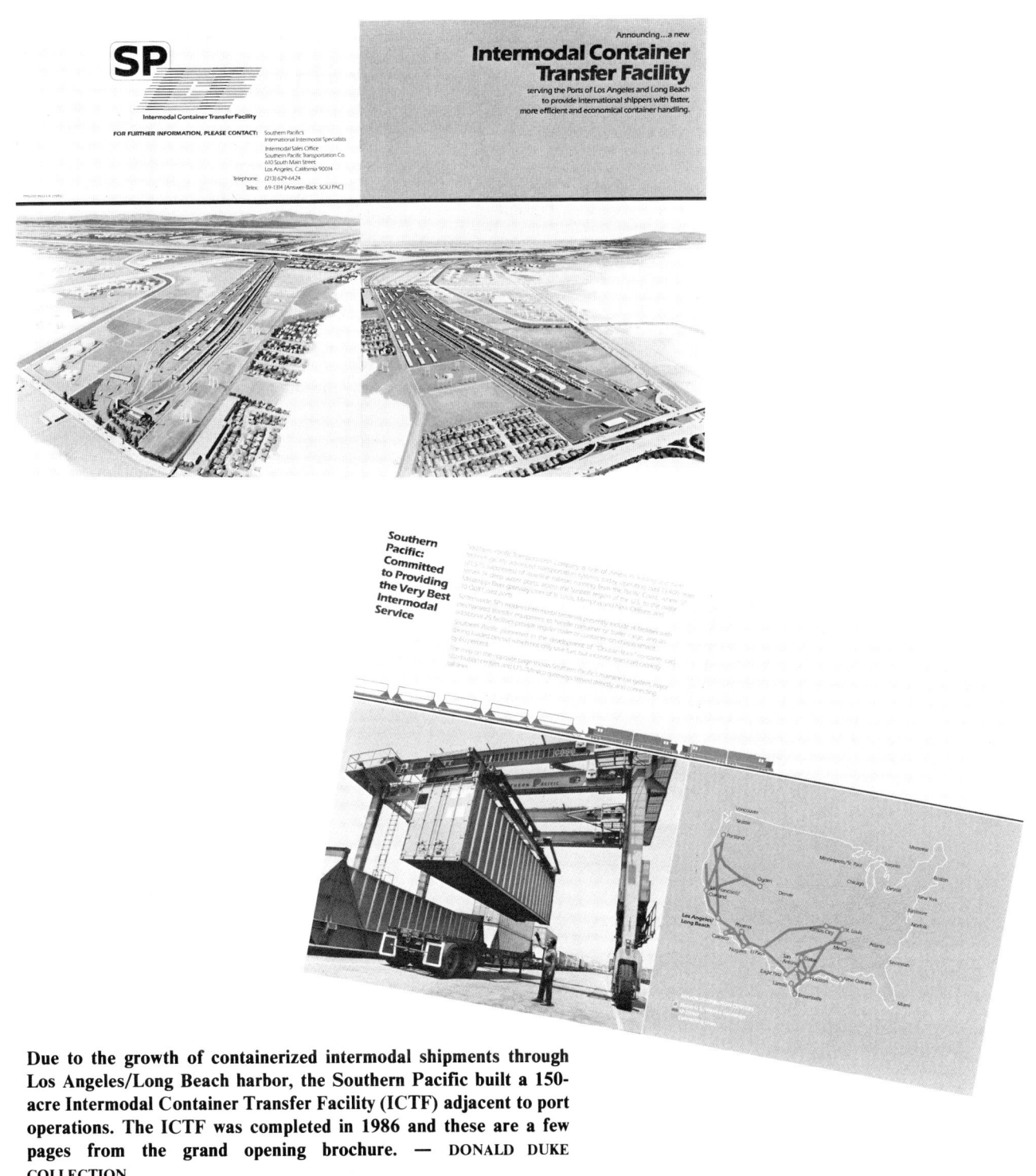

Due to the growth of containerized intermodal shipments through Los Angeles/Long Beach harbor, the Southern Pacific built a 150-acre Intermodal Container Transfer Facility (ICTF) adjacent to port operations. The ICTF was completed in 1986 and these are a few pages from the grand opening brochure. — DONALD DUKE COLLECTION

SILVER KING PIN AWARD RECIPIENTS

Dec. 1977	Ray Ascencio		May 1983	Reggie Short
May 1978	Al Grassmuck		Sept. 1983	Scott Corbett, Jr.
Aug. 1978	John Allen, Sr. (posthumously)		May 1984	P.L. Cowling
Jan. 1979	Roy Hayes		Sept. 1984	G.A. Volkers
May 1979	Pete Keenan		Jan. 1985	Robert H. Maisch
Sept. 1979	Larry Cena		Sept. 1985	E.W. Frey
Jan. 1980	Tom Fante		Feb. 1987	George Page
May 1980	No Award		Sept. 1988	Wayne Daugherty
Sept. 1980	C.T. Groton (posthumously)		Feb. 1989	Jack Lanigan
Jan. 1981	Eugene Ryan		Sept. 1989	Bob Krehmeyer
May 1981	Charles Larkin		Jan. 1990	Nat Welch
Sept. 1981	Lester Robinson		Feb. 1991	Don Orris
Jan. 1982	Paul Johnston		Sept. 1991	William Greenwood
May 1982	Charles Kaye		Feb. 1992	C.B. "Chico" Clark
Sept. 1982	J.P. Newell (posthumously)		Feb. 1993	Frank Richter
Jan. 1983	Rocky Canzoniero		Feb. 1994	Ralph Muellner

INTERMODAL ACHIEVEMENT AWARD

1986	Thrall Car Manufacturing Co.		1990	(no award presented)
	Gunderson Car Building Co.		1991	The Hub Group, Phil Yeager
1987	United Parcel Service		1992	Mi-Jack Products, Jack Lanigan
1988	American President Companies		1993	Santa Fe Railway
1989	International Intermodal Expo., Nat Welch			

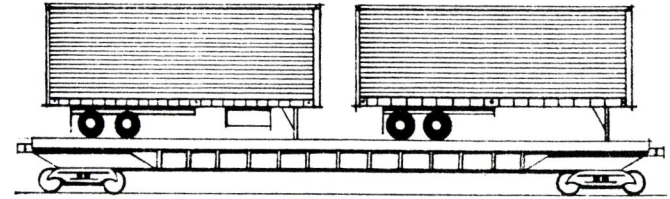

Appendix

Abbreviations

AAR	Association of American Railroads	FRA	Federal Railroad Administration	OOCL	Overseas Orient Container Line
ACF	American Car & Foundry	FTL	Flying Tiger Line	O-T	Operations Transportation
ACL	Atlantic Coast Line Railroad				
AEIL	American Export Isbrantson Line	GATX	General American Transportation Leasing	PC	Penn Central
APD	American President Domestic			PIE	Pacific Intermountain Express
APL	American President Lines	GBRX	Greenbrier Intermodal Leasing	P&LE	Pittsburgh & Lake Erie Railroad
ATA	American Trucking Association	GE	General Electric	PMT	Pacific Motor Trucks
AT&SF	Atcheson, Topeka & Santa Fe Railway	GM	General Motors	PR	Public Relations
		GMAC	General Motors Acceptance Corporation	PRR	Pennsylvania Railroad
AX	All-Purpose Car			PS	Pullman Standard
		GMD	General Motors Diesel of Canada Limited	PTL	Pennsylvania Truck Line
B&A	Boston and Albany Railroad			P&WV	Pittsburgh & West Virginia Railway
B&M	Boston and Maine Corporation	GM&O	Gulf, Mobile & Ohio Railroad		
BN	Burlington Northern Railroad	GN	Great Northern Railway	Q	Chicago, Burlington & Quincy Railroad
BNA	BN America	GNP	Gross National Product		
B&O	Baltimore and Ohio Railroad				
		hp	horse power	R&D	Research & Development
CAB	Civil Aeronautics Board	H-PIT	High Productivity Integral Train	RDG	Reading Railway
CB&Q	Chicago, Burlington & Quincy Railroad	HQ	Headquarters	REA	Railway Express Agency
				RF&P	Richmond, Fredericksburg & Potomac Railroad
C&EI	Chicago & Eastern Illinois Railroad	IANA	Intermodal Association of North America		
				RPC	Ropco Corporation
CEO	Chief Executive Officer	IBM	International Business Machines		
CF	Consolidated Freightways	IBT	International Brotherhood of Teamsters	SAL	Seaboard Air Line Railroad
C of G	Central of Georgia Railway			SCL	Seaboard Coast Line
CGW	Chicago, Great Western Railway	IC	Illinois Central Railroad	SLSF	St. Louis-San Francisco Railway (Frisco)
CMO	Chief Mechanical Officer	IBC	Interbox Connector		
CMSP&P	Chicago, Milwaukee, St. Paul & Pacific Railroad (Milwaukee Road)	ICC	Interstate Commerce Commission	SOIC	Steamship Operation Intermodal Committee
		ICG	Illinois Central Gulf Railroad		
		ICI	Intermodal Concepts, Inc.	SP	Southern Pacific Railroad
CN	Canadian National Railways	ICTF	Intermodal Container Transfer Facility	SRS	Southern Railway System
CNJ	Central Railroad of New Jersey			SS of A	Stevedoring Services of America
C&NW	Chicago & Northwestern Railway	IMA	Intermodal Marketing Association	SSW	St. Louis Southwestern Railway (Cottonbelt)
C&O	Chesapeake and Ohio Railway	ISO	International Standards Organization		
COFC	Container On Flat Car			Susie Q	New York, Susquehanna & Western Railroad
CP	Canadian Pacific Railway	ITA	Intermodal Transportation Association		
CPR	Canadian Pacific Railway			SV	Super Van
CR	Conrail (Consolidated Rail Corporation)	KATY	Missouri-Kansas-Texas Railroad	TEA	Traffic Executive Association
		KCS	Kansas City Southern Railway	TL	Truck Load
CRI&P	Chicago, Rock Island & Pacific Railroad			TLDX	Pullman Standard Leasing Subsidiary
CSLI	CSX Sealand Intermodal Company	LA	Los Angeles		
CSX	Merger of Chessie System (Chesapeake & Ohio, Baltimore & Ohio and Western Maryland) and Seaboard Coast Lines (Seaboard Air Line and Atlantic Coast Line)	LATC	Los Angeles Transportation Center	TOFC	Trailer on Flatcar
		LCL	Less-Than-Carload	T&P	Texas & Pacific Railway
		LIRR	Long Island Rail Road	TP&W	Toledo, Peoria & Western Railroad
		L&N	Louisville & Nashville Railroad	TT	Truc Train
		LTL	Less-Than-Truckload	TTAX	Trailer Train All Purpose Car
				TTX	Trailer Train
CTC	Centralized Traffic Control	MH5	International Standards Committee		
		MIS	Management Information System	UIIA	Uniform Intermodal Interchange Agreement
D-F	Damage Free	MKT	Missouri-Kansas-Texas Railroad (Katy)		
D&H	Delaware & Hudson Railroad			UP	Union Pacific Railroad
DL&W	Delaware, Lackawanna & Western Railroad	MOL	Mitsui O.S.K. Line	UPS	United Parcel Service
		MOP	Missouri Pacific Railroad	U.S.	United States
DOT	Department of Transportation	MP	Missouri Pacific Railroad	USRA	United States Railway Administration
D&RGW	Denver & Rio Grande Western Railroad	m.p.h.	miles per hour		
		M of W	Maintenance of Way	UTU	United Transportation Union
DT&I	Detroit, Toledo & Ironton Railroad				
		NP	Northern Pacific Railway	VCA	Voluntary Coordination Agreements
		NRIA	National Railroad Intermodal Association	VP	Vice President
EIA	Equipment Interchange Association			VPO	Vice President of Operations
E-L	Erie Lackawanna Railroad	NRPA	National Railroad Piggyback Association		
EMD	Electro Motive Division of General Motors			W&LE	Wheeling & Lake Erie
		NS	Norfolk Southern	WM	Western Maryland Railroad
		N&W	Norfolk & Western Railway	WP	Western Pacific Railroad
FAK	Freight-All-Kinds	NYAB	New York Air Brake	WWII	World War II
FEC	Florida East Coast Railway	NYC	New York Central System		
feu	forty foot equivalent unit	NYC&StL	New York, Chicago & St. Louis Railroad (Nickel Plate Road)		
FMC	Federal Maritime Commission				
FMC	Food Machinery Corporation	NYSW	New York, Susquehanna & Western Railroad (Suzie Q)		

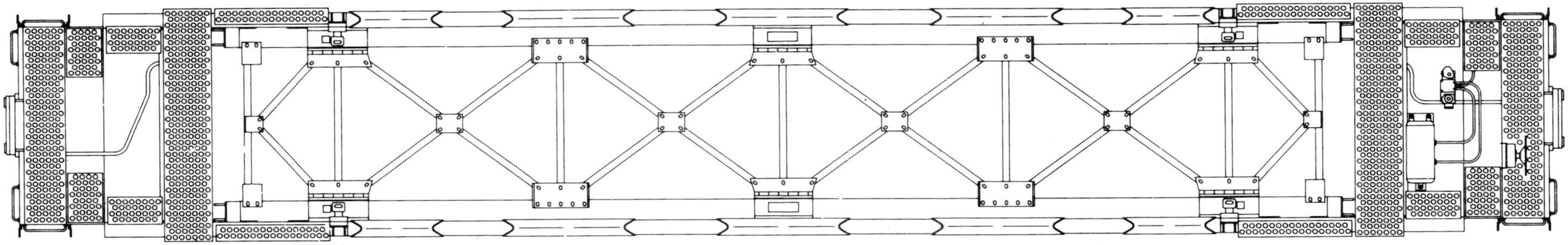

TOP VIEW

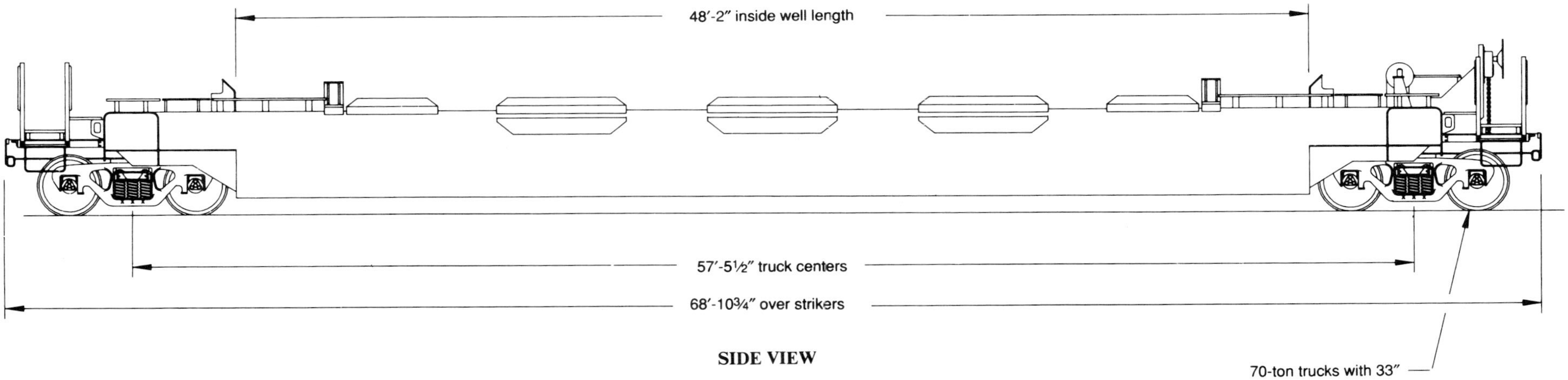

48'-2" inside well length

SIDE VIEW

57'-5½" truck centers
68'-10¾" over strikers
70-ton trucks with 33"

TRAILER TRAIN "Husky Stack" Well Car

Nos. DTTX 56000-56149 class GWF-10 built by Gunderson, Inc. 1991
Drawn by Bruce Keating to HO Scale 3.5mm = 1'0"; 1:87.1

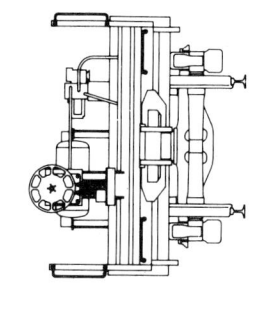

8'-6½" rotators out
8'-0½" rotators in
7'-5" between container stacking cones

END SECTION OF WELL

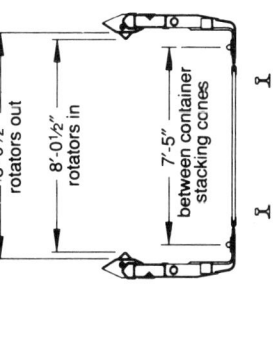

5'-3¼"
4'-9⅜"
9⁷⁄₁₆" light car
9'-11½" outside width
8'-11¼" inside width

CENTER SECTION OF WELL

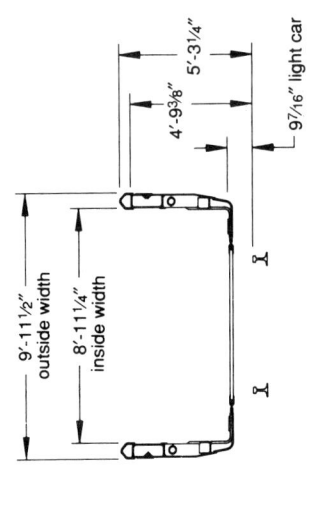

END VIEW

This drawing is through the courtesy of James Panza of Trailer Train. The drawing originally appeared in *Railroad Model Craftsman* for July 1992, together with a feature article.

TRAILER TRAIN 70-ton 3-Unit Well Car
Nos. DTTX 25018-25067; DTTX 25128-25202 class TWG-30 built by Thrall Mfg. Co. 1991
Drawn by Bruce Keating to HO Scale 3.5mm = 1'0"; 1:87.1

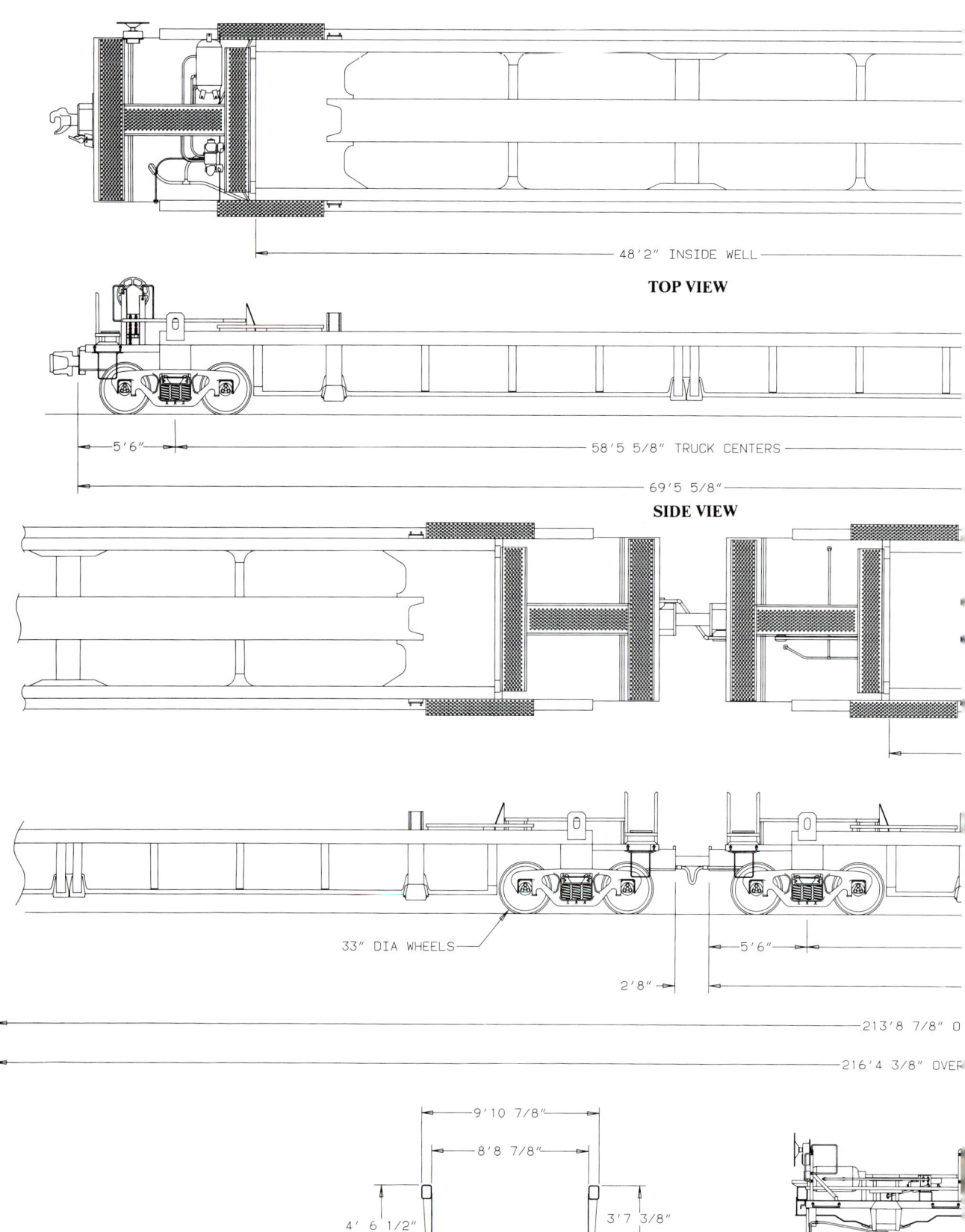

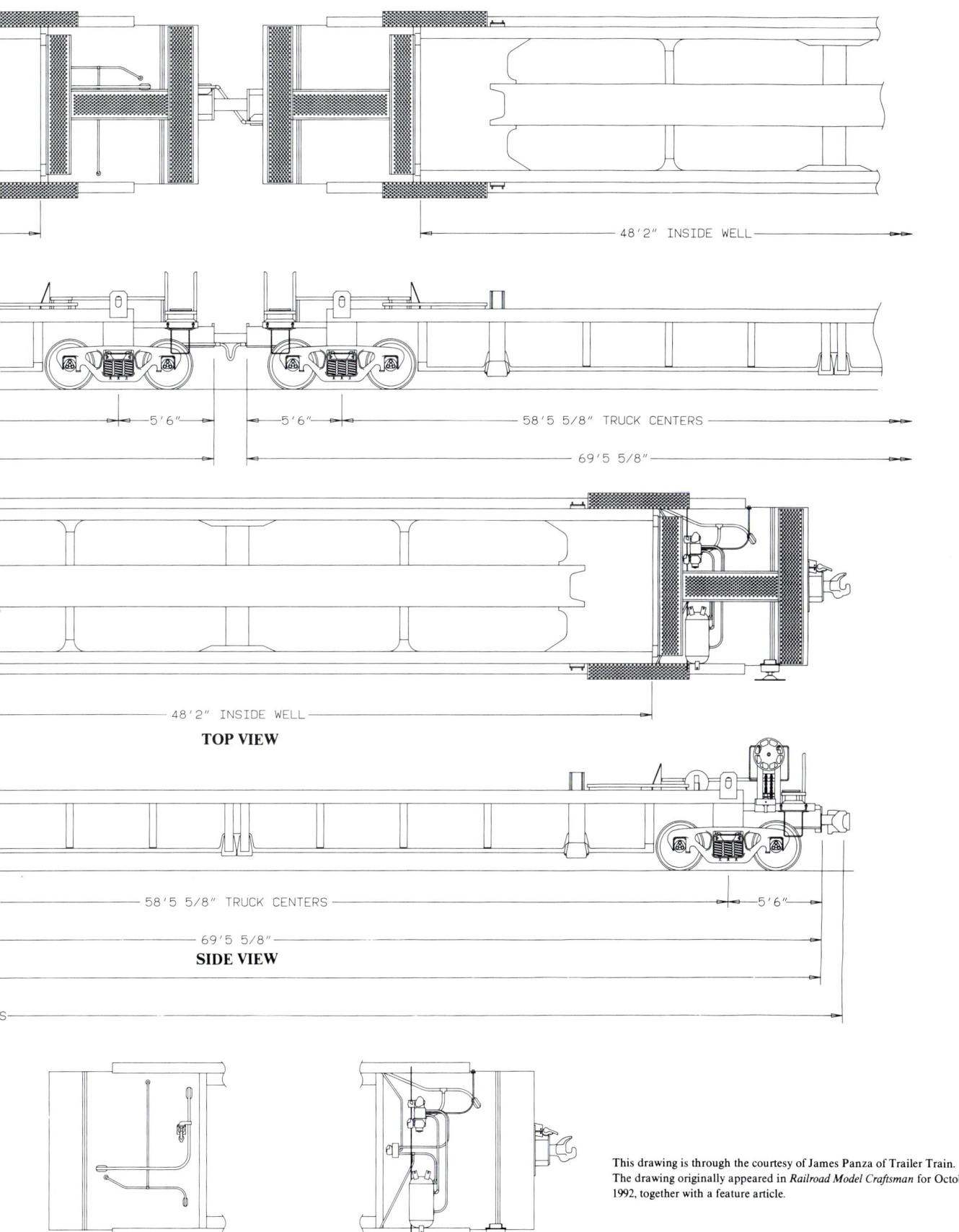

TOP VIEW

SIDE VIEW

AIR BRAKE UNITS AT A AND B ENDS

This drawing is through the courtesy of James Panza of Trailer Train. The drawing originally appeared in *Railroad Model Craftsman* for October 1992, together with a feature article.

Bibliography

Books

Armstrong, John H. *The Railroad: What it is, What it Does*. New York: Simmons-Boardman Books, Inc., 1977.

Ball, Don. *Pennsylvania Railroad: 1940-1950*. Chester: Elm Tree Books, Inc., 1986.

Booz, Allen Hamilton. *Piggyback: The Efficient Alternative For The 80's*. New York: TransAmerica Interway, 1980.

Buford, Curtis D. *Trailer Train Company, A Unique Force In The Railroad Industry*. Newcomen Society in North America, 1982.

Bryant, Keith. *History of the Atchison, Topeka & Santa Fe Railway*. New York: Macmillan Publishing Co., 1974.

Bryant, Keith (Editor). *Railroads in the Age of Regulation: Encylcopedia of American Railroad Business History and Biography 1900-1980*. New York: Facts on File, 1988.

Containerization, Rail System Management Association Proceeding, 1972.

Council of Economic Advisors. *Improving Railroad Productivity - Final Report*. Washington, D.C., 1973.

Davis, Burke. *The Southern Railway: Road of the Innovators*. Chapel Hill: University of North Carolina Press, 1985.

Domestic Containerization, Intermodal Transportation Associations Proceedings, 1986.

Farewell, R.C. *Rio Grande: Ruler of the Rockies*. Glendale: Interurban Press, 1987.

Farrington, S. Kip, Jr. *Railroading the Modern Way*. New York: Coward-McCann, Inc., 1951.

Farrington, S. Kip, Jr. *Railroads of Today*. New York: Coward-McCann, Inc., 1959.

General Electric, *Technical and Economic Feasibility Study of the Coaxial Train*. Erie, PA., 1973.

Grant, Roger H. *The Corn Belt Route: A History of the Chicago Great Western Railroad Co.* DeKalb: Northern Illinois University Press, 1984.

Henry, Robert Selph. *This Fascinating Railroad Business*. New York: Bobbs-Merrill Co., 1942.

Hilton, George, and Due, John. *The Electric Interurban Railway in America*. Stanford: Stanford University Press, 1960.

Hofsommer, Don. L. *The Southern Pacific 1901-1985*. College Station: Texas A&M Press, 1986.

Impacts of an Improved Truck/Rail Operation: A Case Study. Greenwich: Reebies Associates, 1975.

Mahoney, John H. *Intermodal Freight Transportation*. Westport: Eno Foundation, 1985.

Manalytics, Reebie Associates, *Containerization*, Washington, DC: U.S. Maritime Administration 1969.

Mann, Dick. *From Camels to Carloads - And Beyond: A History of the U.S. Freight*. Unpublished Manuscript, 1982.

McKenzie, David R., North, Mark C. and Smith, Daniel. *Intermodal Transportation: The Whole Story*. Omaha: Simmons-Boardman Books, Inc., 1989.

Middleton, William D. *North Shore: America's Fastest Interurban*. San Marino: Golden West Books, 1964.

Middleton, William D. *South Shore: The Last Interurban*. San Marino: Golden West Books, 1970.

National Transportation Policy. [Doyle Report], U.S. Senate, 1961.

Newland, D.E., Cassidy, R.J. *Fundamental Design Considerations For Multi-Wheeled Flexible Railway Vehicles*. ASME, 1970.

Overton, Richard D. *Burlington Route*. New York: Alfred A. Knopf, 1965.

Rath, Eric. *Container Systems*. John Wiley & sons, 1973.

Reebie Associates. *National Intermodal Natural Flexibility Study*, Vol. I-IV, U.S. DOT, 1976.

Road-Rail Systems, The: A Discussion and Description. St. Louis: American Car & Foundry Co.

Salsbury, Stephen. *No way to Run a Railroad*. New York: McGraw-Hill, 1982.

Short, John G. *Piggyback and the Future of Railroad Transportation*. Washington: Public Affairs Institute, 1960.

Short, John G. *Progress in Piggyback and Containerization*. Washington: Public Affairs

Institute, 1961.

Study and Plan: Conrail Bi-Modal and Intermodal Operation. Greenwich: Reebie Associates, 1975.

Systems Engineering for Intermodal Freight Systems (Volumes 1, 3 and 4). Chicago: A.T. Kearney, 1978.

Systems Engineering for Intermodal Freight Systems (Volume 2). Peat Marwick Mitchell, 1978.

Tuggle, Kenneth H. (Chairman of the Interstate Commerce Commission). *The Role of Cargo Containers in Integrated Transportation.* Address before Truck Manufacturers Assoc., July 14, 1959.

U.S. Department of Transportation. *A Prospectus For Change In The Freight Railroad Industry.* Washington, DC, 1978.

U.S. Military Traffic Management Command. *Military Applications of Double Stacking Railcars.* Newport News, VA, 1988.

Periodicals

"A Prospectus for Change in the Freight Railroad Industry." *U.S. Department of Transportation*, 1978.

"ACF's Hitch Hiker Flatcars." *Model Railroader*, April 1968, pp. 38-41.

"After 17 years, piggyback is alive and well and still growing fast on Southern Pacific." *Southern Pacific Bulletin*, March 1969, pp. 2-3.

"AT&SF Develops Container Ten-Pack." *Railway Age*. July 13, 1981, p. 4.

"Can the land-bridge be built?" *Railway Age*, June 5, 1968, p. 31.

"CB&Q's rail-air experiments aim at the future." *Railway Age*, May 29, 1967, pp. 58-59.

Cena, Larry. "Santa Fe's answer to the double-stack." *Railway Age*, June 1985, pp. 54-55.

"Chicago: The Hub of Hubs." *Railway Age*, November 1984, p. 3.

"Containers Boost World Trade..!" *Santa Fe Magazine*, April 1968, pp. 16-19.

"Container System Creates Freight Service." *Railway Age*, February 25, 1922, pp. 475-476.

"Containerization." Rail Systems Management Association - *Proceedings*, 1972.

Cook, James. "Trains of the highway." *Forbes*, November 26, 1990, pp. 167-168.

DeBoer, David J. "The Stack Car Revolution." *Traffic World.* March 17, 1986, pp. 54-56.

Dezendorf, Nelson. "Rail Highway Coordination." *Electro-Motive Division of General Motors*, 1953, pp. 2-20.

Dozell, Gary W. "The Train They Call Sprint." *Trains*, April 1981, pp. 26-33.

Ericksen, Helen. "Only Five U.S. Railroads Involved in FRA Project." *Journal of Commerce*, June 20, 1977.

"For Intermodal, the Fuel Crisis May Have an Upside." *Distribution*, October 1990, p. 18.

Frailey, Fred W. "Super C: Hottest of the Hotshots." *Trains*, May 1986, pp. 42-53.

"Freight Container in 1846." *Railway Age*, October 29, 1927, p. 857.

"From Santa Fe, the container that does it (almost) all." *Railway Age*, July 26, 1982, pp. 16-17.

Gallagher, John S., Jr. "Even highway trailers are going by rail." *Trains*, August 1952, pp. 24-27.

_____. "Piggyback: boom or bust?" *Trains*, March 1954, p. 21.

Grant, H. Roger. "The Chicago Great Western Railroad: Piggyback Pioneer." *Trains*, pp. 30-34.

Howard, F.H. "Piggyback and the Portager Dream I and II." *Trains*, April 1977, pp. 44-51; May 1977, pp. 44-51.

_____. "Circus Loading is for Elephants." *Trains*, April 1977, pp. 44-51.

"How KCS Will Expand Piggyback." *Railway Age*, February 13, 1956, p. 55-56.

Hudson, Gardner C. "Trailer Train: A healthy 10-year-old looks confidently ahead." *Railway Age*, February 28, 1966, pp. 30-36.

Ingles, J. David. "Milwaukee Road - Still Sprinting Along." *Trains*, September 1983, p. 17.

"Intercity Freight Movement by Rail and Highway." *Transportation Board of Record*, No. 511.

"Intermodal Continues to Make Inroads." *Distribution*, May 1991, pp. 63-65.

"Intermodal: Evolution and a Revolution." *Railway Age*, July 28, 1980, pp. 24-30.

"Intermodalism Tomorrow." *Progressive Railroading*, November 1983.

"Iron Highway fills a Gap: This throw-back 'Circus Loading' concept could open rail Intermodal to traffic it can't handle today." *Railway Age*, May 1991, pp. 48-49.

"Itel and Thrall Deliver Test Cars to Trailer Train." *Railway Age*, October 25, 1982, pp. 22-23.

Keefe, Kevin P. "A Horse of a Different Color."

185

Trains, June 1989, pp. 34-37.

Kirchner, H.W. "Economic Advantages of the Unit Container Car." *Railway Review*, November 19, 1921, pp. 682-683.

Kneiling, John G. "Next-generation train technology on a shoestring." *Trains*, August 1976, pp. 41-47.

Malone, Frank. "Commodities by Rail." *Railway Age*, November 24, 1980, pp. 16-23.

Margetts, F.C. "The Marriage of Road and Rail: Trains for Tomorrow." *Trains*, April 1976, pp. 40-47.

Middleton, William D. "Second Morning Chicago." *Railway Progress*, July 1957, pp. 16-23.

_____. "True-train tip-off." *Trains*, March 1971, pp. 24-28.

Miller, Luther. "Piggyback in Perspective." *Railway Progress*, pp. 16-22.

"Milwaukee campaigns for more container-shipment trade with Japan." *Railway Age*, June 5, 1967, pp. 16-17.

Morgan, David P. "Coaxial...as in Cable." *Trains*, December 1969, p. 3.

_____. "Piggyback Gets a Shot of X-15972." *Trains*, December 1953, pp. 6-7.

_____. "Piggyback: The Most Realistic Approach" *Trains*, May 1955, p. 7.

_____. "The Paraphernalia of Piggyback." *Trains*, June 1960, pp. 37-45.

_____. "The RoadRailer Rationale." *Trains*, November 1982, pp. 3-4.

_____. "34 Hours and 35 Minutes 40 Seconds." *Trains*, April 1968, pp. 3-4.

_____. "What Price Piggyback? Is the Union of truck trailer and flatcar a happy one?" *Trains*, May 1960, pp. 30-42.

"Move Over, Super Chief." *Trains*, August 1967, pp. 12-13.

"New Business Means New Equipment." *Railway Age*, July 31, 1967, pp. 43-44.

"New Generation of Cars." *Railway Age*, September 1983, pp. 41-47.

"New Plan Provides Piggybacking Without the Wheels." *Railway Age*, November 26, 1956, pp. 30-31.

"New York Central Won't Carry the Wheels." *Railway Age*, April 8, 1957, pp. 57-58.

"1953's Sizzling Question - Piggyback - How? and When?" *Railway Age*, January 11, 1954, pp. 136-138.

Odegard, Gordon. "Santa Fe 10-Pack." *Model Railroader*, September 1982, pp. 58-61.

Overby, Daniel L. "Piggyback: Where do we go from here?" *Trains*, February 1986, pp. 40-47.

Panza, Jim. "Thirty-five years of Trailer Train." *Railroad Model Craftsman*, July 1990, pp. 72-79.

_____. "Thirty-five years of Trailer Train - Part II." *Railroad Model Craftsman*, August 1990, pp. 74-84.

_____. "Trailer Train's Spine Car." *Railroad Model Craftsman*, July 1989, pp. 60-65.

"Perlman's Piggyback." *Trains*, October 1957, p. 6.

"Piggybackers all fall down but railroads look for a pickup." *Business Week*, November 22, 1969, p. 158.

"Piggybacking Booms." *Railway Age*, December 5, 1955, pp. 36-39.

"Piggyback kept 2.7 million trailers off the highways last year..." *Modern Railroads*, May 1967, p. 13.

"Piggyback Minus the Back." *Trains*, June 1956, p. 6.

"Piggyback: Progress has its Problems." *Railway Age*, May 31, 1965, pp. 54-66.

"Quantum Intermodal Sales Force Changes." *Distribution*, April 1991, p. 18.

"Rail Container Traffic: New Plug in power for piggyback cars." *Railway Age*, September 25, 1967, pp. 25-26.

"Railroads lose court decision in piggyback case." *Railway Age*, June 5, 1967, p. 12.

"Railroads turn idle cars into new TOFC cars." *Railway Age*, July 1983, p. 23.

"Railway Age Special Report: A Look at TOFC Service Today." *Railway Age*, December 5, 1955, pp. 37-64.

"Revenue test due for AT&SF container." *Railway Age*, July 1983, p. 25.

"Roadrailer, nee Railvan." *Trains*, October 1977, pp. 7-8.

"Rock Island's Convert-A-Frate." *Railway Age*, January 23, 1956, p. 7.

Ryan, Eugene F. "Piggyback can beat its Growing Pains." *Modern Railroads*, August 1967, p. 91.

"Santa Fe expands double-stack service." *Railway Age*, August 1986, p. 24.

"Santa Fe: High on the Ten-Pack." *Railway Age*, February 27, 1978, p. 86.

"Santa Fe, OOCL sign double-stack pact." *Railway Age*, April 1991, p. 21.

"Santa Fe Super Train Set to Roll." *Railway Age*, December 18, 1967, p. 11.

"Seeking all-purpose TOFC/COFC cars." *Railway, Locomotives and Cars*, February 1967, pp. 25-27, 56.

Shedd, Tom. "A Decade of Trailer Train: TTX Booms into Second Decade." *Modern Railroads*, March 1966, pp. 120-130.

Sims, Donald. "Espee's Piggyback Lane." *Railway Progress*, pp. 32-36.

"Southern Pacific's Double-Stack." *Model Railroader*, October 1983, pp. 92-94.

"SP Sees Continuing Intermodal Growth." *Railway Age*, February 1991, p. 7.

Sperandeo, Andy. "Santa Fe piggyback conversions." *Model Railroader*, December 1984, pp. 104-109.

Stauffer, Fred B. "If you can't lick 'em..." *Railway Progress*, November 1953, pp. 16-21.

_____. "Report on Piggyback." *Railway Progress*, January 1955, pp. 16-21.

"Super C Challenges Air Freight." *Modern Railroads*, March 1968, pp. 74-76.

"Super C proves the long haul can pay." *Railway Age*, October 28, 1968, pp. 11-12.

"Super C: Santa Fe claims it has world's fastest freight train." *Railway Age*, January 29, 1968.

"The Bi-Modal RailRoader." *Model Railroader*, pp. 62-63.

"The Box Worth Millions." *Forbes*, April 1, 1968, pp. 30-39.

"The Central Calls it Flexi-Van." *Railway Progress*, pp. 32-35.

"The Railvan." *Modern Railroads*, June 1956.

"The Super C'...just like a Champion!" *Santa Fe Magazine*, February 1968, pp. 8-13.

"TOFC/COFC: Competition will pick a winner." *Railway Age*, May 30, 1966, pp. 18-24.

"TOFC/COFC Hits Its Stride Again." *Railway Age*, May 29, 1972, pp. 27-31.

"TOFC/COFC: Why the future looks to good." *Railway Age*, May 29, 1967, pp. 28-41.

"TOFC - Helping Hand for Box Cars." *Railway Age*, August 8, 1955, pp. 46-47.

"TOFC Innovations." *Trains*, September 1961, p. 11.

"TOFC Points Toward Profits." *Railway Age*, December 12, 1956, p. 1057.

"TOFC Potential Called Unlimited." *Railway Age*, May 21, 1956, p. 110.

"TOFC: Standards and Equipment." *Railway Age*, December 5, 1955, p. 35.

"TOFC: What's Ahead for Intermodal Cooperation." *Railway Age*, pp. 32-42.

"Tomorrow's fast freight? The Coaxial train, now only a scale model, would offer high speed and a smooth ride." *Railway Age*, September 15, 1969, pp. 38-40.

"Tractors and Trailers Used by North Shore Line." *Railway Age*, October 22, 1927, pp. 807-809.

"Trailer Train: Getting a grip on the future." *Railway Age*, November 1984, pp. 40-42.

"Trailer Train to Begin Service about March 1." *Railway Age*, January 16, 1956, p. 8.

"Transport: The Container Revolution." *Newsweek*, September 1, 1969, pp. 62-63.

Treiman, Larry. "Containers instead of a New Canal: The Ultimate Land-Bridge." *Trains*, May 1975, pp. 36-39.

"Truck Size Container Enters Piggyback' Field." *Railway Age*, April 11, 1955, p. 12.

Welty, Gus. "Intermodal equipment: A time for testing." *Railway Age*, March 1983, pp. 28-31.

_____. "Lines on Labor, Slingshot Takes Aim." *Railway Age*, December 8, 1975, pp. 16-18.

_____. "Special Piggyback Report TOFC/COFC: Trailer Train Approves an all-purpose car." *Railway Age*, November 27, 1967, pp. 33-41.

_____. "The Intermodal Revolution: The message is clear - if railroads are to grow, they have to win traffic from the highways." *Railway Age*, May 1984, pp. 35-38.

_____. "The Rack Car Fleet: Shrinkage in Size Growing in Quality." *Railway Age*, October 26, 1981, pp. 22-26.

_____. "TOFC/COFC: Setting the pace for recovery." *Railway Age*, November 1983, pp. 44-45.

_____. "You've Come a Long Way, Piggy." *Railway Age*, April 24, 1978, p. 24.

"West Coast Ports vie for lead in intermodal race." *Railway Age*, February 1985, p. 21.

White, John H., Jr. "The Magic Box: Genesis of the Container." *Railroad History*, Spring 1988.

"Whoever Thought Piggyback was New?" *Railway Age*, March 21, 1955.

Biographical Index

Allyn, Henry, Jr., 106-107
Angold, John, 135
Aramian, Sy, 55
Ascenico, Ray, 159
Austill, Bob, 154

Bakka, Charlie, 143
Bang, Arnie, 121
Banner, Paul, 143
Barnes. Duane, 75
Barnum, John, 127
Barnum, P.T., 11
Barriger, John W., 21, 25, 106
Barrow, Keith, 75
Baughan, Ed, 157
Bayer, Palmer, 79, 80
Beck, Dave, 45
Behrend, Dick, 137-138, 153
Berry, Arthur, 67
Berry, Bill, 168
Bevan, David, 44, 67, 68, 105, 107
Biaggini, Ben, 114
Billingsley, Bob, 139
Bourque, Bill, 121, 154
Breakiron, Larry, 100
Brodeur, Rene, 122, 138
Brosnan, Bill, 89, 90
Brown, Virginia Mae, 123
Browne, Ken, 54, 55, 129
Budd, John, 25
Budorick, Bob, 80, 81
Buford, Curtis D., 106, 122, 138, 140
Burkhart, Ed, 152
Burton, Raymond C., Jr., 140

Canzoniero, Rocky, 23, 55, 80, 81
Carpi, Fred, 44, 67, 70, 106
Cena, Larry, 91, 101, 112, 115, 120, 121 122, 123, 135, 136, 141, 142, 156
Chamoff, Phil, 86
Clark, Chico, 87, 88, 93, 96, 97
Clejan, Deodat, 51, 54, 65
Collins, Dan, 121, 124
Cooper, Howard, 92
Corbett, Scott, 87, 88, 97
Cordani, Eugene, 139
Coulson, Dave, 87
Cowling, Laurin, 74, 88, 101, 125
Crane, Stan, 89, 90, 120, 122, 123, 135
Cripe, Alan, 129
Crowe, Pat, 74
Curry, Tom, 107
Cruikshank, Paul, 126
Cunningham, Jim, 74, 75, 103
Cutler, Guy, 175

Day, Milt, 75
Dancu, Ted, 153
DeBoer, David J., 11
Degan, Thomas J., 31
Dezendoff, Nelson, 27
Domigez, Dan, 138
Donohue, Kevin, 133
Dunlap, Dick, 120

Edson, Bill, 120. 121, 122
Eliscu, Avery, 75
Engle, Tom, 144

Farish, James, 75
Farley, Jim, 23
Fante, Tom, 74, 86, 120, 124, 139, 154
Ferren, Norm, 154
Finkbiner, Tom, 133
Forgash, Morris, 70, 106
Forbes, Robert, 75
Forrer, John, 58
Fox, Bob, 90
Fox, Herb, 90
Franklin, Dick, 90
Fraser, Donald V., 35
Frick, Dick, 159
Frey, Ed, 91, 97
Fruehauf, Roy, 79, 86, 107, 109
Furlow, Wayde, 142
Furman, Bill, 154

Galbraith, Bill, 154
Garin, Paul, 139
Gaskins, Darius, 148

Goebel, George, 23
Golden, Sam, 21-22
Goldsmith, Clarence, 125
Goodwin, Robert, 75
Gould, Jay, 107
Gray, John, 95, 153
Green, Charlie, 153
Greenwood, Bill, 143, 167
Greer, Dave, 74
Groton, Charley, 74, 90, 103
Grygiel, John, 111, 114
Gruca, Joe, 45
Gunn, Dave, 112, 115

Hagen, Jim, 138
Harvey, Scott, 144
Harley, Tom, 165
Hasselman, Bob, 103
Hauck, Ken, 74, 75
Hawkins, Roger, 154
Hayes, Roy, 101
Head, Jim, 77, 91
Hennessy, Jim, 142
Hill, E.V., 38
Hoffman, Wayne, 129
Hulick, Bob, 164

Icahn, Carl, 154
Ingram, Bob, 97, 139, 156-157, 161, 162, 167
Insull, Samuel, 17

Jackson, James, 75
Jenks, Downing, 23
Jimenez, Jim, 162
Johnson, Al, 46
Johnson, Bill, 80, 81
Johnson, Paul, 103, 107
Joyce, Patrick, 21

Kaleta, Gary, 162
Kearney, A.T., 108
Keenan, Pete, 101
Keoughan, Larry, 46, 74, 121
Kirk, Bill, 88
Kirwan, George, 142
Kloss, Les, 62
Kneiling, John, 108
Kohout, Howard, 46, 48
Kreyling, Ed, 133
Kudick, Selwyn, 77

Landregan, Bob, 54
Lanigan, Jack, 91, 92, 96
Lawson, E.C., 96
Lenz, Dick, 154
LeTourneau, L.G., 87, 93, 94
Little, Arthur D., 80
Loftus, Bill, 119
Lynch, Jack, 153

McClellan, Jim, 112, 144
McClellan, P.M., 113, 114
McDonald, Jack, 153
McInnes, Don, 76
McInnes, Milton, 107
McLean, Malcolm, 11, 56-57, 89
McKnight, Dan, 100, 101
McQuaid, John, 75, 76
Macomber, Frank, 62, 108
Maisch, Bob, 100, 101, 103
Manos, Dr. Bill, 122, 123, 135
Marden, Bob, 75
Marino, Dominic, 75
Martin, Ed, 68
Mascaro, Al, 75
Mason, Ted, 136, 144
Matney, R.C., 75, 156
Menk, Lou, 94
Middleton, Don, 75
Miller, Gordon, 80
Moir, G. Russell, 106
Moore, Joe, 90
Mueller, Fred, 46
Muellner, Ralph, 167
Murphy, John, 75

Nankivell, Jim, 103
Nash, Joe, 101
Nations, Lloyd, 139
Neff, P.J., 58

Newell, Jim, 44, 46, 67-68, 70, 74, 105
Novas, Peter, 129
Nueschel, Bob, 111

O'Neal, Dan, 147, 148, 149
Orris, Don, 151, 152-153, 155, 156, 157, 158, 167
Osburn, Cy, 28
Osburne, Buddy, 75
Overmeyer, D.H., 108

Paton, Neil, 136
Patterson, J.M., 96
Paul, Bill, 115, 121-122
Pavlick, Mike, 137, 153
Peoples, Bill, 114
Perlman, Alfred E., 31, 63, 89, 114, 135
Pogue, Walter, 142
Porter, McNeil, 157

Quinn, Frank, 93, 94
Quinto, Frank, 105

Reebie, Bob, 129, 130, 131
Reed, George, 139
Reed, John, 114, 115
Reifler, Monte, 131
Reistrup, Paul, 120, 123
Richards, Dennis, 153
Robinson, Les, 45-46, 48, 55, 80, 120
Rosner, Bernie, 75
Russell, Donald J., 35
Ryan, Gene, 27, 31, 38, 44-45, 48, 51, 62, 65, 67-68, 70-71, 77, 96, 105, 107-109

Sanders, Mac, 138
Sarrenbetz, Warren, 80, 81
Saunders, Stuart, 67, 75, 105-106
Saxton, Greg, 154
Sheffield, Connie, 76
Schramm, Ken, 94
Schuller, Jim, 153
Seaton, Bruce, 156
Seel, Max, 46
Shafer, Fred, 101
Sheer, Maury, 75
Sherbourne, Jack, 86-87
Shively, Guy, 101
Short, Reggie, 121, 123
Shum, Don, 152
Sims, Roger, 143
Smith, Alfred H., 15, 30
Smith, George, 100
Smutny, Rudy, 67
Spence, Dick, 120, 123, 138
Stafford, George, 147
Steins, C.K., 46
Stern, George, 121, 123
Stubbs, Troy, 75
Sullivan, Jim, 114
Sullivan, Pat, 97
Sundel, Dan, 23, 35
Sutherland, Frank, 101
Swanson, Don, 103
Symes, James M., 34, 44, 48, 68, 105

Tackberry, Ron, 109
Talbot, Russ, 75
Taylor, Bill, 95
Terlecky, Boris, 59, 138, 140
Thomford, Bill, 139, 163
Thompson, Bill, 123
Thull, Bob, 147
Tippet, Ray, 88
Tomm, Carl, 77
Tonsager, Gene, 100
Turner, Paul, 28, 70

Ventre, Frank, 77
Volkers, Gordon, 70, 74, 96, 152

Wade, Dick, 54, 153
Wade, Ted, 135
Wagner, P.R., 58
Walters, Ed, 74
Ward, Bruce, 154
Wayman, Frank, 75
Welch, Nat, 154
White, John, 13
White, William, 30-31
Wightman, J.E., 71

Williams, Bob, 107
Williams, John, 120, 144
Wogan, Gene, 103
Wright, Jim 152

Wyckoff, Ray, 100
Yates, Bob, 154, 163
Yeager, Phil, 75

Young, Robert R., 30-31, 44, 54

Zimmerman, Edwin, 75

General Index

Adapto System (see American Car & Foundry)
American Car & Foundry Co., 138; absorbed by Carl Icahn 154; builds collapsible trailer hitch, 46 48; designs Adapto container system, 59, 176; develops 40-foot well car, 154; develops Southern Pacific double-stack container car, 139; establishes Road-Rail system with new tie-down device, 58; Lo-Deck car devised, 121
American President Lines, brings double-stack technology into spotlight 155; cars stuck in Chicago snowstorm 151; contract made with Union Pacific for "hook and haul" service, 153; establishes Southern Pacific - Sea-Land connection, 152; "Liner Train" starts service, 152; orders box containers, 169; Orris sold on inter-box connector stack concept, 153; Orris takes over APL intermodal, 151; test stack-container stability by setting dining table inside a container, 169; Thrall builds IBC-Inter-Box Connector car, 153; Union Pacific willing to work with APL regarding stack train concept where SP and AT&SF refused, 152-153; unable to establish container rate with AT&SF, 152; was pioneer container carrier, 151
American Trucking Assn., 74
Amtrak, 99, 130
Association of American Railroads, 73-74, 120, 129, 144, 153
Atlanta Intermodal Expostion, 154-155, 162, 169
Atlantic Coast Line R.R., 100, 107
Baltimore Ohio R.R., 61, 120-121; begins piggyback service, 43; establishes container service called TOFCE, 58; rail bogie units tested, 142
Banner Bogie, 62, 143
Bi-Modal Corporation, established to build Road-Railer 192; Illinois Central Gulf and Union Pacific test RoadRailer, 130-131; Illinois Central calls RoadRailer service "Supermode," 130; prototype of Mark IV RoadRailer built, 129; "Triple Crown Service" established on Norfolk Southern using Road-Railer, 168
Birmingham & Derby Junction Ry., 13
Boston & Maine R.R., 77
Boston & Worchester R.R., 17
Boxcar syndrome, 175
Budd Company, 136; builds 6 prototype cars, 137; Budd trailers, 129; designs Lo-Pac 2000 container car, 136; Lo-Pac design considered by American President Lines, 153; purchased by Thyssen Industries, 136; test BUDX-2000 cars, 137
Burlington Northern R.R., 94, 125, 131, 167; "BN America" uses lightweight containers, 168; control center established in Seattle, 168; develops 28-foot "pup" container, 161; flirts with RoadRailer, 167

Chassis Railer (see C&O Ry.)
Chesapeake & Ohio Ry., 54, 57, 63; becomes CSX Sea-Land Intermodal, 157; buys Sea-Land service, 157; Railvan system established, 129; sets up domestic and international Chassis Railer System, 133; "Triple Crown Service" established using RoadRailer, 168
Chicago & Eastern Illinois R.R., 22, 25, 101; begins piggyback service, 25
Chicago & North Western Ry., 55, 125, 126; begins piggyback service, 43; establishes "Global One" state-of-the-art intermodal terminal in Chicago, 97, 158; leases trailers from Trailmobile, 77
Chicago, Burlington & Quincy R.R., 25; used pioneer loading cranes, 93-94; was a pioneer in container and piggyback service, 25
Chicago-Dubuque Motor Transportation Co., 22
Chicago Great Western R.R., 11, 21, 23, 24, 25, 27, 33, 34, 38,39, 55, 65, 71, 99, 176; pioneer American piggyback hauler, 11; screw jack/chain and binders system was a pioneer piggyback fastener system, 43; served common carrier truckers, 35
Chicago, North Shore & Milwaukee R.R., 17, 18, 21, 28; pioneered rail trailer service between Chicago and Milwaukee in 1920's, 17-18
Chicago, Rock Island & Pacific R.R., 23, 147; initiates Convert-A-Frate service, 59
Chicago, South Shore & South Bend R.R., 19, 21
Cincinnati & Lake Erie R.R., 17
Cincinnati, Lawrenceburg & Aurora Ry., 17
Circus loading, 11
Clark Equipment Co., builds forklift loader called "Trailoader," 29
Clejan car, 54
Consolidated Freightways, 45, 75
Containers, American Car & Foundry develops Adapto System, 59; Burlington Northern designs 28-foot "pup" container, 161; box without wheels concept, 111; capital cost per day for various containers, 172; container concepts, 10; development of highway-rail-sea box, 56; International Standards Organization (ISO) to oversee containers established, 65; Malcolm McLean establishes ship containers, 56-57; New York Central develops Flexi Van container system, 63, 65; Rock Island establishes Convert-A-Frate container, 59; pioneer container system, 15; Southern Railway container system, 90
CXL Sea-Land Intermodal System (see Sea-Land)

Delaware, Lackawanna & Western R.R., begins piggyback, 43
Denver & Rio Grande Western R.R., 22-23, 31, 147, 151; tests piggyback early, 22
Detroit, Toledo & Ironton, 125
Electro-Motive Division of General Motors (see General Motors)
Equipment (see Rolling Stock)
Erie, R.R., 107; begins piggyback in 1954, 43
Erie-Lackawanna R.R., 103, 107
Evergreen Container Service, 159

FAK (Freight-All-Kinds), 15, 34, 35, 112
Federal Maritime Commission (FMC), 57
Federal Railroad Administration (FRA), 92, 119-127; agency created in 1967, 119; Chicago-Twin Cities route on Milwaukee Road selected for "Sprint" demonstration, 126; establishes relationship with Intermodal Steering Committee, 120; explores potential intermodal routes for "Sprint" test, 123; Intermodal Network Study established, 129; Milwaukee Road becomes test railroad, 125; mission was established to assist and promote railroads, 119; working relationship with Operating Transportation General Committee for intermodal set up, 120; "Slingshot" operation on ICG, 123; studies new intermodal rolling stock, 136; test of "Sprint" on Milwaukee Road a success, 127
Flexi Van (see New York Central)
Florida East Coast Ry., 100
Flying Tiger Line, 159
Fruehauf Trailer Mfg Co., leases trailers for piggyback, 77; purchase Paceco Crane Co., 86; Ryan makes contact with Fruehauf, 107

General American Transportation Co., 51; builds Clejan cars, 54; Clejan cars produce tracking problems, 54; establishes rental car pool fleet, 70; flatcar pool disbanded, 71; GATX car code established, 176; invents G-85 piggyback car, 54
General Motors - Electro-Motive Division, devises Trailer Transport Terminal for piggyback, 30; EMD X-15972 depressed center car devised, 29, 51, 176; exhibits at 1952 Railroad Mechanical Officers Convention, 30; Gene Ryan hires out to Chevrolet Truck Division, 27; G.M Diesel of Canada designs "Portager" car, 60-61, 62; GMDX-401 car, 61; GMDX-405 and GMDX-406 cars, 61-62; organizes Rail-Highway Coordination Program to sell piggyback, 28; Pennsylvania Railroad studies GM piggyback car, 44; T-40 piggyback car, 60; Trailer Transport System established, 28, 30, 51, 58
Grand Trunk Western Ry., 126; initiates "Expeditor" piggyback service, 131
Great Northern Ry., 112, 126; begins piggyback service, 43
Georgia Railroad, 147
Greenbrier Intermodal, builds "Husky" container car, 163; Greenbrier Leasing purchases FMC Corporation Marine-Rail Division, 154; produces GBRX-1984 5-unit bulkhead articulated double-stack car, 154; standardizes on 5-unit articulated cars, 160

Hawaiian Merchant (Matson Navigation Co.), 57
Hitches, 46; American Car & Foundry hitch, 54, 58; collapsible hitch born, 48; "kingpin grabber" designed, 46, 48; knock-down hitch, 48
Hoffman & Hilsabeck (securement device), 22
Hunt, J.B., conversion from piggyback to container and double-stack service, 169; offers quality trailer service called "Quantum," 169

Ideal-X, first container ship, 57
Illinois Central (Illinois Central Gulf), 120-123, 125; begins RoadRailers "Supermode" trains, 130; "Slingshot" trains, 123; starts piggyback service, 43; test Flexi Van units, 65
Illinois-Minnesota Motor Carriers Conference, 22
International Brotherhood of Teamsters, 16, 18; Ryan proves Teamster cooperation would increase employment, 45; would fight piggyback, 45
International Standards Organization (ISO), 65, 91, 167
Intermodal (definition of), 10; box without wheels, 111; established as a result of "20 Questions Case," 39; tariff plans Plan I through Plan V, 38-41
Intermodal Association of North America, 76
Intermodal Concepts, Inc. (Rail Bogie), 142-143; initial test of "Pogie Bogie," 143
Intermodal Marketing Assn., 74
Intermodal Steering Committee, 56, 73
Intermodal Transportation Assn. (ITA), 74
Inter-Rail Xpress, 130
Interstate Commerce Commission (ICC), 15, 34, 35, 48, 57, 75, 99, 105 147, 149, 167, 177; "20 Questions Case" (Movement of Trailers by Rail), 38; determines railroads do not require truck certificate for TOFC, 38, 41; improvements made for TOFC/COFC regulation, 148; Intermodal Plans, 40, 107
Interstate Highway Act, 68
Iron Highway, 62, 144
Itel, uses containers, 169

K-Line, 159
Kansas City Southern R.R., begins piggyback, 43
Kearney cars, designed early stacked container car, 62; "Minipiggi" trailer car introduced, 62
Keystone Container Co., 15; was part of Pennsylvania Railroad system, 15

LCL Corporation, 15
LCL (Less-Than-Carload), 13-16, 23, 30, 33, 34, 73
Lehigh Valley R.R., begins piggyback service, 43
Lift Equipment - Loaders, J.I Case Co. purchases Drott Co., 91; Clark Co. develops "Trailoader," 29; Drott Co. builds PRR's Kearney Yard cranes, 85, 90; Drott Co. develops overhead cranes, 85; Drott expands into marine cranes, 91; electric vs hydraulic cranes, 94; Fruehauf purchases Paceco, 86; Hostler Tractor produces "The Monster," 55; LeTourneau builds yard machine called "Letro-Jib," 93; Mi-Jack establishes loader dealership, 91; Mi-Jack "Translift" is top-lift machine, 92, 93; Missouri Pacific uses freight cranes for intermodal, 86; Nelson Equipment Co. modifies log loader into intermodal "Piggypacker," 88; P&H Crane Co. builds overhead cranes, 93; Paceco builds caniltever cranes for PRR, 86; Paceco builds Matson dockside crane, 85; Paceco span crane called "Transtainer," 86; Penn Central purchases 14 "Piggypackers," 88; Pettibone makes trailer forklifts, 85; Raygo-Wagner purchases "Piggypackers" patents, 92; Raygo-Wagner builds hydraulic cranes, 94; Ropco Corp. develops top/bottom lift machines, 89; Southern Ry. builds homemade stationary cranes for intermodal, 90; spreader cranes used to lift containers on and off ships, 89; Taylor Machine Co. builds top-pick machines, 94-95; Travelift Engineering Co. builds boat cranes for intermodal use, 91; Travelift purchased by Drott, 91; Wagner Tractor builds hydraulic cranes, 87; Wagner Tractor "Lumber jack" rebuilt to handle containers, 87; Western Pacific acquires a large "Transtainer," 86
Liverpool & Manchester Ry., 10
Long Beach Container Terminal, 97
Long Island Rail Road, 13, 38, 143
Louisville & Nashville R.R., begins piggyback service, 43
LTL (Less-Than-Truckload), 16, 173

Maersk Line, 159
Matson Navigation Co., 57; *Hawaiian Merchant* handles containers first, 57; inaugurates container service from Hawaii and Orient to West Coast, 57
McDonough of Union Pacific develops container spine car concept, 163

189

McDowall-Ferris Trucking Co., 107
McKinsey & Co., 111
Milwaukee Road, 22, 101; purchases first production "Piggypacker," 126; selected for FRA "Sprint" demonstration test, 125-126, "Sprint" test proves a success, 127; tests Flexi Van, 65
Minipiggi (see Kearney Co.)
Minneapolis Traffic Assn., 22
Missouri-Kansas-Texas R.R., 35; begins piggyback service, 43
Missouri Pacific R.R., 61; establishes container and piggyback service handling both in gondola cars, 58; uses freight cranes for intermodal service, 90
Moore McCormick Lines, 56
Motor Carriers Act, 22, 38
Motor Transportation Advisory Committee, 73

National Association of shippers, 75
National Intermodal Network Study, 121
National Piggyback, 156
National Railroad Intermodal Assn., 74, 97, 143
National Railroad Piggyback Assn., 74
Navajo Freight Lines, 113
New Haven Line (New York, New Haven & Hartford R.R.), 23, 24, 27, 35, 38, 55, 99, 101; buys Clejan cars, 54; files "20 Questions Case" before ICC, 38; initiates Trainliner service, 24; leases trailers, 77; offers piggyback service, 24; purchases first piggyback cars, 24
New York Air Brake Co. (see Iron Highway)
New York Central R.R., 15, 17, 22, 35, 61, 105, 112, 120, 129, 176; buys "Piggypackers" to handle Flexi Vans, 88; establishes Flexi Van container service, 63-65; establishes "Star" service, 31; gets into TOFC service, 65; joins Trailer Train, 105; makes Flexi Van test across U.S. with Santa Fe, 63; owns U.S. Freight, 33; Perlman cancels Ryan's Rail-Trailer contract, 31, 44; Ryan approaches NYC's William White with trailer plan and signs contract, 30; Robert R Young takes over NYC, 31; Young hires Al Perlman as NYC president, 31
New York, Susquehanna & Western R.R., 156
Nickel Plate Line (New York Chicago St. Louis R.R.) 71; begins piggyback service, 43
Norfolk & Western Ry., 105, 120-122, 123
Norfolk Southern Ry., 131; acquires North American Van Lines, 133; home-built cranes, 133; sets up "Triple Crown" RoadRailer service, 133
North American Car Co., 61, 129; enters bankruptcy, 131
North Shore Line (see Chicago, North Shore & Milwaukee R.R.)
NYK Line, 159

OSK Line, 159
Overseas Orient Container Line, 159

Pacific Intermountain Express (PIE), 45
Pan Atlantic Steamship Co., 57
Panama Canal, 11, 111
Penn Central Co., 101, 103, 119
Pennsylvania Railroad, 15, 17, 101, 105, 106; acquires Paceco lift crane, 86; begins piggyback, 43, 44; develops double trailer on flatcar plan, 44; establishes Trailer Train, 67-68; orders trailer-carrying flatcars, 35; owns Penn Truck Line, 75; purchases cantilever unit crane for Kearny, New Jersey yard, 86; Ryan launches Truc-Train service, 46-48; Ryan sets up piggyback terminals at Kearny, New Jersey, and Chicago, Illinois, 48; study of Ryan's Rail-Trailer plan, 44
Piggyback, definition of, 10
Piggyback, Inc., 54; leases Clejan cars, 54
Pogey Bogie (see Walter Pogue)
Pullman-Standard Car Mfg. Co., builds 2-trailer cars, 51; develops box girder car called "Land Bridger," 122, 135, 136; Gene Ryan becomes piggyback car consultant, 27

Quantum (see J.B. Hunt Co.)

Rail-Trailer Co., 34; approaches New York Central regarding piggyback, 30; depressed well cars developed, 108; establishes Con-Bak container stacking, 108; established Reefer Leasing, 107; establishes Van Car to purchase GM designed trailer cars, 31; finances New York Central terminals, 31; Fruehauf leases trailers to Rail-Trailer, 107; Fruehauf takes back leased trailers, 109; obtains concessions with Teamsters, 45; obtains car financing from New York Life Insurance Co., 44-45; Robinson develops collapsible trailer hitch, 46; Ryan drops out of Rail-Trailer Co., 109; Ryan sets up Pennsylvania Railroad terminal in Jersey and Chicago, 48; Ryan to build cars and finance NYC terminals, 31; sets up Truc-Train services, 46; shippers agents and freight forwarders become major players in intermodal game, 108; U.S. Van Lines becomes subsidiary, 107; Van Car orders cars, 45
Rail Systems & Management Assn., 112
Railiner System (see Southern Car & Mfg. Co.)
Railvan, 176; coupler problems,. 54; derailment of Railvans, 54; developed by Chesapeake & Ohio, 54; eliminates use of flatcars, 54; single-axle rail wheels drop down to track, 54
Railway Express Agency (REALCO), 106, 173, 176; leases trailers from Van Pool, 80; maintained nationwide network of repair depots, 80; REA becomes Van Pool contract repairman, 80; REALCO sold to Transamerica Corp., 81; REALCO Trailer Leasing established, 80; tests Steadman system, 60
Ramps, P.T. Barnum Circus used end ramps, 11; circus loading techniques, 21; circus ramps become a burden, 90; large concrete ramps, 90; loading ramps 1-8 tracks wide, 48; piggyback ramp at plants, 43; ramp crews, 48; shippers used own drivers to back up loads at ramps, 39; small ramps led to poor service, 83; ramp reductions, 89; ramp-to-ramp service, 39; ramps sprung up everywhere, 71; stub track ramps 88 tie-pile ramps, 71
Ringling Brothers and Barnum & Bailey Circus, 21, 22
Richmond, Fredericksburg & Potomac R.R., 129, 130
RoadRailer (see also Chesapeake & Ohio) capital costs per unit are high, 172; cost 43 cents per mile to operate, 173; trains limited to 75 RoadRailer units, 172
Rock Island Line (see Chicago, Rock Island & Pacific R.R.)
Rockford & Interurban Ry., 17
Rolling Stock, 40-foot well car developed, 154; all-purpose spine car technology, 165; A-Stack containers developed by Santa Fe, 141; American Car & Foundry designs 40-foot well car, 154; American Car & Foundry develops 3-unit double-stack car, 139; Banner Bogie, 62, 143; Budd Lo-Pac 2000 car designed, 136; Clejan car, 54, 126; container cars settled into Types I, II and III car, 161; container car floor failures, 164; development of 48-foot 2-platform car called "4-Runner," 140; development of single-axle container car called "Front Runner," 141; EMD X-15972 depressed center car designed, 29; FMC produces 5-unit bulkhead double-stack car, 159; G-85 car, 54; GBDX-401 car, 61; GBDX-405 car, 61-62; GBRX-1984 5-unit articulated car designed, 154; Greenbrier builds "Husky" stack car, 163; Gunderson builds bulkhead container cars, 160; Gunderson designs Maxi-III car, 162; Intermodal standardizes on 5-unit articulated container carrier, 159-160; Iron Highway (see New York Air Brake); Lo-Deck car (see American Car & Foundry); Lo-Pac 2000 container car (see Budd Co.); Mark IV RoadRailer (see Bi-Modal); *Minipiggi* (see Kearney Co.); "Pogie Bogie" (see Intermodal Concepts); "Portager" car developed by General Motors, 60-61; Pullman-Standard designs "Land-Bridger," 122; Rail Bogie (see Intermodal Concepts); RailTrailer develops depressed well car, 108; RoadRailer (see Bi-Modal Corp.); Santa Fe designs spine car, 135; Santa Fe develops 6-pack car, 135; Santa Fe develops 10-unit articulated unit called "Fuel Foiler," 135; Southern Pacific builds prototype stack car, 154; Southern Pacific designs double-stack container car, 138-139; T-40 piggyback car, 61; Tare weight for 6,000-foot train, 172; Thrall and Trinity build interbox container car, 160; Thrall builds IBC cars for American President Lines, 153; trailer spine car, 135; Trailer Train builds all-purpose container/trailer car, 106; Trailer Train designs single-axle trailer car, 140, 163; Trailer Train introduces 2-platform car called "4-Runner," 140, 163; Union Pacific shops build container spine car, 153; Youngstown Steel Door builds trailer well car, 137
Santa Fe Railway (Atchison, Topeka & Santa Fe Ry.) 10, 103, 111-115, 120, 123; begins piggyback service, 43; BN extends container service into Los Angeles via Santa Fe, 168; builds 3 fiberglass and metal A-Stack containers that overlap each other, 141; builds 10-unit intermodal cars called "Fuel Foilers," 135; coaxial train developed by General Electric, 117; Corwith Yard at Chicago becomes intermodal testbed, 91; decides trailers are more efficient than containers, 156; designs A-Stack containers, 141; develops trailer spine car, 135; establishes micro-bridge service, 112; establishes rail bridge across continent, 111; Hobart Yard in Los Angeles places second Drott unit into service, 91; Matson Navigation, American President Lines and Sea-Land become important customers, 91; mini-bridge (port-to-port) service makes container movement by rail possible, 112; New York Central - Santa Fe coast-to-coast test train with Flexi Van equipment used, 112-113; operates "Land Bridge," 111; Reed established "Super C" to replace dead New York Central cross-country connection, 114; seek ship ports of call terminals, 112; shop forces build six-pack, 135; Southern Pacific complains to NYC over test plan with Flexi Van cars, 114; "Super C" train inaugurated, 115; tests Flexi Van across the U.S.A. with New York Central, 63, 65
Sea-Land Container service, 11, 151; becomes aggressive in double-stack service, 156; becomes CSX Sea-Land Intermodal, 157; begins handling tank containers, 173; builds terminal in Little Ferry, New Jersey, 157; maintains nationwide offering of international and domestic containers to and from the eastern seaboard, 168; negotiates rate concessions with American President Lines, 152; purchased by CSX Corporation, 157; puts trainload rates into effect for containers, 112; Sea-Land services offered, 111
Sea Train, 111
Seaboard Air Line R.R., 100, 101, 107, 129, 130; tests Flexi Van, 65
Sears, Roebuck & Co., 18
Seatrain Lines, 58
Smith Transport (Canadian), 60
South Shore Line (See Chicago, South Shore & South Bend R.R.)
Southern Car & Mfg. Co., establishes Railiner system, 59
Southern Pacific Company, 38, 39, 112, 120, 147, 151; acquires prototype "Piggypacker," 88; buys Clejan cars, 54; develops double-stack container car, 138-139; embarked on piggyback services between Los Angeles and San Francisco, using Pacific Motor Trucking trailers, 35; FMC builds prototype stack car, 154; handles Pacific Motor Trucking trailers, 35; Southern Pacific's intermodal service placed under "Freight Protection, Merchandise & Station Department," 86
Southern Ry., 61, 112, 122. 147; builds homemade cranes to handle containers, 90
Staggers Rail Act of 1980, 148
Standard Steel Car Co., 21
Steadman System, used Canadian road chassis and transfer chassis, 59-60; used by Canadian National system, 60; was a side loader, 63
Steamship Operations Intermodal Committee (SOIC), 57
Stoughton Trailer, 162
Strick Division of Fruehauf, 63
Suez Canal, 111
Supermode trains (see Illinois Central)

Teamsters (see International Brotherhood of Teamsters)
Thrall Car Co. build IBC car for American President Lines, 153; purchases RoadRailer concept, 131
TOFC (Trailer-on-Flatcar), 11
TOFC, Inc., 55, 107
Trailer Railer (see Intermodal Concepts)
Trailer Train, 119, 176; 41 railroads join Trailer Train between 1955-1964, 70; 15,000 cars in TTX fleet by 1963, 70; board cancels advertising campaign, 106; brought industry into second generation of intermodal equipment, 83; Curtis Buford becomes president, 106; develops all-purpose container/trailer car, 106; designs single-axle trailer car, 140; establishes subsidiaries Railbox and Railgon, 140; gets together with car builders, 68; heavy into research and development of trailer and container cars, 119; initiates retrofit program, 145; introduces 48-foot two-platform car called "4-Runner," 140; major freight forwarded U.S. Freight joins Trailer Train, 70; makes it easy for railroads to obtain cars, 77; Pennsylvania Railroad driving force behind pioneer years, 65,105; Pennsylvania Railroad control severed, 107; promotes longer cars, 68; Raymond C. Burton, Jr. becomes president, 140; rebuilds short trailer cars into container cars, 145; single-axle car named "Front Runner," 141; Southern Pacific joins Trailer Train system, 54; Trailer Train established, 67, 80; Van Pool established to lease trailers, 77
Trailers, Association of American Railroads (Mechanical Committee) set trailer standards, 56; Fruehauf leases trailers for piggyback service, 77; REALCO leases trailers for piggyback service, 80; tank, flatbed and bulk trailers developed, 56; TOFC standards set, 56; Trailermobile leases trailers to C&NW, 55; used standard highway trailers for piggyback service, 55
Transamerica, buys Railway Express (REALCO), 81; joins container service, 169
Transportation Act of 1920, 16
Transportation Research Forum, 112
Truck Ferry Service (see Chicago, South Shore & South Bend R.R.)

Unit Pak (see Railway Express Agency)
United Parcel Service, 99-103; becomes prime nationwide delivery service, 99; brown delivery vehicle called "Package Car," 100; establishes UPS trains, 101; flexibility with Teamsters, 101; key sort centers

established, 103; "Martrax" service started, 103; organized in Seattle initially, 99; tackles United States Post Office parcel delivery, 100; UPS becomes largest freight transportation company in America, 103
Union Pacific R.R., establishes Mark V RoadRailer service, 133; shops at Omaha built container spine car, 153
United States Railroad Administration (USRA), 16, 126, 129

United Transportation Union, 121, 130
U.S. Freight (see New York Central)
U.S. Lines, 56

Van Car (see Rail-Trailer Co.)
Voluntary Coordination Agreement (VCA), 168

Wabash R.R., begins piggyback service, 43
Waterman Steamship Co., 57
Western Pacific R.R., acquires Paceco crane, 86

Western Railroad Trunkline Assn., 57

XTRA, 176; begins to use containers, 169; per diem relief for trailer leasing, 80; was established to lease trailers, 77-78
Yale & Towne, 62; develops loader for General Motors Diesel of Canada, 61
Youngstown Steel Door, 136; develops trailer well car, 137

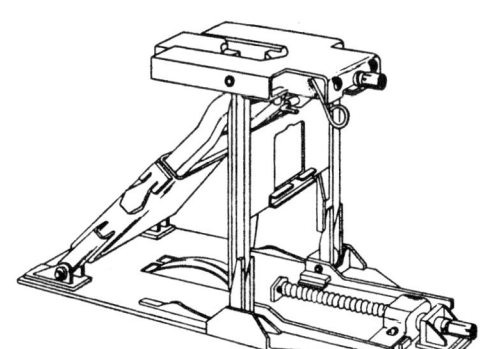